D0087811

CONSULTANT EDITOR: NICOLAS TREDE[

Published

Forthcoming

Peter Childs	The Fiction of Ian McEwan
Peter Dempsey	The Fiction of Don Delillo
Michael Faherty	The Poetry of W. B. Yeats
Matthew Jordan	Milton: *Paradise Lost*
Merja Makinen	The Novels of Jeanette Winterson
Stephen Regan	The Poetry of Philip Larkin
Susie Thomas	Hanif Kureishi
Angela Wright	Gothic Fiction

**Palgrave Reader's Guides to Essential Criticism
Series Standing Order
ISBN 1–4390–0108–2**
(outside North America only)

You can receive future titles in this series as they are published by placing a standing order. Please contact your bookseller or, in the case of difficulty, write to us at the address below with your name and address, the title of the series and the ISBN quoted above.

Customer Services Department, Palgrave Macmillan Ltd
Houndmills, Basingstoke, Hampshire RG21 6XS, England

Twentieth-Century War Poetry

EDITED BY PHILIPPA LYON

Consultant editor: Nicolas Tredell

First published 2005 by
PALGRAVE MACMILLAN™
Houndmills, Basingstoke, Hampshire, England RG21 6XS and
175 Fifth Avenue, New York, N.Y. 10010
Companies and representatives throughout the world

PALGRAVE MACMILLAN is the global academic imprint of the Palgrave
Macmillan division of St. Martin's Press, LLC and of Palgrave Macmillan Ltd.
Macmillan® is a registered trademark in the United States, United Kingdom
and other countries. Palgrave is a registered trademark in the European
Union and other countries.

ISBN 1–4039–3963–2 hardback
ISBN 1–4039–1316–1 paperback

This book is printed on paper suitable for recycling and made from fully
managed and sustained forest sources.

A catalogue record for this book is available from the British Library.

Library of Congress Cataloging-in-Publication Data

Twentieth-century war poetry / edited by Philippa Lyon.
    p.cm.—(Readers' guides to essential criticism)
  Includes bibliographical references and index.
  ISBN 1–4039–3963–2 (cloth) – ISBN 1–4039–1316–1(pbk.)
    1. War poetry, English – History and criticism. 2. English poetry –
20th century – History and criticism. 3. War and literature –
Great Britain – History – 20th century. 4. World War, 1914–1918 –
Great Britain – Literature and the war. 5. World War, 1939–1945 –
Great Britain – Literature and the war. 6. Solidiers' writings,
English – History and criticism. I. Lyon, Philippa, 1968– IL Series.

PR605.W3T94 2004
821'.9109358—dc22   2004052829

10 9 8 7 6 5 4 3 2 1
14 13 12 11 10 09 08 07 06 05

Printed and bound in China

CONTENTS

An overview of the current status of the genre and an examination of war poetry's relationship to the literary canon. This chapter also considers the idea of war poetry as bearing a 'special' relationship to the history of wars and looks at the biographical emphasis of criticism.

This examines a number of key literary contexts and political and intellectual debates from which war poetry emerged in the First World War. The rise of Brooke and the soldier-poet figure is examined.

Here, the changing perceptions of war poetry and war poets are assessed in the context of a rise in pacifism and developments in English Literature. This chapter considers the popularity of Owen in the 1930s and the place of the Spanish Civil War poets in the developing war poetry genre.

The lesser-known poetry of the Second World War is discussed. The burgeoning of war poetry in the early 1940s is set against contemporary debates about the meaning and purpose of art in wartime. This chapter considers the continuing influence of First World War poetry models and the development of new poetic approaches.

This chapter traces developments in critical thought about war poetry since the end of the Second World War. Discussions focus on a range of key approaches from the construction of the genre as 'anti-war', to the persistence of patriotic anthologies and the development of feminist and cultural-historical studies.

A NOTE ON DATES

When an author or other significant figure is mentioned for the first time in the Guide, birth and, where appropriate, death dates have been supplied, but in some cases these are not available.

ACKNOWLEDGEMENTS

The editor and publishers wish to thank the following for permission to use copyright material:

Anon, for an extract from a review of *Poems by Contemporary Women*, compiled by Theodora Roscoe and Mary Winter Were, *Times Literary Supplement*, 29 April 1944, by permission of the Times Literary Supplement.

Roy Campbell, for an extract from *The Flowering Rifle: A Poem from the Battlefield of Spain*, Longman Green (1939) Ad Donker Publishers, by permission of Jonathan Ball Publishers (Pty) Ltd.

John Cornford, for an extract from 'To Margaret Heinemann' from *Collected Writings* by John Cornford, by permission of Carcanet Press Ltd.

Robert Graves, for an extract from 'A Dead Boche' from *Complete Poems* by Robert Graves, by permission of Carcanet Press Ltd.

Sydney Keyes, for an extract from 'War Poet' from *Collected Poems of Sydney Keyes*, Routledge, by permission of David Higham Associates Ltd on behalf of the Estate of the author.

Rudyard Kipling, for an extract from 'Tommy' from *The Complete Barrack-Room Ballads of Rudyard Kipling*, Methuen & Co (1973), by permission of A P Watt Ltd on behalf of the National Trust for Places of Historic Interest or Natural Beauty.

C. Day Lewis, for an extract from *A Hope For Poetry* (1939) pp. 14–17, by permission of Blackwell Publishing Ltd; and 'Where are our War Poets?' from *The Complete Poems* by C. Day Lewis, Sinclair-Stevenson (1992). Copyright © 1992 in this edition, and the Estate of C. Day Lewis, by permission of Random House Group Ltd.

Herbert Read, for an extract from 'To a Conscript of 1940' from *Selected Poetry* by Herbert Read, Random House, by permission of David Higham Associates Ltd on behalf of the Estate of the author.

Siegfried Sassoon, for an extract from 'October' from *Collected Poems of Siegfried Sassoon*. Copyright © 1918, 1920 by E. P. Dutton, copyright © 1936, 1946, 1947, 1948 by Siegfried Sassoon, by permission of The Barbara Levy Literary Agency on behalf of George Sassoon and Viking Penguin, a division of Penguin Group (USA) Inc.

Robert Service, for an extract from 'The Volunteer' from *The Rhymes of a Red-Cross Man*, Fisher Unwin (1916), by permission of the Estate of the author, c/o M Wm Krasilovsky, Agent, NY.

Philip Tomlinson, for an extract from 'To the Poets of 1940', *Times Literary Supplement*, 30 December 1939, by permission of the Times Literary Supplement.

John Williams, for material from *Twentieth-Century British Poetry: A critical Introduction*, Edward Arnold (1987), pp. 13, 27, 35, 65, by permission of Hodder Arnold.

Every effort has been made to trace the copyright holders but if any have been inadvertently overlooked the publishers will be pleased to make the necessary arrangement at the first opportunity.

Introduction

W hy should we want to read poetry about war? After a turbulent twentieth century marked by bloody conflict, affecting nations across the globe, is it strange – perverse, even – that there is a reading public still so preoccupied and fascinated by war poems? As we know, the new millennium shows every sign of continuing with a cycle of war, as hostilities both between and within nations erupt into military action. What, then, is the purpose of creating art out of a phenomenon that wields such terrible power; that has such destructive force? Does war poetry simply record the gruesome progress of the development, advance and cessation of wars throughout history? These questions have haunted many poets and anthologists in the very act of writing and collecting war poetry.

The business of war poetry has often seemed to be closely related to telling stories, and relating histories, of wars. At the beginning of the twentieth century, some of the most popular military or battle verse often gave colourful accounts of specific episodes or heroic figures, as in 'The Charge of the Light Brigade' (1854) by Alfred Lord Tennyson (1809–92) or 'A Ballad of Agincourt' (about 1605) by Michael Drayton (1563–1631). Both of these poets portrayed an image of conflict they had not themselves witnessed: before long, however, readers would be expecting their poets of war, or 'soldier-poets', to have come directly from the battlefield to the pen. The desire for a connection between war poetry and the 'real' experience of war is still very strong. Pick up a war poetry anthology in a bookshop or library, and you are likely to see book jackets illustrated with scenes of battle devastation, poems punctuated by images of poets in uniform or forewords by the veterans of war.

Is, then, war poetry simply about the experiences of fighting men? Despite the fame of particular soldier-poets, the answer to this is, in many senses, no: a huge amount of war poetry has been written by women from many walks of life, and much poetry has been written by individuals (both male and female) who were not necessarily in the thick of battle. Equally, war poetry is not always seen simply as personal suffering made into art: in several of the critical extracts in this Guide, the poetry poses direct questions about motivation, intent and fairness; that is to say, about the nature, morality and politics of war.

As the genre of war poetry has developed in relation to major histor-ical events, it is important to consider much of the essential criticism through a period perspective. The structure of the guide will not, however, be exclusively chronological.

In the first chapter there is an overview of the significance of the genre today, leading into some of the key themes and theoretical issues that can be traced through the Guide. The subsequent three chapters will navigate the reader around the genre in historical context, through a chapter each on the respective world wars, and a chapter on the key developments of the interwar years. The 1930s are discussed in some detail, as this was a period in which the war poetry canon was substantially modified and the association of poetry with war became even stronger. It was also a period in which expectations that war poets would deliver a particular kind of anti-war 'message' became more entrenched. In each of these three period-based chapters more recent criticism is woven in to put the development of the 'war poetry' concept in clearer perspective. The fifth chapter, starting from the end of the Second World War, surveys major critical developments and tendencies in relation to wider academic contexts and social and political debates.

In the course of this Guide, we will be considering not only critical texts that have emerged from academia and literary journalism, but poets' personal papers and memoirs and the editorial comments of anthologists. Part of the Guide's method, therefore, is to suggest to the reader that a fuller understanding of the war poetry genre can be gained from considering the views and ideas of poetic practitioners alongside those of career critics; another aspect of this method is to indicate how often the roles of poet and critic overlap. Throughout the Guide, the aim is to focus upon the developing idea of what 'war poetry' is, and what it signifies in a number of key historical settings, whilst reminding the reader of the extent to which these ideas have continued to be challenged and adapted.

Any glance through the current war poetry volumes available will demonstrate that the genre did not stop at the Second World War, and that the Vietnam, Korean, Falklands, Gulf and Balkan wars have all elicited their poetic responses. It would not be possible to cover these in sufficient depth in this book, as each needs to be viewed with some sensitivity to its specific socio-historical and political context. The Guide will therefore concentrate mainly on the two world wars on the basis that they are the most significant in shaping the genre, and are the focus of most of the available war poetry criticism. The aim of the Guide will be to equip readers with an understanding of key approaches, so that they can read further into the topic with a critical awareness of the development of the genre.

CHAPTER ONE

Navigating the Genre

LITERARY AND CULTURAL STATUS

War poetry is one of the most popular contemporary poetry genres and has generated a vast body of anthologies and critical texts. Today, the most minimal of poetry stocks in bookshops tend to include at least one or two war poetry anthologies, and there is an extensive choice of titles in print. Yet evidence of the sustained enthusiasm for war poetry goes well beyond that represented by the sale of popular anthologies.

The connections between poetry and war permeate many aspects of contemporary British culture. When a memorial service was held for British soldiers who died in action in the 2003 Iraq conflict, an excerpt from a poem formed one of the readings, and many subsequent media reports of the event used this part of the service for their sound clip.[1] The poem was 'For the Fallen', by Laurence Binyon (poet, art historian and dramatist, 1869–1943) which, having been first published in 1914, was 90 years old. The symbolic value and resonance of this poem is clearly still great; deriving as it does from a long association with consolatory and commemorative remembrance of the First World War. In British culture war poems, particularly of the First World War, are continually reactivated as symbols of bereavement, commemoration and patriotic pride; they are regularly reinvested with significance as cultural signs of respect for deaths in military conflict. The historian J. M. Winter writes in *The Experience of World War I* (1995):

■ One of the most extraordinary features of World War 1 was the extent to which it gave birth to a special literature of commemoration: a body of soldiers' and ex-soldiers' memoirs and fiction which has come to be termed 'war literature'.[2] □

As we will go on to see, however, many of the key terms in Winter's description beg further questions, and a more extensive analysis. For example, some of the war poetry celebrated today is by individuals who had never been soldiers, or who had been soldiers but had seen little or no combat, and later chapters in this Guide will look at the role and contribution of non-combatant poets to the genre in much more detail. Also relevant, however, is the oft-cited status of war poetry as 'special'.

If war poetry is 'special', is this intended to suggest that it is more special than other categories of poetry we might consider? Or does it rather suggest that it cannot be studied or evaluated on the same terms as other kinds of poetry? The idea of war poetry as bearing a peculiar relationship to history and the commemoration of wars has produced a range of difficult and, some would argue, anomalous judgments about poetic quality. The literary critics Dominic Hibberd, Bernard Bergonzi and Kelsey Thornton have all, for example, commented on the 1985 memorial to the poets of the First World War in Westminster Abbey.[3] As these critics all point out in their different ways, the memorial is a cautionary tale of the changing nature of cultural and literary evaluation and selection. In his essay, 'The Problem of War Poetry' (first delivered as the Byron Foundation Lecture for the University of Nottingham, 1990), Bergonzi writes:

> ■ Academic practices have, in fact, become fused with the national mythmaking that led, in 1985, to the unveiling of a monument to the poets of the First World War in Westminster Abbey. Dominic Hibberd has remarked, 'Imagine a monument there to the Metaphysical Poets or the Restoration Dramatists or the Victorian Industrial Novelists', adding that at least half of the sixteen poets commemorated are in his view distinctly second-rate.[4] □

Bergonzi, in his discussion of Hibberd, is highlighting the tendency of late twentieth-century critics and readers alike to reiterate the traditional rankings and honours accorded to war poets, without, perhaps, subjecting them to sufficient scrutiny. As we will see in the subsequent sections of this chapter, the idea of war poetry as a 'special' kind of literature arises from the close association that has developed between war poetry and ideas of history and personal experience, particularly in relation to the First World War.

In Westminster Abbey, then, the poets' names engraved upon the memorial stone of the Great War are: Richard Aldington (1892–1962); Laurence Binyon; Edmund Blunden (1896–1974); Rupert Brooke (1887–1915); Wilfrid Gibson (1878–1962); Robert Graves (1895–1985); Julian Grenfell (1888–1915); Ivor Gurney (1890–1937); David Jones (1895–1974); Robert Nichols (1893–1944); Wilfred Owen (1893–1918); Herbert Read (1893–1968); Isaac Rosenberg (1890–1918); Siegfied Sassoon (1886–1967); Charles Sorley (1895–1915) and Edward Thomas (1878–1917). Many of these names will appear later in the Guide and several of them are examined in some depth. It is worth reflecting, as you consider the discussions that follow, how these names came to be selected and in what sense they can be considered to constitute an adequate 'memorial' to the First World War poets as a whole. Is this list the result of a consensus among literary academics; a list with a specific representative agenda; or a reflection of popular taste? If such a memorial tablet were to be redesigned today, how might would it differ?

The relationship of war poetry and war poets to memorial culture is long established. Statues dedicated to the dead of the world wars, for example, frequently incorporate poetry quotations, as do Armistice Day events and memorial services. War poetry has seeped into other cultural forms, too. In 1991, the novelist Pat Barker (born 1943) published her novel *Regeneration*, followed by the two further, related novels, *The Eye in the Door* (1994) and *The Ghost Road* (1995). This trilogy, set in the First World War, featured imaginative projections of Siegfried Sassoon and Wilfred Owen, based on elements of biographical evidence about their wartime lives. In *Regeneration*, Barker concentrates in particular upon the period of time spent at the Craiglockhart War Hospital where the two poets met, using this as a means of exploring the nature of the psychological traumas of trench warfare on the Western Front, and disjunctions between public discourses, private relationships and poetic representations in wartime. A cinematic interpretation of the narrative, *Regeneration*, directed by Gillies Mackinnon, was released in 1997. The casting and styling of the poet-characters in this film bears a close relationship to the photographic images of Owen and Sassoon used in a number of poetry anthologies. As we will see later in this Guide, the interest in a small number of war poets as mythic, suffering-hero figures has been perpetuated through the selective use of text and image in anthologies and in critical studies.

Regeneration is, of course, an example of a retrospective analysis and re-construction of the significance of First World War poets from a late twentieth-century perspective. During the Second World War, film had become a popular mass form of entertainment and cinematic representations of the war were being produced and consumed during the conflict itself. As we will consider in Chapter Four of this Guide, a huge amount of war poetry was written in the Second World War, and one of the most popular and commercially successful of these poets, John Pudney (1909–77), was even commissioned by the RAF to produce a poem to mark its 25th anniversary. One of Pudney's poems, 'For Johnny', was also used in the film released in 1945, *The Way to the Stars*.[5] The subsequent profile of Second World War poetry has been far lower than that of the First, however; whilst a small number of specific poems are well known through frequent anthology appearances (for example, 'Lessons of the War' by Henry Reed (1914–86)), no Second World War figure equivalent to Brooke, Owen or Sassoon has taken hold in the popular imagination. The individuals who constitute the Second World

War poetic 'canon' in professional literary terms, and whom we will discuss later, are not widely known.

One of the major routes through which our contemporary ideas of war poetry have taken root in the last few decades of the twentieth century has been that of secondary education. Since the 1960s, as discussed in Chapter Five, teachers and anthologists have seen the war poetry genre as presenting an opportunity to engage young people's interest in issues of direct political and social relevance. Working in the practical criticism tradition developed by the Cambridge-based critics I. A. Richards (1893–1979), F. R. Leavis (1895–1978) and others, educationalists have tended to select poetic material that lends itself to detailed classroom discussion, where formal techniques can be identified and the representation of points of view about war debated. For many British citizens of the 'baby boom' generation (and subsequent generations), this is the first overt contact with a genre that has become deeply embedded in our culture. As we will consider in Chapter Five, the use of war poetry in education has been an important part of the process of genre development, leading to a liberal and anti-war emphasis in the selection and analysis of poems.

The unusual level of interest and affection in which war poetry is held even beyond compulsory education seems to derive partly from an idea that it offers a means of re-exploring history, of identifying previously obscured narratives or new perspectives upon well-established narratives. The Imperial War Museum, for example, holds a large collection of war poetry, including the Salamander Oasis Trust archive, which consists of thousands of poems (both published and unpublished) by ordinary servicemen and women of the Second World War.[6] War poetry is, in this way, often constructed as primarily historical and experiential through the acts of institutional collection and collation. For the many individuals who access the archive, war poetry is not simply about public history, however, but is profoundly implicated within traditions of personal and familial remembrance. These traditions are also still actively continued through the writing of retrospective war poetry, such as *The Invasion Handbook* (2002) by the poet and critic Tom Paulin (born 1949), and by the many non-professional poets who produce privately published collections.

WAR POETRY AND THE CANON

If, as we saw in the J. Winter quotation in the previous section, war poetry has a 'special' status as literature, we might imagine that its primary proponents would be firmly established within the poetic canon. By a poetic canon, we tend to mean a relatively small group of writers and texts judged to be of high status and superior quality by a consensus of literary opinion. This notion of a canon requires us to comply with an allied belief, that particular individuals are justified and qualified in offering such literary opinions. It requires us to accept that they are, on the whole, better able than others to judge literary quality due to the breadth and depth of their knowledge, and the sophistication of their critical skills. There is also often a sense that to be truly 'canonical', individual poets and poetic texts should sustain this good opinion over a long period of time. Yet, as we will see throughout this Guide, war poetry has had a fraught relationship to the canon, and many critics have contented themselves with devising, modifying and reproducing an implicitly distinct pantheon of war poets.

An important part of this discussion is the fact that the canon itself has become a notoriously problematic and contentious evaluative framework for academic English Studies over the last 20 to 30 years. During this period, developments in critical thinking began to relate evaluations of 'high' cultural products much more directly to questions of cultural, political and social inequality. For some critics and students of literature, a white, middle-class Western male perspective seemed to have dominated the development of the literary canon. The growth in cultural studies and in historically oriented literary studies led to a further questioning of both the processes and location of cultural authority: who has the right to judge what is best; and how can a group of socially and culturally privileged individuals act as arbiters of quality for others? How far do socially marginal voices, those without the same level of access to educational and publishing opportunities, achieve a fair trial in the courts of literary fame? It is not the intention here either to produce a new, definitive list of canonical war poetry or poets, or to argue against canonical thinking. Rather it is important to be aware, in reading the Guide, that these are fruitful questions. Most of the quotations selected for discussion in subsequent chapters are placed in historical and social context, so that you can make your own judgements about how taste and opinion about war poetry has been formed, articulated and changed.

War poetry, as has already been mentioned, tends not to be judged primarily in literary terms, and this further complicates its relationship to the already fraught notion of the canon. Many anthologists and critics write of war poetry in terms of its 'truth' to experience or its 'authentic' representation of the history and experience of war, particularly combat experience. This, as we will explore later in the Guide, can be a limiting, even circular approach to the genre. What type of 'experience' are we registering as 'real' or 'true', if we have not ourselves been in combat, let alone the combat of 60 or 90 years ago? Our understandings of the 'experience' we so often seek in war poetry derive from historical and biographical narratives, or, indeed, cinematic representations of war, yet we do not necessarily question or investigate the nature of these representations.

The fascination with 'experience', then, is deeply embedded within the genre and within other forms of representation of war in British culture; we will look at further implications of this in the subsequent sections in this chapter on representation and on biography. As a genre, war poetry has been both celebrated and despised for its supposed 'special' relationship to the gritty and bloody experience of battle, and this is a dichotomy we will also consider. Critics have used the idea of 'experience' in war poetry to formulate quite distinct views about individual poets, and the genre as a whole. Thus we see C(ecil) Day Lewis (1904–72),[7] in Chapter Three, elevating Owen, whom he describes as having been 'made a poet by the war', to the loftiest poetic heights. W. B. Yeats (1865–1939), by contrast, uses the centrality in Owen's work of war's 'pity' as a reason for omitting him from the 1936 *The Oxford Book of Modern Verse 1892–1935*.[8]

Having recognized these various theoretical and methodological problems, therefore, the Guide will not only consider how and why certain individuals and poems have been selected for canonical treatment, but will also discuss some of the ways in which the war poetry genre as a whole has been positioned within, at the margins of, or even outside the poetry canon. This positioning will be evident from a range of texts, including many different types of anthology and specialist war poetry study, and critical surveys of twentieth-century poetry. As the field of literature available is so substantial, the reader is liable to find further examples with which to compare, extend or contest the analysis in this Guide.

In John Williams's chronological survey, *Twentieth-Century British Poetry* (1987), to take one initial example, war poetry is first dealt with in a chapter entitled 'Modernism 1900–1930'. As the chapter title shows, the emphasis is on the influence of the radical formal experiments and self-conscious aestheticism that have come to be associated in particular with Modernist poets such as Ezra Pound (1885–1972) and T. S. Eliot (1888–1965).[9] The earliest moves towards what we now call Modernism were, according to Williams, interrupted by the 1914–18 conflict:

■ The course of events [that is, the development of literary Modernism] was undoubtedly influenced by the First World War, which was responsible for creating a situation where the persisting class distinctions within British society were subjected to a uniquely close scrutiny. Distrust and suspicion of those traditionally in positions of power was confirmed by the wartime image of the bungling statesman and the incompetent or callous General who kept well clear of the trenches. At the front it became possible for those of both high and low estate to experience a situation where peacetime class consciousness was replaced by the practical distinction between those who fought and those who stayed at home. This temporary realignment of allegiance was widely enough experienced to ensure that it would never be possible to return to anything like the situation as it was before the war, though it was by no means radical enough to initiate revolutionary changes in the social structure.[10] □

Williams describes the First World War as, in a sense, causing a rupture in the pre-war cultural landscape. The war, he suggests, largely supplanted awareness of class distinctions with the newly urgent issue of whether one was a combatant or non-combatant. Whilst the precursor of Modernism, Imagism (discussed further in Chapter One), continued to influence poetry, it was modified during the war into a hybrid form through the conjunction with 'Georgian sensibilities', including the nostalgic longing for an English rural past.[11] The war, as Williams goes on to write, was 'undoubtedly responsible for a major disruption of continuity in the development of poetry'.[12] For many critics, it was only after the 'disruption' of the First World War that Modernism developed fully, and by the Second World War it was on the wane.

What does it mean, then, for war poetry to be framed as having 'disrupted' the progress of a literary Modernism? Williams certainly indicates, through his analysis of work by a number of specific poets (Aldington, Owen, Sassoon and Rosenberg) that, despite faults and problems, some First World War poetry has been established as of the first rank. Yet the issue of the special or different status of war poetry persists in his analysis. Discussing poetry of the Second World War, in the chapter 'Post-Modernist Poetry 1930–1950', Williams writes:

■ Despite the fact that in 1939, by way of contrast to 1914, the whole nation found itself potentially on the firing line, the effect on poets was to some extent comparable with 1914–18. The existence of a single, dominating event brought together and tended to remould the variety of styles and schools that had developed between the wars. There is also the fact that the First World War naturally offered itself as a model of how 'war poetry' might be written. One crucial difference was the emergence of a common, widely understood 'cause' to be fought for in 1939. The effect of both world wars in the twentieth century was to create a sense of a temporary but profound disruption if not cessation of the accepted moral and social order.[13] □

Williams portrays poetry, in both world wars, as having broken the chain of pre-war developments, 'remoulding' the styles and approaches of existing schools: there is a sense that the poetry produced in the conditions of war cannot quite be like, or perhaps, cannot quite be compared with, peacetime poetry. We will see other versions of this type of thinking later in the Guide, in which war is positioned as a period of literary history to be kept in brackets, slightly apart.

In discussions of the relative standing of the poetry of the two world wars, Second World War poetry has sometimes been judged the poorer, being characterized as a period of romantic excess; an inexplicable and unattractive detour in British poetry. It is perhaps partly for this reason that 1945, the end of the war, rather than 1939, is so often used to iden-tify the starting point for anthologies and literary studies. For many other critics, however, the significance of literary development in the Second World War has been conceptualized quite differently. In *Modernism in the Second World War: the Later Poetry of Ezra Pound, T. S. Eliot, Basil Bunting and Hugh MacDiarmid* (1989), for example, K. Alldritt argues that Modernist approaches continued to develop throughout the Second World War, using the four eponymous poets as the key instances.

As we will see in Chapter Five, following the substantial growth of interest in both world wars in the 1960s and 1970s, critics and antholo-gists with specialist war poetry interests developed a range of alternative perspectives. Increasingly, critics of the Second World War argued for it to be understood as offering a wealth of literary innovation and a poetry in which many voices and troubled and fragmentary identities are explored. As Adam Piette argues, for example, in *Imagination at War: British Fiction and Poetry 1939–1945* (1995), there are many contrasts and faultlines to be investigated between the public narratives of the war, and the private recollections and testimony of individuals. The record of what Piette refers to as 'the private imagination' has been 'skewed', he writes, by factors such as:

■ ... the mechanical way in which Alun Lewis [1915–44], Sidney Keyes [1922–43] and Keith Douglas [1920–44] have been canonized and dubbed the only war poets, thereby obscuring not only the witness of those who felt differently, but also the very witness of the three poets themselves.[14] □

What Piette suggests here is that Second World War poetry critics have conceded to a perceived pressure to supply canonical figures who echo Brooke, Sassoon and Owen. As we can see from this observation, whilst the construction of a set of canonical poets is one of the important ways through which a genre can gain in stature and renown, it can also risk 'skewing' or over-simplifying the full complexity of a field of literature. These are themes that will be returned to regularly, as we examine the different periods in which the war poetry genre developed.

REPRESENTING WARS

In this Guide, we will consider the development of the war poetry genre in the twentieth century primarily in relation to the two world wars. Both wars continue today to generate a vast quantity of academic inquiry, documentary investigations and fictional reconstructions (in poetry, prose, film and drama). Overall, it is the poetry of these wars that has continued to attract the majority of literary critical attention, both through single-war studies and, in smaller number, comparative studies of the poetry of each war. It is also the case that the poetry of the two world wars has stimulated the most popular interest, and we will explore examples of this throughout the chapter.

In the subsequent chapters of this Guide, we examine contemporary attitudes to the poetry of war during the conflicts themselves, and investigate how readers, anthologists and critics have developed a range of retrospective understandings of war poetry from the standpoint of years or decades later. War poetry tends to be (although is not always) stimulated by a particular war: to this extent we need an awareness of some of the key historical determining forces, intellectual debates and literary conventions and influences at play in the poet's contemporary environment.

In Chapter One, for example, we note the gradual genesis of the terms 'war poetry' and 'soldier poetry' during the 1914–18 war. We also consider some of the critical pamphlets produced at the time that discussed war poetry in terms different to those that predominate today. One of these, *Poetry in the Light of War* (1917) by Caroline Spurgeon (1886–1942), discusses war as a phenomenon that reinforces the intrinsic worth of poetry as an art form: the more modern notion that poetry should incorporate issues or observations of the war from a distinct moral position is not apparent here.[15] By Chapter Four, however, the conceptual distance travelled becomes very clear: the categories of 'war poetry' and 'war poet' are extremely well known and much debated having become, in the interwar years, closely associated with a certain type of poetry and poet of the First World War. Yet, whilst it can be seen from contemporary sources of the 1940s that 'war poetry' had become a recognizable literary category, it was still a highly contested one. Many of the Second World War poets keen to represent ideas about the philosophy, ideology and experience of war were just as keen not to be pigeonholed as 'war poets' for fear of being judged by comparison with Owen and others.

We have already touched upon the idea, at the beginning of this chapter, that war poetry has gradually become constructed as one of the means through which personal war experiences and familial and national histories of war can be accessed and even imaginatively re-experienced. This construction is sometimes based upon a simple, referential understanding of war poetry as reflecting an external historical reality: according to this thinking, representations of war in poetry are seen as uncontestable and authentic. Some anthologies and critical studies of war poetry have also taken a similar view through the privileging of 'realist' war poetry: this is discussed as 'truly' reflecting war experience, perhaps because the conventions and tropes of poetic realism bear a resemblance to prosaic representations of war in history, memoir and journalism. War poetry has also frequently been presented as a natural and inevitable companion to war and in Chapter Five there are examples of post-war anthologists such as Richard Eberhart and Selden Rodman who, in *War and the Poet: an Anthology of Poetry Expressing Man's Attitudes to War From Ancient Times to the Present* (1945), comment: 'The fact that men have written in all ages on war is as natural as that they have written on love, or death.'[16] Similarly, Catherine Reilly introduces her *English Poetry of the Second World War: A Biobibliography* (1986) with the observation: 'War, like love, is a constant theme in poetry.'[17]

As we will see later in this Guide, the view that war and war poetry are, in a sense, naturally occurring phenomena has been incorporated into a range of different cultural–political positions. For example, some critics present it as natural that war poetry should reflect or represent pride in one's nation, others as 'natural' that war poetry should display the pity or horror of armed conflict.

Other critics and poets have discussed war poetry not as authentic and natural but as a highly mediated and coded form of literary representation, in which images of war are selective and explicitly constructed. The emphasis on the consciousness (or self-consciousness) of the poetic act has not only referred to the way in which particular observations, perceptions and beliefs about war are formulated and represented, but also to how these are placed in relation to other poems and to deeper underlying cultural myths and stories. This can be seen, for example, in Chapter Three where T. S. Eliot makes the following point in his 1963 introduction to *In Parenthesis* (1937) by the poet and artist David Jones (1895–1974):

■ Here is a book about the experiences of one soldier in the War of 1914–18. It is also a book about War, and about many other things also, such as Roman Britain, the Arthurian Legend, and diverse matters which are given association by the mind of the writer. And as for the writer himself, he is a Londoner of Welsh and English descent. He is decidedly a Briton. He is also a Roman Catholic, and he is a painter who has painted some beautiful pictures and designed some beautiful lettering. All these facts about him are important. Some of them appear in his own Preface to the book; some the reader may discover in the course of reading.[18] □

Here Eliot emphasizes the 'writerly' complexity of Jones's text, the aesthetic sophistication, the layers of mythic association and historical allusion which result from the connections of the poet's consciousness, and which 'may' (or may not) be discovered by the reader. Whilst Eliot, too, emphasizes the need to relate to 'experience' later in this piece, there is a distinct sense that such experience needs to be understood through reference to the ancient, as well as the recent past, and to myth as well as memory.

The notion that war poetry reflects history or portrays an individual's original and authentic war experience leads us to a further area for discussion. In the first section of this chapter we began to note how the world wars are marked out by quite distinct traditions. These can be sketched in very rudimentary terms: with the First World War, there is often an emphasis placed on the initial idealism and innocence of the volunteers, the shock of combat conditions, the gradual bitter awareness of military bungling and the unimagined scale of losses; the archetypal figure in this scenario is the mud-bound trench soldier. In the Second World War, there is often a fundamental acceptance of the necessity for war, and a desire to celebrate the stoicism and heroism of the ordinary soldier or citizen. These, of course, are very broad frameworks and there are a good number of alternative representations and revisionist readings of the wars that work against the grain. In Chapter Five we will consider some important critical analyses that explore how memories and myths about wars are constructed and articulated in literary form.

Throughout the Guide, and in relation to several different periods in the twentieth century, we will be considering the relationship between established conceptions of war poetry and the challenges regularly made to such orthodoxies. Again, the aim of this Guide is not to discredit any particular approach but to raise questions in the reader's mind. In an article by Tim Kendall in *PN Review* (September–October 2003), ' "The Pity of War"?', for example, Kendall shows how the Second World War poet Keith Douglas was both highly aware of, and influenced by, the poetic models that had gone before him, and how he was determined to avoid any simple repetition of them.[19] Whilst Douglas identified the experience of battle as central to war, thus fulfilling one of the most fundamental existing requirements of the war poet, he was at the same time resolved to avoid some of the most famous moral and emotional responses of the poets of the Western Front. In particular, Kendall writes, Douglas did not wish to repeat the famous compassionate tone of Owen:

■ When Douglas admits to a reaction characteristic of Owen, as he does on one occasion in *Alamein to Zem Zem* [1946] looking at a soldier's corpse, he says that the scene filled him 'with useless pity' – a description which conveys the passivity of pity and raises awkward questions for Owen and his armchair descendants: what exactly are the uses of pity? Who benefits from it? According to Freud, the chief beneficiary is the pitier: pity constitutes a 'reaction-formation' against the sadistic drive, disguising, in a more amenable form, the pleasure we derive from the sufferings of others. Douglas refuses to saccharine his responses in this way: 'We see him almost with content,' he writes in '*Vergissmeinnicht*', as he examines the corpse of a three-week-dead German soldier.[20] ☐

Kendall points out here that Douglas attempted to exert a conscious degree of control over the type of First World War influences that might emerge in his work. As this quotation suggests, Owenesque pity was clearly seen by many of Douglas's contemporaries as central to representation of First World War suffering. Douglas, however, resisted this in the interests of exploring the far less palatable and socially acceptable emotion of cold curiosity. Many other examples of continuity and change in poetic approaches to war will be found throughout the Guide.

But what, then, of other major conflicts of the twentieth century: the Spanish Civil War, for example, or the Vietnam War? Both wars had a substantial impact upon public opinion in Britain, and certainly influenced literary and political thinking. In Chapter Three, we will consider British poets who volunteered to fight in Spain, mainly for the Republican cause, and whose poetry often aimed to sustain and perpetuate the belief-systems that had caused them to fight; in Chapter Five, the Vietnam War is discussed as a factor in the critical shift towards anti-war readings of war poetry. Yet neither of these wars absorbed British society as totally as the world wars, nor was perceived to have threatened the basis of 'civilized' British life in the way that the two world wars were. Furthermore, and perhaps more problematically, both wars tend to be perceived as ideological in a way quite different to the First and Second World War. As we will see in more detail in Chapter Three, the poetry produced during the Spanish Civil War was viewed by many critics as overly weighted by specific political standpoints, triggering debates about the compatibility between ideology, poetic form and aesthetic pleasure.

THE BIOGRAPHICAL

For many years, there has been a fascination with the figure of the war poet, and much interest in war poetry is expressed through the selection and investigation of the lives, attitudes and experiences of particular poets. A number of organizations have been established that aim to appreciate and promote the life and work of war poets: the Wilfred Owen Association, the Edward Thomas Fellowship and the Ivor Gurney

Society to name but a few. Among the large body of war poetry studies that has accumulated, there is also a substantial number of biographies, autobiographies and memoirs of individual poets. Indeed, one of the first texts of the post-1945 period to take First World War poetry as a subject for serious, book-length scholarly study was Dennis Welland's *Wilfred Owen: A Critical Study* in 1960.[21]

Since the expansion of academic interest in war poetry in the 1960s and 1970s, many critics and scholars works have drawn on poets' biographies to focus, frame or fundamentally inform their work in a variety of ways. The influential study of First World War poetry *Out of Battle* (1972) by the poet and critic Jon Silkin (1930–97) is structured through a series of analyses of individual poets and their writings, and most of the poets are introduced with basic biographical information.[22] This tends to include the dates they joined up, their military role and their attitudes to war, usually gleaned from personal letters and memoirs. Writing of Charles Sorley, for example, Silkin quotes a letter from Sorley that describes a deep ambivalence about the war's 'cause' and his allegiance to middle-class England, and makes these comments upon the letter:

■ This is a courageous expression of some of the pressures under which he enlisted, although it disposes of any patriotic reasons to which his enlisting may at the time have been attributed. What Sorley is committed to is a scrupulous honesty.[23] □

In this way, Silkin uses biographical materials to produce a working assumption about Sorley that he then applies to Sorley's poetic method. By implication, readers are also being encouraged to approach his work in this spirit: to treat it as a scrupulously honest attempt to represent his attitudes, perceptions and experience. In relation to several other poets, too, Silkin draws together strands of information, motivation, belief and outlook from personal papers in building a critical framework to analyse war poetry.

The type of biographical approach exemplified by Silkin also involves readings made by other critics, however, and establishes connections between a poet's personal experience or attitudes and their social and cultural contexts. Thus, when discussing the specific tone used by Edmund Blunden towards nature in his war poems, he elaborates his point with reference to the impact of increasing urbanization. He extends this further with reference to the poetry collection *Death of a Naturalist* by Seamus Heaney (born 1939):

■ Seamus Heaney's *Death of a Naturalist* (1966), makes precisely the right point in that, whereas his father's generation was connected with the land because they farmed it, he has a naturalist's concern; he is an observer of, and perhaps an inquirer into, nature, but he does not depend on it for his livelihood. His connection with it is less intimate. Blunden's difficulty as a poet, inasmuch as he is a poet of nature or uses nature as the propulsion for his feelings, lies precisely here. And this may provide an even more profound reason for the literary quality in some of his perceptions of nature. The difficulty works in two directions. It is not merely *his* connection that is not vital, as a farmer's is. The audience he could count on to read his poetry was also either urban or composed mainly of people who had a 'naturalist's' connection with nature.[24] ☐

In this piece of commentary Silkin is still using a biographical focus, yet drawing out many connections from contemporary and historical sources and showing how these potentially affect readings of Blunden's poetry. This is useful not only in pointing to the changing social patterns during the period in which Blunden was writing, but also in exposing the complexities involved in referring to a poet's use of 'nature'. We will consider the uses of nature and the pastoral tradition in war poetry further in subsequent chapters.

For Linda Shires, too, in *British Poetry of the Second World War* (1985), biographical details are interwoven with critical commentary and analysis of the work of individual poets. Discussing the changes in the poetry of Dylan Thomas (1914–53) brought on by the advent of the war, Shires writes:

■ In autumn 1940 Thomas moved from Laugharne [in Wales] to London and began a job with Strand Films. During this time he also wrote scripts for the BBC. The war did not find its way into the foreground of Thomas's poems. Shocked and amazed by it, he was especially moved by a film assignment concerning bombing raids. That horror remained engraved in his mind. According to G. S. Fraser [1915–80] and Stephen Spender [1909–1995],[25] war helped Thomas' poetry by giving him a theme without harmfully altering his imagery. Providing background for several of his most magnificent poems, including 'A Refusal to Mourn the Death, By Fire, of a Child in London', war did seem to steady the groundings in reality Thomas had already made.[26] ☐

As this excerpt shows, Shires examines the poetry written during the war years and compares it with Thomas's pre-war styles and themes. The war, Shires comments, provided 'background' for some of Thomas's best poems along with a sense of horror that was firmly fixed in his mind. As the work of Silkin and others also demonstrates, there is a sense in which this kind of critical commentary is directed towards the biographical image of the poet as well as the poetry itself. Indeed it is possible to see that in some cases, critical readings of war poetry are deployed as evidence for the character or beliefs of the poet; that is to say, they are used to draw conclusions about a poet's 'psychology'.

The interest in individual war poets has been evident in discussions and anthologies of war poetry throughout the twentieth century. Later in this Guide we will look, for example, at the First World War, considering how the initial interest generated by established, mainly non-combatant poets with consciously propagandist agendas began to transfer to 'soldier poets'. During this period, Rupert Brooke was constructed as the archetypal aesthetic warrior figure, lauded for his personal beauty, poetic creativity and apparent eagerness for the patriotic fray. The fame accorded to individual war poets, based as it often is on particular biographical constructions, has a tendency to fluctuate with changes in perceptions of war and literary tastes. As we will note in Chapter Three, the late 1920s and early 1930s saw a particularly marked shift in attitudes to war, resulting in a favouring of more compassionate poet-figures. New research and scholarship can also stimulate revisions of the reputations of individual poets: the First World War poets Isaac Rosenberg and Ivor Gurney both became better known long after the war had concluded, for this reason.

As the example of Brooke suggests, however, the use of biography as a primary means for interpreting war poetry raises several theoretical issues. Brooke's early image as a martyred hero belied his lack of combat experience in the First World War, as we will see later in this chapter, and the continued biographical interest in this poet has transformed the original idea of the 'golden-haired Apollo' into a much more unconventional, complicated, satirically minded and often inconsistent figure.[27] The important general point is that, whilst biographical contexts can be extremely interesting and illuminating, the biographical narratives upon which reputations and literary judgements are built can also be partial, misleading or simply highly selective. Biography needs, therefore, to be scrutinized and interrogated rather than treated as an external, uncontestable reality against which to measure or interpret the poetry.

Equally, it is possible to see that there are problems in overemphasizing particular types of poetic lives and creating stock biographical structures that we expect to see repeated. Arguably, the enthusiasm for the 'stories', personal suffering and poetry of individuals such as Brooke and Owen has been partly responsible for the common assumption, still very much evident today, that war poetry is the business of male combatants. We can see that some studies of the poetry of the Second World War are preoccupied with identifying analogous poetic figures to those of the First World War, or perhaps failing to take into account the long-range view, the civilian perspective or retrospective poetic accounts of war. Women poets, in particular, have often been excluded on this basis, resulting in more recent efforts to bring them out from the margins of the war poetry genre.

SELECTIVITY, PACKAGING AND PUBLICATION

When we read a war poem, we do not tend to encounter it as an isolated piece of text. More often than not, we are reading it within a collection of poetry, perhaps a generic anthology of English verse or a volume of war poetry (of which, as already noted, there is a wide variety). Does this context make any difference to our assumptions about the poem, or the sense we make of it?

The term anthology derives from the Greek '*anthos*', flower and '*-logia*', collection. On one level, therefore, the anthology can be understood as a gathering together of choice poems, the best of a particular genre or the best according to the anthologist's personal taste. In order to produce an anthology, the poetry has to be selected from the vast number of texts in circulation, organized into a particular running order and placed within an overall structure or framework. Frameworks vary enormously, from the simple logic of chronological or alphabetical order to the genre-oriented or thematic approach. The juxtaposition of poems, the construction of the overall text and the presentation of a rationale for the collection are carried out by an anthologist or editor, and such anthologists or editors are quite often poets or publishers themselves.

Editors and publishers are often influenced by ideas about poetic form, function and value, but also by the prospect of an anthology's commercial success. The publisher of a new anthology has to consider the marketability of a particular theme or genre and how best to present the anthology to ensure it sells as well as possible. In many ways, therefore, anthologies are highly mediated texts: they have a dimension of literary and cultural significance that is more than simply the sum of the poems included. Anthologies can, for example, offer useful insights into the poetic experiments and preoccupations of a particular era, or indicate some of the ways in which poetry represents, or emerges from, specific socio-historical and cultural conditions. This Guide treats the whole anthology as a text for analysis: where appropriate and helpful, we will be considering how anthologists have both responded and contributed to critical debates through their approach to selecting and presenting war poetry, and what this might suggest to us about the significance and value of the genre at different points in the twentieth century.

As we noted at the beginning of this chapter, war poetry is one of the more popular poetry genres. It was recently possible to find, for example, in Marks and Spencer's, a pocket-sized volume entitled *The Little Book of War Poems* (2001), edited by Nick de Somogyi, on a stand along with confectionary and other last-minute purchase items.[28] The volume is made with good quality paper, using a decorative typeface and the emblematic red poppy symbol on the book jacket. It appears to be designed for the gift market, and covers centuries of poetry, from Ovid

(43 BC–AD 18) to Thomas Hardy (1840–1928), with the emphasis on pre-twentieth-century work. The introduction points out:

> ■ The war poems in this collection are organized into five sections, like the five acts of a classical tragedy. Each section is named after a military command, in honor of the many poets included here who themselves saw active service. The following pages advance from the onset of war ('Forward March'), via the eve of battle ('Who Goes There?'), to the catastrophe of the Front Line ('Charge!'); then return, with the veterans, to the fears and uncertainties of the Home Front ('Stand at Ease'); and close at last in the aftermath of remembrance ('Fall Out').[29] □

Here, Somogyi refers both to the classical idea of tragedy, with its associations of nobility, and a selection of military commands as a means of structuring his anthology, so that each anthology section represents a distinct and predictable phase or stage of war. Within this scheme, military service is presented as courageous despite, or perhaps even because of the likelihood of 'catastrophe' ensuing. Interestingly, the references to front line disasters and the use of the poppy book jacket design both provoke distinctive associations with the First World War. Although the anthology includes poetry addressing many different conflicts, it displays, as do many other volumes, the extent to which the narratives, symbols and poets of the First World War have come to set the terms of reference for the genre.

The passage quoted from Somogyi's introduction is also influenced by myths of soldierly survival against the odds. The 'Charge!' section of the anthology, we are told, deals with 'the catastrophe of the Front Line', yet this is closely followed by a 'return' home. Whilst many of the poems in the anthology consider the significance of battle deaths, therefore, the underlying narrative of the anthology offers the more consolatory, if questionable, impression that the distress of battle is followed quite naturally by a return to the home front and the recuperations suggested by 'Stand at Ease'. As Somogyi writes:

> ■ Aristotle considered that Tragedy cleanses our spirits by the emotions it evokes in us of pity and fear. Many of the poems that follow may act in a similar way, and (in Donne's words) 'breed a just true fear' in us, 'a mingled sense' (in Wordsworth's) 'Of fear and sorrow'.[30] □

Somogyi proposes that readers progress through a ritualized acknowledgement of the horrors of war; he suggests to readers of his anthology that they may achieve a type of catharsis (a purgation of emotions) through the poetry.

Somogyi's introduction, in the context of the book's design and packaging, clearly pays court to the idea of a soldier's courage. Other recent anthologies have foregrounded war poetry far more overtly as a means through which soldierly values are acknowledged and honoured by society. In *The Happy Warrior: An Anthology of Australian and New Zealand Military Poetry* (2001), for example, edited by Paul Barrett, Warrant Officer Class 2, and Kerry B. Collison, the packaging of the book makes the military historical agenda prominent. A romantic, soft-focus, sepia-toned photograph of an Australian soldier is again bordered with the design of the red poppy, and a gold star on the rear of the book jacket announces that there is a foreword by Lieutenant General Peter Cosgrove. Barrett and Collison's anthology incorporates a body of work by, as they put it, individuals who are not professional or established poets:

> ■ The people within these pages represent the thousands who have given of themselves so generously towards Australia's heritage, our traditions and our hope for the future. So this anthology is of a special kind, with a special purpose. It is partly to entertain. It is also partly to provide insight into the minds and hearts of soldiers, sailors and airmen and women who have served or are still serving their country, thus to reach those little aware of their effort and sacrifice.[31] □

One of the purposes of the anthology, the editors continue, is not only to respect and understand the efforts of military personnel in a range of conflicts, but also to raise money for ex-servicemen and women. Among the critical comments quoted on the book jacket is one by Rod Moran, Literary Editor of *The West Australian*. This observation reinforces the role of the poetry in locating the excluded or marginalized voices of ordinary soldiers in history, a theme we will take up again in the course of this Guide: '*The Happy Warrior* is an important work of historical retrieval. The volume returns to these long forgotten rank-and-file bards both their voice and their moral stature in our folk literature.'[32] Despite the explicit way in which Barrett and Collison frame the anthology as one of Australian and New Zealand experience, the volume is prefaced with the British poet Laurence Binyon's 'For the Fallen' – the same poem that, as we saw at the start of this chapter, provided an excerpt for the 2003 Iraq memorial service for British soldiers – and takes its title from 'Character of the Happy Warrior' by the major British Romantic poet William Wordsworth (1770–1850). To the 'uplifting message' of this much older work of English poetry, the editors note, Australians add their own 'unique character'.

In *A Happy Warrior* the poems themselves are arranged into sections according to themes designed to reflect not only the major wars, but also a cross-section of military roles and sensibilities about war. A very different approach to structure is evident in the anthology *101 Poems*

Against War, edited by Matthew Hollis and Paul Keegan (2003).[33] Here, there is no explicit organizational framework: an ancient poem in translation is followed by a nineteenth-century American work; Yeats's First World War poem, 'An Irish Airman Foresees His Death' is juxtaposed with the contemporary poem 'Phrase Book' by Jo Shapcott (born 1958). There is, therefore, a lack of grouping or phasing to guide the reader through historical periods, national boundaries or different attitudes to conflict. Some of the conjunctions between poems offer surprising links and connections in the approaches to anti-war thinking; yet there is also the possibility, for the reader who progresses steadily through the book, that the impact is accumulative, pointing to the persistence and cyclical nature of war. This is, perhaps, one of the strategic difficulties faced by anthologists of the modern anti-war tendency: how can the anti-war outlook be squared with the apparently relentless cycle of violence and conflict?

As we have considered in this chapter, war poetry has moved far beyond the bounds of most poetry genres, to take up a place in British cultural memory and in the various histories – both public and private – of wars. It has also been, at times, both written and used as a political and ideological tool, and in Chapters Two and Three we will consider in more detail the question of how war poetry has been used as propaganda. In the subsequent three chapters of this Guide, we will be picking up many of the questions and themes raised in this chapter, and applying them to both the world wars and the interwar period. In Chapter Five, the emphasis shifts slightly, as we consider some of the critical approaches to the retrospective interpretation of world war poetry that have been developed over the last 50 years.

CHAPTER TWO

The First World War

INTRODUCTION

Of all wars, it is still the First World War that dominates the imagination of twenty-first-century readers, when contemplating the war poetry genre. It is often represented as a war of dramatic and emotive images: the extreme youth of soldiers; the mass-volunteering; the hopeful, passionate language of those who believed the war was morally right and necessary; the almost unimaginable level of slaughter during the years of trench warfare. After almost a hundred years, the war is still a subject of intense interest, not only in terms of its place in British history or as the symbolic entry into modernity, but also in terms of familial memory and collective consciousness. Many still research their forebears' regimental history during the war or visit war graves, and through the marking of Armistice Day and the common practice of wearing red poppies in remembrance of the fallen, members of third or fourth post-war generations show the continued traces of the war in our present.

Poetry of the First World War has a significant part to play in the way the war itself is understood and remembered. In one of the most popular collections of First World War verse, *Up the Line to Death: The War Poets 1914–1918*, edited by Brian Gardner and first printed in 1964, the section headings describe the progress of the war.[1] These begin by suggesting the idea of patriotic enthusiasm, 'Happy is England Now', continue with the soldiers' assimilation of combat conditions, 'To Unknown Lands' and 'Death's Kingdom', and conclude with the realization of the horror of war: 'O Jesus, Make it Stop.' This depiction of innocence betrayed is a familiar narrative to many of us who read war poetry in the British state school system, where the ideas of protest poetry and the 'pity of war' have formed the backbone of the study of war poetry.

In this chapter, we will be exploring and questioning how far this 'innocence betrayed' narrative helps us understand the war poetry of 1914–18. We will be moving from the analyses of post-1945 critics back to the accounts of First World War contemporaries, and considering the poetry in a selection of intellectual and historical contexts. We will discuss issues such as: Did 'war poetry' exist in the First World War in the way we understand it today? What made different poets so passionate about their pro-war, or anti-war views? What did the war poets think of each other's work? Through these and other discussions we will begin to open up the complexity and variety of poetry about war as it developed during the 1914–18 conflict.

LITERARY CONTEXT

THE WAR POETRY TRADITION

Associations of war poetry with the First World War have become so deeply embedded in late twentieth-century British culture and popular imagination that it would be easy to assume that the genre was born, fully formed, from the conflict of 1914–18. Indeed, many critics and poets have argued that it was only during this conflict that 'war poetry' emerged in its modern sense, as poetry that expresses a protest against war.

In an afterword for *101 Poems Against War* (also published as an article in the *Financial Times*, 15/16 February 2003) the current Poet Laureate, Andrew Motion (born 1952), argues that it was in the First World War that a 'fundamental' change was brought about:

■ Towards the end of the First World War, amid the squalor and tragedy of the Western Front, something fundamental changed. Wilfred Owen, Siegfried Sassoon, Ivor Gurney and Isaac Rosenberg – along with less famous others – began writing in ways which not only questioned the purpose of war, but also challenged previous poetic orthodoxies. The patriotic imperative 'Dulce Et Decorum Est' became 'that old lie', and in the process our sense of 'a war poet' was transformed. ['Dulce Et Decorum Est' is from the *Odes* (Book 3, no.2, line 13) of the ancient Roman poet Horace (65–8 BC). 'Dulce et decorum est pro patria mori' means 'It is sweet and fitting to die for your country']. 'This book', Wilfred Owen wrote about the collection of his poems that he did not live to see published, '[is not] about deeds, or lands, nor anything about glory, honour, might, majesty, dominion or power'. Its subject was 'War, and the pity of War'. It was still possible to celebrate individual acts of courage and to commemorate losses, but not to glorify conflict as such.[2] □

Throughout subsequent wars, Motion argues, we have been able to:

■ ... guess what attitude poets will take to a conflict before we read a line they write about it. Which in turn suggests their poems will be confirmations rather than surprises. Yet in these modern war poems we continue to feel surprised, let alone shocked and appalled. This is because the best war poets react to their experience of war, rather than simply acting in response to its pressures.[3] □

In these extracts, Motion is arguing that the First World War brought about a radical and long-lasting change in the ideological position from which poets would view and represent war. Before 1914, war poets 'wrote about war as they did about any other subject – from a variety of angles, and with a wide range of attitudes'. After the war it was no longer possible, he suggests, for poets to 'glorify conflict'.[4]

As we will discuss in depth in later chapters, many subsequent war poets were deeply influenced by the poetic examples of the First World War, and particularly by the liberal humanist emphasis on the 'pity of war' exemplified by Wilfred Owen. Other recent critics, too, have represented the genesis and development of the war poetry genre in the way described by Motion, seeing the First World War as a watershed beyond which all war poets assumed a critical stance. Yet for at least a decade after the war, celebratory and idealistic First World War poetry continued to be published and widely read. New expressions of highly politicized military enthusiasm were explored in the Spanish Civil War, and in the Second World War it is possible to see a continuation, in modified forms, of pride in militarism and affirmation of the patriotic wartime spirit. Whilst the angry or empathic 'protest' poems by First World War poets such as Siegfried Sassoon, Isaac Rosenberg, Wilfred Owen and others have often been to the fore in school literature curricula, popular anthologies of war poetry reserve ample space for the enthusiastic volunteer poetry of Rupert Brooke or the battle-lust of Julian Grenfell. The poetic voices which express the honour of sacrificing one's life for one's country continue to be selected by editors and anthologists, and are still part of the representative tradition of the First World War.

What Motion usefully foregrounds in his article is the realist and humanist momentum of the genre over the course of the twentieth century. As we will see in Chapter Five, by the late twentieth century war poetry tends to be viewed as a literary category in which the personal and social cost of war is registered, given especial significance through the poet's wartime experiences, and offered as testimony, warning and commemoration to the poetry-reading public. Not all critics view the First World War as producing the modern understanding of the 'war poetry' genre, however. Other late twentieth-century anthologists, poets and critics, whilst sharing aspects of Motion's general outlook on the social and cultural value of the genre, have argued that war poetry emerges from, and is profoundly interconnected with, a much longer literary tradition.

One of these is the poet Jon Silkin in his influential 1972 critical study *Out of Battle: The Poetry of the Great War* which has already been quoted in Chapter One. In this study, Silkin looks at the relationships between some of the First World War poets and Thomas Hardy, Alfred Lord Tennyson, William Wordsworth and Samuel Taylor Coleridge (1772–1834):

■ I shall suggest that some of the forces which developed in the nine-teenth century emerged in the First World War and influenced the poets. ... I shall read their poems partly by evaluating those forces of which the war itself was a product. In so far as I can evaluate the poems, I will sometimes prefer those which seem to emerge from the generalized consciousness of their period and change or modify the prevailing attitudes. Modifying those attitudes, such poems modify ours, and in such a way as to dislodge the idea that there is one literature of the past and another of the present. Even where a poem's subject may not now be ours, the poet's response to his subject and his situation may well be relevant to our own.

This is as true of certain poets writing near the end of the eighteenth century as of the poet of the First World War, and I begin by briefly consider-ing Wordsworth and Coleridge because both were intermittently, but inten-sively, concerned with the problems of the revolutionary and Napoleonic periods.[5] □

As indicated in this passage, Silkin makes a detailed analysis of a num-ber of key Romantic poets' involvement with the revolutionary politics of their day.[6] Whilst the parallel between the Romantics and the First World War poets is on the whole implied rather than explicit in this introduction, the interest and continuing literary importance of both groups is seen as emerging from their relationship to the 'generalized consciousness of their period'. Silkin foregrounds the poet's 'response' to his subject, discussing the way in which the creative individual is able to be both 'of' their historical and cultural moment, with the values and attitudes this entails, and to challenge or change such values and atti-tudes through their poetry. At the same time, poets are seen as selecting from, identifying with and adapting other poetic approaches. In taking this theoretical position, and drawing such a prominent link to the Romantic period and poets, Silkin places First World War poetry within a process of socio-political and historical change, as well as within an evolving literary tradition.

Other critics have reached even further back into history to map out a war poetry tradition. The poet Alan Bold (1943–98), in *The Martial Muse: Seven Centuries of War Poetry* (1976), begins his chronology of a war poetry tradition with the poet John Barbour (about 1320–95). Bold includes late medieval, Elizabethan, Augustan, Romantic and Victorian poets in his anthology, although more than half the poems are of the twentieth century and it is the two world wars that feature most prominently. In a detailed and useful introduction to his collection, Bold surveys a myriad of shifts in the poet's relationship to and representation of war, with reference to the changing nature of warfare from the Crusades to the Spanish Civil War. For Bold, the 'war poem' is a broad and accessible literary category, having 'instantly useful artistic currency'. War poetry, like war itself, is seen as an inevitable feature of every historical period and one which illustrates the poet's quality and skill:

■ Major poets are usually characterized by their ability to interpret man the warrior – to ignore war would be to opt out of possibly the most significant area of human development. Thus poetry has always been in on the action. Primitive poets were employed to record the exploits of the winning side; Renaissance poets entertained their sophisticated public by questioning the morality of war; Romantic poets felt an obligation to give a personal account of war; modern poets have turned to war as one area in which they can assume a public role – whatever the reasons at any historical moment poetry and war have been drawn together. Poetry, which is ideally the most memorable method of verbal communication, has relished the contrast between war and peace. That there has been a steady change of attitude towards war – from glory to gory – has been partly due to the way in which the insights of the artistic community have educated the emotions. ...

A battle-weary American Civil War General, William Sherman [1820–91] – the man who devastated Georgia in 1864 – is reported as saying 'I am tired and sick of war. Its glory is all moonshine ... War is hell' [address at Michigan Military Academy, 19 June 1879], but the verdict of the reading public has been precisely the opposite. They have accepted war as an activity involving nobility or a rugged recklessness. They have abstracted from the killing and mutilation a simple code of ethics which differentiates organized murder (war) from individual murder, which is socially taboo. War poetry has oscillated between an acceptance of this ethical elevation of war to the realms of nobility, and a conviction that the difference between war and murder is one of degree. The state, for its part, has continued to insist that collective military murder can be justified as something totally different from criminal murder. Some poets accept the state as the supreme arbiter of morality, others do not. Basically that is the difference between the pro-war poet and the anti-war poet.[7] □

For Bold, each of the instances of war and war poetry discussed refer us back to a number of underlying principles, the most fundamental of these being that whilst each war is quite different in cause, method and outcome, war is an intrinsic part of human evolution, and poetry is 'always in on the action'. Whilst Bold identifies Owen as the supreme war poet, he does not accord the First World War a particularly special or decisive place within literary history; he does not view it as radically altering the subsequent representational possibilities for war poets. Long after the First World War, Bold argues, the reading public appears to accept the existence of war and persists in seeing war as an activity that can reveal 'nobility or rugged recklessness'. Indeed, for Bold, even the impact of war on the soldier-poet's sensibility and poetic development can be fleeting, as shown by Sassoon's return to patriotic poetry in the Second World War.[8]

Bold's analysis, written in the mid-1970s in a period of intense debate and fear about the obliterating potential of atomic weaponry, focuses on a conundrum which has preoccupied many critics and anthologists since. As we will go on to consider in greater detail in Chapter Five, the approaches taken by late twentieth-century critics often reflect and refract the social and political issues and debates of their historical contexts. If war appears to be, for Bold, 'part of human nature', he also displays a belief, in the context of post-1960s' debates about the nature of society and the possibility of social and personal change, that the urge to wage war can be controlled or quelled by human effort. As Bold puts it: 'the only way to extinguish the volcano is to discover the source of its energy' and war poetry has a vital role to play in seeking this 'source'.[9] Yet did the First World War poets themselves view their task in this way, and was their poetry treated as part of a project to overcome the causes of war? In the next two subsections, we will identify some of the contemporary critical and literary contexts for the First World War poets, juxtaposed with a selection of late twentieth-century critical perspectives, in order to explore how the genre was framed and developed during the 1914–18 war.

HISTORICIZING THE GENRE

To gain a sense of how poetry about war was viewed during the First World War, it is helpful to begin with a brief examination of the role of pre-1914 poetry, in which influential images of the military and a confident sense of Englishness were portrayed.

One of the poets who can be seen as a precursor of First World War poetry is Rudyard Kipling (1865–1936), particularly in work such as *Barrack-Room Ballads* (1892). In the following example, taken from the first stanza of Kipling's 'Route Marchin', the setting is India, in the era of the British Raj ('raj' is Hindi for 'reign' and this phrase refers to the period of British sovereignty in India):

■ We're marchin' on relief over Injia's sunny plains,
   A little front o' Christmas-time an' just be'ind the Rains;
   Ho! Get away you bullock-man, you've 'eard the bugle blowed,
   There's a regiment a-comin' down the Grand Trunk Road;[10] □

In characteristic *Barrack-Room Ballads* style, the voice here is presented as that of the average British soldier on imperial duties, with an outlook which is crude, partly humorous and more than a little belligerent. Britain had taken over large colonial possessions by the 1890s, and the maintenance and control of these territories was seen as a national duty and, generally, a source of patriotic pride. Kipling's ballads were hugely popular, although some critics worried about what was seen as their vulgarity of language and subject.[11] The sentiments and values displayed in 'Route Marchin', reflecting what the critic Simon Featherstone in his *War Poetry: An Introductory Reader* (1995) calls the 'militarist patriotism' of late Victorian and Edwardian Britain, were not peculiar to Kipling.[12] Other poets such as Laurence Binyon and Henry Newbolt (1862–1938) wrote patriotic ballads prior to the First World War, for example, Newbolt's 'Drake's Drum', published in *Admirals All and Other Verses* (1897).[13]

In 'Route Marchin' and other poems from *Barrack-Room Ballads*, the soldier's experience is presented in the spirit of adventure as well as duty. There is a strong emphasis on the ordinariness of the soldiers and their problems and complaints, whether trivial or serious: acts of bravery tend to be immediately offset by philosophical asides and cynical remarks. The roughness of the speaker's life is presented so as to invite the sympathy of the reader, at a time when to be a private soldier in the army was not necessarily a respectable or popular occupation.[14] In the following quotation from the poem 'Tommy' (an informal term for a British private soldier), the topic is the hypocrisy of civilian society towards the military:

■ We aren't no thin red 'eroes, nor we aren't no
  Blackguards too,
  But single men in barracks, most remarkable like you;
  An' if sometimes our conduck isn't all your fancy paints,
  Why, single men in barracks don't grow into plaster saints;
    While it's Tommy this, an' Tommy that, an'
      Tommy, fall be'ind,'
    But it's 'Please to walk in front, sir,' when there's
      trouble in the wind,[15] □

In this poem, from the soldier's perspective, civilians are seen as abusing and demeaning soldiers, only becoming respectful when a war appears likely. The army is, the poem suggests, a convenient scapegoat for civil society: blamed for wrongdoing in peacetime and sent into danger in times of war. The *Barrack-Room Ballads* display twin concerns with the demotic and the imperial: with the general life, conditions and social standing of the soldier, and with the issues of the colonies. The ballads were extremely influential, as well as popular, tending to overshadow the more equivocal tone of some of Kipling's other poetry, such as 'Recessional' (1897).[16] In his 1978 study, *Drummer Hodge: The Poetry of the Anglo-Boer War (1899–1902)*, Malvern Van Wyk Smith explores the ways in which Kipling's critics often failed to look 'beyond the jingles to the complex moods of his best poems' and notes that 'a host of Kiplingesque imitators' became fixated on 'the obvious attractions of the "barracky" style'.[17]

Neither Kipling, Newbolt nor Binyon were military men: they were, in the main, constructing dramatic scenarios and narratives of military life from their imagination. Indeed at the beginning of the First World War, poetry about war was often written by non-combatants. It was only from approximately 1915 that a combination of events, discussed later in this chapter, led to a fascination with the idea of the soldier-poet and an increase in the amount of poetry written by soldiers being published. Over the second half of the twentieth century much of the interest in war poetry has centred upon protest poetry and the figures of Owen and Sassoon.

However, as discussed in Chapter One, there are several key strands within the war poetry genre that run in parallel. It is possible to see, therefore, how some of the formal and thematic features of a poem such as 'Route Marchin' have been in evidence throughout the twentieth century. There is the focus on the idea of 'Tommy' as an everyday soldier figure; the emphasis on hardship and the hypocrisy of those who send soldiers to wars but distrust them in civilian society; and the juxta-position of humour, cynicism and a rebellious spirit. In Kipling's ballads the speaking voice, although ostensibly that of the soldier, is often caricatured and associated with an earthy outlook at odds with the middle-class values of much of the readership. The 'barracky' tone of 'Tommy's, speech and attitudes is presented in a way that emphasizes the difference and distance between reader and soldier, in a period when soldiers were often distrusted. The fashion for the heroic soldier-poet in the First World War, however, grew out of the mass-recruitment of 'ordinary' men, most of whom were non-professional soldiers, and who were seen as engaged in a noble, sacrificial enterprise on behalf of their country.

The term 'war poetry' itself was not in common use before the First World War, but came into play as the war progressed, along with the terms 'soldier's poetry' and 'soldier poets'. Yet, as a number of contemporary critical sources show, the poetic forms, ideas and values associated with these terms were many and various. Two useful examples of this can be found in a series of pamphlets by the English Association, a body that aimed to promote English as an educational subject and encourage the study of English literature. In *Poetry in the Light of War*, published in January 1917, Caroline Spurgeon describes how the war has led her to question the role and value of poetry. From the first page of the pamphlet, the First World War is represented not as a patriotic adventure, but as the cause of great suffering:

> ■ At first, in the initial shock and horror of August 1914, in view of all that such a war meant and was going to mean in waste and cruelty and suffering, the pursuit of letters seemed futile and unimportant. That very natural feeling has gradually become modified and changed, until to-day, after two years, I have returned to the belief I held before the war, only it is a belief reborn in anguish of spirit, and so intensified and strengthened. It is this: that to attain with some degree of permanence the attitude of mind in which great poetry is understood in its fullness, is one of the ends of life – it is indeed, perhaps, the main end of human life.[18] □

Although Spurgeon talks about the 'waste and cruelty and suffering' of war, she does not attempt to use poetry to elaborate specific objections to, or protests against it. In the passage above, Spurgeon argues that war in fact reinvigorates poetry: the war turns us to spiritual matters, and reminds us that poetry is the zenith of human endeavour and cultural achievement. Poetry is presented both as the ultimate counterpoint to the barbarity of war, and as its essential companion. This approach can be traced through many subsequent decades of war poetry criticism.

In the English Association pamphlet no. 38 *War and English Poetry*, written by R. O. A. Milne and published in September 1917, the *Iliad* (an ancient Greek epic poem about the Trojan War attributed to Homer) is identified as 'the supreme war-poem of the world' and is taken as 'a general standard for reference from time to time during a survey of English poetry related to war'.[19] This needs to be placed in the context of a period in which Classical literature had an important place in school and university curricula and was often viewed as setting the benchmark of poetic excellence. Milne selects examples of what he terms 'war-poetry' from the fourteenth through to the nineteenth century, drawing his survey to a close with a brief reference to the status and significance of the poet's experience of war:

> ■ I do not know whether it is possible, but I doubt it, to draw any dividing line between the war-poetry of the study and that illuminated by personal experience. The rough survey that I have attempted does not point to any such distinction.[20] □

The quotation suggests there is no reason to distinguish between the poet who writes from the battlefield and the poet who conjures the images from reported experience and imagination. Furthermore, in one of the few references Milne makes to the First World War, he writes:

■ ... among the verse written by soldiers in this war it is not surprising to find as many poems recalling loves of home and memories of country days as proclaiming the delight of battle, or even the loftier summons of patriotism and duty. Some of this work of to-day, as we all know, transcends the lyrical faculty which is the frequent appanage [natural accompaniment or attribute] of youth, and reaches the level of true poetry; some of it is made sacred by the death of the writer, and cannot be coldly weighed in the balance.

It may be, perhaps it is bound to be, that of the highest poetry of the world no great part falls within the title of this Address [the pamphlet was first delivered by Milne as a lecture]. 'The infinite variety of shapes and combinations of power' into which, as William Hazlitt [1778–1830, journalist, critic and essayist] says, objects are moulded by the poetic imagination may not be at the ordinary service of those who write of war.[21] □

It is important to note here that in discussing the range of likely topics to be chosen by the war poet, Milne does not refer to the horror of war, the scale of injury and death, or any sense of moral outrage. Despite the date of publication after the disastrous 1916 Battle of the Somme (often cited by later critics as a turning point from early idealism into disillusionment) the 'war poetry' category here is seen as restricted mainly to the expression of heroic or patriotic feeling. As the passage above goes on to explain, the quality of the majority of war poetry is also seen in modest terms: 'of the highest poetry of the world no great part falls within the title of this Address'.[22] The poets who write about war, Milnes argues, have a limited range of material and ideas to draw into their 'poetic imagination'. This claim appears to rest on the assumptions that war is a knowable, containable and largely understood phenomenon, and that war poetry is written to record major conflicts and where appropriate, celebrate victory. The literariness of war poetry, its ability to attain the status of 'true poetry' is, in fact, compromised by the nature of war itself. Many of the ideas put forward by Milne continued to preoccupy many war poets and critics of war poetry throughout the twentieth century, as we will see in later chapters.

LITERARY INFLUENCES

As we discussed briefly in Chapter One, the term 'war poet' is sometimes used to imply that war is *the* central element of the poet's biography, focusing attention on war experience as the defining moment of the poet's working life. Undoubtedly, involvement in the war affected many individuals profoundly, and, for many poets, led to a desire to explore new poetic themes and approaches. Yet too great an emphasis on a poem being the 'direct' result of war experience can obscure the extent to which poets are stimulated and informed by other literary texts, in what is often a gradual process of creative development. Earlier in this chapter, we considered a small sample of alternative perspectives on the idea of the war poetry 'tradition', including Jon Silkin's discussion of the links between the Romantics and some of the First World War poets. Here, we will briefly examine selected aspects of the contemporary literary context from which the First World War emerged, to illustrate some of the poetic models and techniques that individuals took with them on to the battlefield.

When we consider poetry of the period from the turn of the century up to the First World War, it can be difficult to avoid a sense of polarization between 'traditional' and 'modern'. In *Twentieth-Century British Poetry: A Critical Introduction* (1987), John Williams uses these terms to categorize the poetry and poetic groupings of the period, yet stresses the need to understand them in historical and cultural context. Williams points out, for example, that Thomas Hardy combined a traditional approach to form and a concern with the rural past, with an inventive and often original approach to rhyme and metre:

> ■ Hardy's originality, often the object of criticism by contemporary reviewers who understood him to be using the 'old styles' ineptly, made him the object of admiration from two otherwise contrasting poetic movements early in the century.
>
> The first self-consciously 'Modernist' poets in England in the twentieth century, calling themselves Imagists, hailed him as a precursor of Modernism, while the Georgian poets – claiming to be equally modern – viewed Hardy's experimentation in a less iconoclastic light than the Imagists, finding in his work a model for their own reinvigorated style of traditional poetry.
>
> Georgian poetry, established through a series of anthologies edited by Edward Marsh [1872–1953] after 1911, constituted an attempt to revive the popularity of English poetry at a time when Hardy, Robert Bridges [1844–1930] and John Masefield [1878–1967] were generally respected, but no English poet of any comparable stature was emerging to take their place. The title 'Georgian' arose from the association of Marsh's anthologies with the accession of George V on the death of Edward VII in 1910. The general intention of Marsh was to encourage the writing of poetry very much in the spirit of Hardy's comment to Graves. [In *Goodbye To All That (1929)* Robert Graves recalled Hardy telling him as a poet that 'All we can do is write on the old themes in the old styles, but try to do it a little better than those who came before us.'] Among the poets who appeared in the anthologies were Rupert Brooke, Walter de la Mare [1873–1956],

W. H. Davies [1871–1940] and Edmund Blunden. While Georgian poetry was essentially retrospective, drawing for its images on an imagined English countryside of the past containing the predictable landmarks, 'country cottages, old furniture, moss-covered barns, rose-scented lanes, apple and cherry-orchards',[23] it sought to strike a new and energetic note of patriotism. Before long, the already popular theme of a national heritage threatened by urban growth was to be dramatically intensified by the threat of a European war.

  Georgianism was thus a reaction against overly sentimental poetry where it occurred in the mid-Victorian period, and was most certainly set against the aestheticism of the 1890s. At the same time it tended to rein-state a patriotic brand of political conservatism endemic to the work of Wordsworth, Sir Walter Scott [1771–1832], Samuel Taylor Coleridge and Robert Southey [1774–1843], and to bind this in with its determination – also in common with the early Romantics – of re-establishing a wide readership for poetry. On this last count, sales figures for the Georgian anthologies indicate that it was in no small way successful.[24] □

Williams shows here that in literary criticism terms such as 'traditional' and 'modern' are not always rigidly defined; they can be deployed for different cultural and political purposes, depending on the values of the individual or group using them and the historical context in which they are used.

  In what way, then, were the Imagists 'self-consciously' modern in their aims? In as far as there was common ground among the poets included in the 1914 anthology *Des Imagistes*, it was the desire to make a break from the tendency towards lush emotiveness in poetry: to find a greater freedom in the choice of poetic subject and a greater precision in diction and imagery.[25] This was part of a project to be in the vanguard of modernity, to develop new approaches in the arts that would contrast starkly with the elaborate yet vague poeticizations of some of the late Victorian and Edwardian poets. In a subsequent text, *Some Imagist Poets: An Anthology*, published in 1915, a Preface set out the principles underlying the poetry, claiming that they constituted 'the essentials of all great poetry, indeed of all great literature'.[26] Among these were the aim to use 'common speech' and to 'employ always the *exact* word', to create new rhythms and to produce concentrated, 'hard and clear' poetry. Of the poets included in the 1915 anthology, Richard Aldington went on to fight in and write poetry and fiction about the First World War, and some of the poetry of H. D. (Hilda Doolittle, 1886–1961) has recently been considered in relation to the war poetry genre.[27] Herbert Read, poet of both world wars, was also strongly influenced by the emergence of the Imagist school, and wrote of his sympathy with the principles they espoused.

  The poets associated with the *Georgian Poetry* anthologies often asserted their sense of the 'modern' by developing new ways of representing 'traditional' rural life. In the first of these anthologies, *Georgian Poetry 1911–1912*, Marsh's prefatory note illustrates this conjunction of newness with the established literary values of the past:

■ This volume is issued in the belief that English poetry is now once again putting on a new strength and beauty.

Few readers have the leisure or the zeal to investigate each volume as it appears; and the process of recognition is often slow. This collection, drawn entirely from the publications of the past two years, may if it is fortunate help the lovers of poetry to realize that we are at the beginning of another 'Georgian period' which may take rank in due time with the several great poetic ages of the past.[28] □

Here, Marsh's confidence in the 'strength and beauty' of the poetry is based on his prediction that it will be judged equal to previous 'great poetic ages'. Several of the individuals included in his anthology were to become firmly established as 'war poets' in later years, including Rupert Brooke, Lascelles Abercrombie (1881–1938) and Wilfrid Gibson. Siegfried Sassoon was also one of the poets selected by Marsh to be included in a subsequent Georgian anthology, and Sassoon's collection *The Old Huntsman and Other Poems* (1917) juxtaposed war poems with Georgian pastoral poems such as 'October':

■ Across the land a faint blue veil of mist
Seems hung; the woods wear yet arrayment sober,
Till frost shall make them flame; silent and whist
The drooping cherry orchards of October
Like mournful pennons hang their shrivelling leaves
Russet and orange: all things now decay;
Long since ye garnered in your autumn sheaves,
And sad the robins pipe at set of day.[29] □

In this quotation, Sassoon's use of the archaic 'arrayment', 'whist' and 'ye' and his emphasis on romantic images such as the 'blue veil of mist' might initially seem at odds with his approach to diction and metaphor in poems about combat conditions during the First World War. However, several of Sassoon's war poems also deploy traditional verse forms and conventional rhyme schemes: 'To Any Dead Officer', for example, uses octets (verses of eight lines) with abab rhymes.[30] Natural images also seep into Sassoon's war poems, such as 'Prelude: the Troops', where visions of the English countryside throw into relief the barren and relentlessly hostile environment:

■ They march from safety, and the bird-sung joy
Of grass-green thickets, to the land where all
Is ruin, and nothing blossoms but the sky[31] □

Here, the sky 'blossoms' with explosions: this usage of 'blossoms' creates a greater conceptual distance between the destructive activity of the battlefield and the more usual organic, harmonious associations of the verb. Sassoon was able to draw upon elements of a Georgian sensibility and place them in new and unexpected contexts, in order to represent the shock of combat conditions.

Other poets of the war also drew heavily upon pastoral images and language in finding ways to represent and explore the significance of the war: for example, the Irish nationalist poet Francis Ledwidge (1891–1917) in 'A Soldier's Grave', where the poem concludes with the image of the grave 'sweet arrayed, / And there the lark shall turn her dewy nest';[32] and the patriotic English poet Edward Thomas, in 'As the team's head-brass flashed out on the turn', which he wrote before he had experienced combat directly.[33] In these poems, the extensive use of natural imagery can be read in quite different ways: as an avoidance or softening of the full horror of war, for instance; as an affirmation of national or cultural identity in the context of war; or as an expression of the intensity of loss experienced during battle. In each of these cases, a consideration of the literary contexts, influences and traditions that inspired and informed the poets helps us to formulate fuller readings of the poems, and to avoid reducing them purely to an encounter between soldier and war.

PATRIOTISM, PROPAGANDA AND PROTEST

PATRIOTIC ENTHUSIASM

In the previous section, we considered examples of poetry from the late nineteenth and early twentieth centuries that expressed patriotic themes, such as Kipling's *Barrack-Room Ballads* and the *Georgian Poetry* anthologies. As we have also seen, however, patriotism could be associated with different cultural assumptions and political beliefs: for Kipling, in the *Barrack-Room Ballads*, love of country meant, on the whole, support for and pride in Britain's imperialist projects; for Edward Marsh and some of his 'Georgian' poets it was often a more selective attachment to an image of rural England. I. F. Clarke's 1966 study *Voices Prophesying War 1763–1984* describes how patriotic sentiments have also often been formed and expressed in terms of perceived (and, sometimes, actual) military threats from other nations.[34] From the mid-Victorian through to the Edwardian period, a range of texts focused on the risks posed by German aggrandizement: periodicals such as *Punch*; popular novels, for example, *The Battle of Dorking* (1871) by George Tomkyns Chesney (1830–95), which portrayed a German invasion attempt; and daily newspapers, particularly those of the Northcliffe press. Lord Northcliffe (1865–1922) owned several daily newspapers that tended towards an overtly anti-German, pro-war position.

When war broke out in 1914, the army recruitment drive was able to appeal not only to a desire to defend and uphold British interests but also to a widespread public anxiety about the threat from Germany. The freshly intensified sense of patriotic duty inspired by the war revolved in particular around the theological idea of personal sacrifice. Fighting for one's country offered an opportunity for an almost Christ-like personal transformation and the prospect of injury or death was framed in terms of a spiritual cleansing or purification. Contemporary literary instances of this are plentiful, one of the most famous being Rupert Brooke's metaphor in his poem, 'Peace', of 'swimmers into cleanness leaping': the swimmers are the young soldiers who are made pure through their act of faith and devotion to England.[35] In Chapter Four we will consider a retrospective analysis of this mood of patriotic fervour by Robert Nichols, one of the First World War poets to survive the war.

Daily newspapers had a particularly significant role to play in fore-grounding the ideology of patriotic military duty, and frequently used poetry to support this position. From an early stage in the war, *The Times* adopted a squarely pro-war stance. Stories of German barbarism and brutality were given great emphasis and many articles, poems and let-ters focused on a highly romanticized image of the British soldier. The following quotation, from a reader's letter in *The Times* of 20 October 1914, gives some indication of the way in which, from an early stage in the war, poetry had a central role in perpetuating patriotic ideals:

■ Our Poets

To the Editor of *The Times*

   Sir, – Really, these poets! Mr William Watson [1858–1935] says he has yet to learn that Mr. Henry Newbolt 'has ever chosen to enhance with the lus-tre of his pen the fame of the British soldier.' He must know very little of Mr Newbolt's poems. Has he never heard tell of 'Gillespie,' or 'The Ballad of John Nicholson,' or 'The Grenadier's Good-bye,' or 'He Fell among Thieves,' or 'The Gay Gordons' ? Mr. Watson's poems have been my treasured compan-ions in the far places of the earth. They have solaced me on Russian steppes, in African deserts, in the wilds of High Asia, and among the islands of the Eastern Seas. But I have never yet read 'The Grenadier's Good-bye' without tears of pride, and I dare not read 'John Nicholson' late at night – it stirs me so that I lie awake for hours. With all his magical use of words, Mr. Watson never brings the lump in your throat. The other man does, I sup-pose because he is simpler and more unconsciously sincere.

   Yours truly,

   A Roving Briton.[36] □

Here, the letter-writer, who describes himself in anonymous but unequivocally patriotic terms as 'A Roving Briton', engages in a debate about the effectiveness of poems in conveying 'the fame of the British soldier'. Set against Watson's 'magical' poetry is the poetic simplicity and sincerity of Newbolt, seemingly favoured as more in keeping with the life of the ordinary soldier. The soldier, here, is clearly a symbol of considerable British pride; paying homage to the soldier's 'fame' in poetry is a source of competition between poets.

To make sense of the deeply emotive nature of this response to poetic representations of the British soldier, we need to consider further the social standing and symbolic value of youth during this period. In *The Times* of 24 October 1914, an article entitled 'The Day of the Young' was printed, in which the war is presented, without irony, as a blessing and heroic opportunity for the younger generation:

■ The Day of the Young

It's a great war, whatever. Isn't it luck for me to have been born so as I'd be just the right age and just in the right place?

That is how, a correspondent tells us, a young cavalry officer writes from the front; and there are many middle-aged men among us who must envy him. We have lived in our own youth an ordinary life of routine through long inconclusive years; and now suddenly comes a time in which the future of the world is to be made, more even than it was made in the wars a hundred years ago; and we ourselves can have little or nothing to do with the making of it. But this young man, and thousands of others, who were undergraduates, or shopmen, or ploughboys a few months ago, are now making history; and they in their old age will have stories to tell their grandchildren such as no man has ever told before; or they will be remembered as having given their lives for their country in the most momentous of all its struggles. And they have, too, this greatest good fortune of all, that their cause is, beyond all dispute, the best for which England has ever gone to war. The undergraduate who last summer term was playing his pleasant game and making his pleasant little academic jokes, to whom the world was a charming if rather bewildering place, is now suddenly a man with a plain and glorious duty before him, a man like those Greeks who fought at Marathon [490 BC] and Salamis [480 BC], like Aeschylus [525–456 BC] himself, the poet of the great age that was prepared for a victory in which he took his part.[37] □

In this extract the war is considered largely in terms of abstract values: it is history in the making, a time when 'the future of the world is to be made'. Perhaps most dramatically of all, the 'cause' for which the war is being fought is 'the best for which England has ever gone to war'. Through this elevated language, the war is represented as a historical turning point, in which any man would wish to earn his share of the military glory in the tradition of classical heroism.

As the article also emphasizes, it is primarily the male 'youth' of the nation that are recruited for active service in the war: indeed war is to some extent presented as a test of youthful masculinity. The writer of this piece, who declares himself to be 'one of the middle-aged men' who can 'have little or nothing to do' with the war and its outcome, is ostensibly regretful about his own exclusion from it, and admiring and envious of the younger men's involvement.[38] It is not easy to determine whether the older men ineligible for combat genuinely felt such regret; it is clear, however, that the onus was on young men, not only to take part in the war but to do so in a spirit of 'glorious duty'.

The passionately patriotic rhetoric illustrated in the two excerpts above was, however, by no means universally or unquestioningly absorbed or expressed. In a later subsection, we will go on to consider several examples of oppositional voices to the war, some of which were formulated in overtly political or philosophical terms. It is also important to note that those who protested against the war did not necessarily see themselves as unpatriotic: whilst militaristic patriotic rhetoric was deployed forcefully in the public debates about the need for war, some of those who supported anti-war positions retained a strong sense of patriotic identity. On a personal level, duty to country could sometimes be experienced and expressed in far more complex and politically equivocal ways than the pro-war *Times* or *Daily Mail* might suggest. In the following poem by Robert Service (1874–1958), ironic humour and a strong sense of class politics are used to interrogate some of the official assumptions about patriotic duty, and in particular the type of language used on the recruitment posters:

■ The Volunteer
Sez I: My Country Calls? Well, let it call.
I grins perlitely and declines with thanks.
Go let 'em plaster every blighted wall,
'Ere's *one* they don't stampede into the ranks.
Them politicians with their greasy ways;
Them empire-grabbers – fight for 'em? No fear!
I've seen this mess a-comin' from the days
Of Algyserious and Aggydear*
I've felt me passion rise and swell,
But … wot the 'ell, Bill? Wot the 'ell?

Sez I: If they would do the decent thing,
And shield the missis and the little 'uns,
Why, even *I* might shout God save the King,
And face the chances of them 'ungry guns.
But we've got three, another on the way;

It's that wat makes me snarl and set me jor:
The wife and nippers wot of 'em, I say,
If I gets knocked out in this blasted war?
Gets proper busted by a shell,
But ... wot the 'ell, Bill? Wot the 'ell?[39] □

* [Algeciras Conference of 1906 and Agadir Crisis of 1911: these refer to disputes between Britain, France and Germany in the build-up to the war]

Service writes in a vernacular style that would have been familiar to readers of Kipling's soldier's verse, using the rhetorical questions, conversational phrases and colloquialisms of the working man. Here, the strident individualism of the voice appears to deflate the aims and values of the British establishment. The speaker does not want to fight for 'empire-grabbers' or politicians with 'greasy ways'. In the third and final stanza of the poem, however, the voice capitulates to the need to join up, ending on the refrain 'I've gotta go, Bill, gotta go'. It is, primarily, the sight of the injured and traumatized soldiers returning from the front and a sense of solidarity with them that inspires the change, rather than a submission to the ruling class discourse of patriotic duty.

For women poets in the First World War, the general connection being made between patriotism and the sacrifice of young men's lives in the war was problematic in an entirely different way: if the ultimate test of loyalty to one's country was through combat, what value could be placed on the good intentions of the patriotic British female? Women were extensively involved in war work through roles such as munitions worker, or casualty station nurse on the Western Front, and they could often be in great danger. They were not, however, permitted to be in combat. The pro-war rhetoric of patriotism attempted to accommodate and incorporate women, through, for example, the construction of explicitly 'feminine' models of patriotic duty. A number of poems gave tacit recognition to the fact that many women desperately wanted to display their commitment to Britain in wartime, to match the 'sacrifice' being made by young men. In Laurence Binyon's poem 'To Women' (1914), women's suffering through anxiety and loss is figured as a correlative of men's active service: 'From hearts that are as one high heart/ Withholding naught from doom and bale,/ Burningly offered up – to bleed,/ To bear, to break, but not to fail.'[40]

Women who wrote poetry about the war often affirmed the dominant rhetoric of sacrificial service, even writing in coercive terms of the need for young men to join the army, as in 'The Call' by Jessie Pope (1868–1941), discussed in the next subsection.[41] In her Preface to *The Virago Book of Women's War Poetry and Verse* (1997) edited by Catherine Reilly, the poet and short-story writer Judith Kazantzis (born 1940) exposes a problem for many late twentieth-century readers of the anthology.[42] The book itself is

presented as a progressive cultural project by a feminist publishing
company: it is a collection of poetry by women only, which shows previously neglected feminine perspectives on the two world wars. Many of the
First World War poems included in this anthology, however, demonstrate
an uncritical belief in the importance of patriotic duty and the necessity
for, and appreciation of, men's service. As Kazantzis writes:

> ■ This is the poetry of England, inalienable from Honour, Duty, God, Christ
> and Sacrifice. This poetry sees as glorious not war itself but certainly the
> sacrifice of youth. And it accepts that purposeful Sacrifice with enormous
> gratitude. All flows from Duty. That duty is the world task of keeping alive
> English values; and then of guarding the sanctity of the English hearth and
> homeland against the militaristic enemy that threatens all this. If we don't
> remember the archaic glow of belief in the Imperial task, we lose the ideal-
> istic moving force behind 'Lamplight', [...] by May Wedderburn Cannan
> [1893–1970]. If we don't remember that in 1914 middle-class England
> was a Christian country, we lose the numinous glow behind the word
> 'England'. In short, orthodox Great War belief in the English cause against
> the Germans, and in the backing of an English God – and great gratitude to
> the protagonists of all this, the English fighting men – is of the essence in
> many of these poems.[43] □

For many women poets, their ineligibility for active combat meant
exclusion from what was perceived to be the central experience of war.
Their preoccupation with the 'glorious' nature of 'sacrifice' and 'duty'
reflected the orthodoxy of First World War British society, and the poetry
that expressed these values could be a means of asserting patriotism.

PROPAGANDA

By wartime 'propaganda', we do not necessarily refer to all official representation of war aims but rather to concerted and organized attempts,
from any source, to propagate a particular doctrinal view of the war, in
order to bolster or sustain support. As we noted in Chapter One, it is
important to make some distinction between the design and use of literature as propaganda. It might be possible, in some instances, to argue that
a writer or poet intended to produce a piece of literature with some propagandist intent. This might be due to their involvement with pro-war
campaigns or to the blunt, coercive messages that they convey, as we will
consider below. More often than not, such intent is not demonstrable, and
it is not possible to identify authorial motivation or aims. The political and
propagandist *uses* of literature, however, can be quite distinct from intent.
    The Government called on literary figures to assist with its propa-
ganda campaigns from an early stage in the war, through the work of

the Secret War Propaganda Bureau. In his study *Minds at War: The Poetry and Experience of the First World War* (1996), David Roberts gives an account of the scope and outcomes of the Bureau's project.[44] In the following quotation, Roberts begins by pointing out that some writers such as Robert Bridges, the Poet Laureate, and the novelist John Galsworthy (1867–1933), quickly demonstrated that they were prepared to speak up on behalf of the Government's war policies, and that others soon responded to the Bureau's initiative:

■ Clearly, writers in the same frame of mind as John Galsworthy and Robert Bridges needed little encouragement to write supporting the war effort. However, the Government did not leave the matter to chance. At the end of August [1914] Sir Edward Grey [1862–1933, Foreign Secretary, 1905–16] and Lloyd George [1863–1945, Chancellor of the Exchequer 1908–15, Minister of Munitions 1915–16, Secretary of State for War 1916, Prime Minister 1916–22] took the initiative in setting up a department of propaganda, The Secret War Propaganda Bureau, whose offices were established in Wellington House, Buckingham Gate, London. The Bureau was put in the hands of Charles Masterman, a member of the Cabinet.

One of his first ideas was to encourage sympathetic, famous, and influential writers to use their pens in support of the war effort and in particular to spread the 'British viewpoint' in America where there was little understanding of the British Government's actions.

He called a meeting of 'well-known men of letters' at Wellington House on 2nd September 1914. To this day no official departmental papers relating the activities of the Wellington House Propaganda Department are available in the Public Records Office, but from the personal papers of some participants quite a lot is known. Those present included, Thomas Hardy (then 74), H. G. Wells [1866–1946, novelist], Arnold Bennett [1867–1931, novelist and playwright], John Galsworthy, John Masefield, Robert Bridges [the Poet Laureate], Conan Doyle [1859–1930, novelist], Owen Seaman [1861–1936, poet and editor of *Punch*], J. M. Barrie [1860–1937, playwright], G. K. Chesterton [1874–1936, novelist, essayist and poet], Israel Zangwill [1864–1926, novelist and playwright], G. M. Trevelyan [1876–1962, historian] and Gilbert Murray [1866–1957, Greek scholar and translator]. Rudyard Kipling, unable to attend, sent a message of support. Laurence Binyon was soon to be associated with the group.[45] □

From this meeting, Roberts goes on to argue, literary forms of propaganda were fairly promptly formulated by many of those present:

Inspired by the meeting, many of those present rapidly set to work to provide the literary help requested by the Government. – Hardy's poem was quickly taken up by the British and American press: published in the *Times Literary Supplement*, on 10 September, and *The New York Times* on 11 September.

■ Men Who March Away
(Song of the Soldiers)

What of the faith and fire within us
Men who march away
Ere the barn-cocks say
Night is growing gray
Leaving all that here can win us;
What of the faith and fire within us
Men who march away?

Is it a purblind prank, O think you,
Friend with the musing eye,
Who watch us stepping by
With doubt and dolorous sigh?
Can much pondering so hoodwink you!
Is it a purblind pranks, O think you,
Friend with the musing eye?
Nay. We well see what we are doing,
Though some may not see –
Dalliers as they be –
England's need are we;
Her distress would leave us rueing:
Nay. We well see what we are doing,
Though some may not see![46] □

As this extract shows, Roberts argues that this and a number of other poems written by those present at the Bureau's meeting can be situated within an explicitly propagandist framework. Other poets and writers, too, were commissioned to produce histories, journalism or poems that would validate the Government's actions in going to war. The poet John Masefield was even placed on the Government payroll in order to carry out a pro-war lecture tour.[47]

Yet an overtly 'propagandist' poem such as that by Hardy, in the extract above, could be very close in ideology and impact to poems written quite independently of Government departments or campaigning groups. Rupert Brooke's hugely popular collection *1914 and Other Poems*, discussed later in the context of the rise in soldier's poetry, contained poems which seem as though they could have been commissioned by the Government's propaganda department. Julian Grenfell's 'Into Battle', too, portrays a similar idea to Hardy's 'faith and fire' and represents death in battle as an enhancement of nobility, a patriotic reward:

■ And life is colour and warmth and light,
    And a striving evermore for these;
And he is dead who will not fight;
    And who dies fighting has increase.[48] □

Neither Brooke nor Grenfell's work was written under the auspices of any official propagandist organization, but was clearly shaped by the discourses of militarist patriotism discussed earlier in this chapter. These discourses were absorbed and assimilated by individuals, to be expressed sometimes in strident, overtly controlling terms. This type of expression is evident in Jessie Pope's 'The Call':

■ Who's for the trench –
  Are you, my laddie?
Who'll follow French –
  Will you, my laddie?
Who's fretting to begin,
Who's going out to win?
And who wants to save his skin –
  Do you, my laddie?[49] □

The poem overtly targets young men and interrogates their motives and intentions. The questions are framed to show that those avoiding call-up will not only attract society's opprobrium but also be faced with their own sense of cowardice and failure.

The Times, as we have already seen in the discussion of patriotism, offered a ready outlet for those wishing to affirm the pivotal historical significance of the war, or to applaud the bravery of British soldiers. In some articles it is possible to see an attempt to inflate readers' enthusiasm through the incorporation of literary texts or fragments into a jingoistic stance. The following excerpt from *The Times* of 8 September 1914 illustrates this:

■ A Call to Arms
UNPUBLISHED FRAGMENT BY TENNYSON
At a large patriotic meeting held last night at Freshwater, LORD TENNYSON quoted some lines by his father, not printed in the published works, but preserved in his (the present Lord Tennyson's) memory. They seem, he said, to have been written for the present crisis:

O who is he the simple fool
Who says that wars are over?
What bloody portent flashes there
Across the Straits of Dover?
Are you ready, Britons all, to answer foes with thunder?
      Arm! Arm! Arm!
Nine hundred thousand slaves in arms

> They seek to bring us under –
> But England lives, and still will live –
> For we'll crush the despot yonder –
> Are you ready, Britons all, to answer foes with thunder?
> Arm! Arm! Arm![50] □

In this extract, the ideological orientation of the article is highlighted both through the title 'A Call to Arms' and the description of the 'patriotic' meeting at which Tennyson's son spoke. The reference to his father, the previous Lord Tennyson, who had been Poet Laureate from 1850–92, appears calculated to bring to mind the poem 'The Charge of the Light Brigade', and to conjure up rousing images of soldierly sacrifice.[51] Indeed elements of this fragment echo the better-known poem: the phrasing of the line 'Nine hundred thousand slaves in arms', for example, is reminiscent of the 'rode the six hundred'. Yet, as the article clearly states, the poetic fragment foregrounded here is not only 'unpublished', it exists purely in the memory of the poet's son. In mentioning the fragment in this way and at this point in time, as the prophetic words of a poet of the English battle poem tradition, the article seems to suggest that the late Lord Tennyson himself would have given the present war his support (thus co-opting him posthumously into the war effort).

PACIFISM AND PROTEST

Alongside the propagandist efforts discussed in the previous subsection, there were a number of prominent individuals who viewed the war in quite different terms. For example, the prominent playwright, novelist, critic and journalist George Bernard Shaw (1856–1950) was absent from the list of literary figures invited to the 1914 meeting hosted by the Secret War Propaganda Bureau, because of his known anti-war views.[52] Shaw believed that war obstructed the 'life force', which he associated with the development of ideas, the exertion of the human will and the power of rational thought. The philosopher Bertrand Russell (1872–1970) also made public not simply his opposition to the war, but his theories concerning the role of war in the nation state.

In his book *Principles of Social Reconstruction* (1916), Russell expounded a theory of the 'psychology of war fever'. Russell discusses his theory of war as a social phenomenon rather than in relation to the poetic representation of war, and he focuses in particular on the rousing of the 'ordinary wage-earner' to enthusiasm for war. He offers, however, an important alternative perspective upon the wartime discourse of militant patriotism. In the following extract, Russell argues that behind the political and practical rationales put forward by governments, war is driven by a conjunction of state needs, the psychological impulses of individuals and inadequate social structures:

■ Besides the conscious and deliberate forces leading to war, there are the inarticulate feelings of common men, which, in most civilized countries are always ready to burst into war fever at the bidding of statesmen. If peace is to be secure, the readiness to catch war fever must be somehow diminished. Whoever wishes to succeed in this must first understand what war fever is and why it arises.

The men who have an important influence in the world, whether for good or evil, are dominated as a rule by a threefold desire: they desire, first, an activity which calls fully into play the faculties in which they feel that they excel; secondly, the sense of successfully overcoming resistance; thirdly, the respect of others on account of their success. [...]

The same desires, usually in a less marked degree, exist in men who have no exceptional talents. But such men cannot achieve anything very difficult by their individual efforts; for them, as units, it is impossible to acquire the sense of greatness or the triumph of strong resistance overcome. Their separate lives are unadventurous and dull. In the morning they go to the office or the plough, in the evening they return, tired and silent, to the sober monotony of wife and children. Believing that security is the supreme good, they have insured against sickness and death, and have found an employment where they have little fear of dismissal and no hope of any great rise. But security, once achieved, brings a Nemesis of *ennui* [Nemesis is the ancient Greek goddess of retribution; ennui is listlessness and dissatisfaction arising from boredom]. Adventure, imagination, risk, also have their claims; but how can these claims be satisfied by the ordinary wage-earner? Even if it were possible to satisfy them, the claims of wife and children have priority and must not be neglected.

To this victim of order and good organization the realization comes, in some moment of sudden crisis, that he belongs to a nation, that his nation may take risks, may engage in difficult enterprises, enjoy the hot passion of doubtful combat, stimulate adventure and imagination by military expeditions to Mount Sinai and the Garden of Eden. What his nation does, in some sense, he does; what his nation suffers, he suffers. The long years of private caution are avenged by a wild plunge into public madness.[53] □

Here, Russell elaborates upon his idea of war as a type of recurring social pathology, 'a wild plunge into public madness', in which institutions of government and individuals collude, albeit irrationally, to sanction war. War is viewed by Russell partly as a wish-fulfilment, a vicarious acting-out of the frustrated desires of daily life through the military engagements of the nation. This theoretical formulation recognizes not only the importance to individuals of 'belonging', but also the irrepressible attraction to the 'hot passion of doubtful combat' and 'adventure'.

Russell was unusual in mounting and sustaining such an individualistic, public and polemical critique of war during the conflict itself. His views caused outrage at Trinity College, Cambridge University, from which he was sacked in 1916, and he was imprisoned in 1918 for writing an article 'insulting to an ally'.[54] There were many other types of oppositional voice during the war, such as Quakers, who testified their commitment to peace as part of their faith. Those who wished to be exempted from military service on religious or political grounds were put before tribunals, whose job it was to establish whether they were genuine Conscientious Objectors.[55] It is important, however, to distinguish between such concerted stances against the war and the various critical positions taken by contemporary poets.

When we read about the better-known First World War poets today, as we saw in the first subsection, we tend to expect a discussion of their 'anti-war' orientation and their legacy to anti-war thought and poetry throughout the twentieth century. The gradual process of critical alignment between the canon of First World War poetry and anti-war thinking will be dealt with again later in this Guide, particularly in Chapters Three and Five. Yet this alignment often needs to be examined carefully, and considered in relation to a number of quite distinct anti-war beliefs. 'Pacifism', for example, is defined as a belief that all war is fundamentally wrong. As we will see, the nature and extent of poets' protests was often fragmented, inconsistent or episodic; sometimes protests were made specifically in relation to the First World War, rather than all war.

Siegfried Sassoon made one of the most high-profile protests of all the First World War poets when, in 1917, he wrote a letter to his commanding officer voicing his concerns about the progress of the war. Having served, he wrote, in what he initially understood to be 'a war of defence and liberation', he now believed that the Government's policy was 'prolonging the War by failing to state the conditions of peace'.[56] Sassoon's letter gained a great deal of attention, even prompting a question in the House of Commons, and resulted in much debate in the press. Yet Sassoon was very far from being a convert to pacifism. He did not believe that it was wrong in itself to take up arms, and, as he emphasized in his letter, he was not protesting against the conduct of the war, despite his satirical comments concerning the callousness and incompetence of the senior military officers in poems such as 'The General'.[57]

Sassoon's declared objection was that the war's aim had shifted; being no longer a war of defence, the sacrifice and sufferings of his fellow soldiers were, in his eyes, unjustifiable. In addition, as testified by those who fought alongside him or witnessed his character in action, Sassoon was capable of courage, even wild disregard for his own safety on the battlefield, and he was awarded a Military Cross.[58] Even for Wilfred Owen, compassionate observer and advocate of war's 'pity', it is not at all clear that the deep repugnance towards the suffering caused by war was analogous with pacifism. For Owen and Sassoon, the desire to see the war ended was superseded by the sense of the officer's duty and loyalty towards his men; both poets wrote of their determination to return to the battlefield after their respective periods of invalidity.

Some poets, such as Charles Sorley, Edward Thomas and Isaac Rosenberg, displayed a wariness of pro-war rhetoric at an early stage in the conflict. They anticipated the suffering and destruction that the war would bring about, yet still volunteered for action. Despite the tendency of some popular anthologies to represent the poet's experience in the First World War as a trajectory from innocent enthusiasm to the horror of experience, arrival at the trenches did not always precipitate a shock of disillusionment. Edward Thomas, for example, wrote most of the poems in which he deals with the loss of war before he arrived at the battlefield. It is also important to note that during the war, Sassoon's protest was not necessarily viewed as having been authenticated or justified by the poet's combat experience. Some critics distrusted the value of poetry written in the midst of war, believing poets suffered from a lack of distance or perspective. As we will consider further in the next section, for some commentators, the protest poetry of poets such as Sassoon or Owen did not so much represent a brave stance against orthodoxy, as a surfeit of self-concern.

DISSEMINATION AND RECEPTION

SOLDIERS' POETRY

In the first year of the conflict, as we have seen, much of the poetry about war was written by non-combatants. By the time Rupert Brooke's *1914 & Other Poems* was published in June 1915, shortly after the poet's death from septicaemia, Brooke was already known for his 1911 collection *Poems* and for his involvement with Edward Marsh's *Georgian Poetry* anthologies.[59] The posthumous publication of Brooke's war sonnets, '1914', attracted an even wider audience and became a cornerstone of Brooke's reputation.[60] Contemporary reviewers wrote in rapturous terms of these poems, as can be seen in the following extract from a review in *Times Literary Supplement* (11 March 1915), quoted in the 1917 impression of *Poems by Rupert Brooke*:

■ It is impossible to shred up this beauty for the purpose of criticism. These sonnets are personal – never were sonnets more personal since Sidney [Sir Philip Sidney, 1554–86, prose writer, critic and poet] died – and yet the very blood and youth of England seem to find expression in them.

They speak not for one heart only, but for all to whom her call has come in the hour of need and found instantly ready. The words pause and break, as thought and feeling falter for very fullness, like the song of a bird faced with all a summer's loveliness and with but one brief dusk wherein to sing. No passion for glory is here, no bitterness, no gloom; only a happy, clear-sighted all-surrendering love.[61] ☐

Brooke's poetry had, by 1915, already begun to acquire an aura of almost mystical perfection, as indicated by the phrase 'it is impossible to shred up this beauty'. A number of associations had also accumulated around the figure of Brooke himself. In the quotation above, the reference to 'blood', for example, gestures on the one hand to Brooke's status as a soldier who died in the course of the war, and on the other to Brooke's symbolic value as a representative of all young English men killed in the war, in whose poetry ' the very blood and youth of England seem to find expression'.

Brooke's experience as a soldier was in fact limited to an unsuccessful campaign in Belgium, and his death did not result directly from enemy action, but the public was keen to take up the legend of the heroic soldier-poet. In the introduction to his 1981 study *Poetry of the First World War: A Casebook*, Dominic Hibberd summarizes Brooke's significance to the wartime public:

■ The vogue for poetry by the men who were actually doing the fighting was given force by Brooke's death in 1915; in his *1914* ['1914'] sonnets he seemed to have come closer than anyone to speaking as the national war poet. Although some people were privately sceptical about his achievement, his public image was defined by Winston Churchill in an eloquent obituary in *The Times* [an excerpt from this is discussed in the final subsection of this chapter]. Hundreds of soldier-poets were discovered in the middle years of the war, and often introduced to the public in extravagant terms, although the verse in their slim volumes was rarely of the smallest literary merit.[62] ☐

The interest in the poetry by 'men who were actually doing the fighting' went beyond Rupert Brooke. As Hibberd goes on to discuss, the war poetry of Siegfried Sassoon and Robert Nichols was also widely read during the war years. Both poets had work included in the *Georgian Poetry* anthology covering the years 1916–17, and were seen as broadly in the same category of soldier-poet as Brooke.

Sassoon's war poetry developed a cynical and sometimes satirical tone as he became increasingly disaffected with the war's progress. In post-First World War criticism, Brooke and Sassoon were often placed in distinct categories: Brooke as the naïve idealist, Sassoon as the stern protest figure. During the war, as Hibberd observes:

■ Sassoon's war poems aroused adverse criticism but fewer hostile reactions than we might expect. Some critics suggested that this young officer had suffered too much to be able to write without bias, and the critic, essayist and autobiographer Edmund Gosse (1849–1928) commented that such verse would tend to weaken the war effort. There was general respect for Sassoon's burning honesty, but also agreement that, whatever he had written, it was 'not poetry'. In making this complaint, most reviewers seem to have meant that Sassoon's subject-matter was too violent and his rhythms too prosaic.[63] □

Thus some of his contemporaries implied that the traumatic nature of Sassoon's experiences placed both his poetry and his views about the war in question. Many critics (and, indeed the public) wished to see soldier-poets as noble figures but found this difficult to square, in Sassoon's case, with the vehemence of his protest. In the next chapter we will consider an example of the way in which Sassoon's poetic critique of the war was marginalized within a 'patriotic' 1920s anthology.

The treatment of Sassoon can perhaps be better understood in the context of wartime expectations of the 'soldier poet' or the 'war poet', as explored and expressed in a number of wartime anthologies. In the introduction to his 1917 anthology, *A Treasury of War Poetry: British and American Poems of the World War 1914–1917*, the editor George Herbert Clarke (1873–1953) incorporates a detailed description of the role and value that the war poet figure holds in wartime culture:

■ For the most part, the poetry of war, undertaken in this spirit, has touched and exalted such special qualities as patriotism, courage, self-sacrifice, enterprise, and endurance. Where it has tended to glorify war in itself, it is chiefly because war has released those qualities, so to speak, in stirring and spectacular ways; and where it has chosen to round upon war and upbraid it, it is because war has slain ardent and lovable youths and has brought misery and despair to women and old people. But the war poet has left the argument to others. For himself, he has seen and felt. Envisaging war from various angles, now romantically, now as the contemplative interpreter, but always in a spirit of catholic curiosity, he has sung the fall of Troy, the Roman adventures, the medieval battles and crusades, the fields of Agincourt and Waterloo, and the more modern revolutions. Since Homer [presumed author of the ancient Greek epics *The Iliad* and *The Odyssey*], he has spoken with martial eloquence through the voices of Drayton, Spenser [1552–99], Marlowe [1564–93], Webster [about 1578–1632], Shakespeare [1564–1616], Milton [1608–74], Byron, Scott, Burns [1759–96], Campbell [1777–1844], Tennyson, Browning [1812–89], the New England group, and Walt Whitman [1819–92] – to

mention only a few of the British and American names, – and he speaks
sincerely and powerfully to-day in the writings of Kipling, Hardy, Masefield,
Binyon, Newbolt, Watson, Rupert Brooke, and the two young soldiers – the
one English, the other American – who have lately lost their lives while on
active service: Captain Charles Hamilton Sorley, who was killed at Hulluch,
October 18, 1915; and Alan Seeger [born 1888], who fell, mortally
wounded, during the charge on Belloy-en-Santerre, July 4, 1916. □

Clarke here represents the war poet role as 'envisaging the war from
various angles' and he refers to a broad spectrum of examples leading
up to the time of writing. According to Clarke's analysis the individual
poets, historical circumstances and viewpoints (romantic, curious and
so on) may change, but the war poet role is based on a profound sense
of continuity and non-partisanship: 'the war poet has left the argument
to others'.

Whilst many poets were published with greater ease due to the
vogue for soldier-poets after Brooke's death, some poets who went on
to become regular fixtures of anthologies and critical studies in the second half of the twentieth century were little known during the war
itself. The work of Wilfred Owen, for example, was only brought to the
attention of a substantial reading public well after the end of the war.
Poems by Wilfred Owen was published in 1920 and was well received by a
small number of writers and literary critics, including the poet, editor,
critic and performer Edith Sitwell (1887–1964) and the editor and critic,
John Middleton Murry (1889–1957).

It is also important to remember that despite the wartime popularity
of soldier poetry and the literary canonization of Brooke, the conceptu-
alization of war poetry during and immediately after the war period did
not fall neatly into pro- and anti-war categories. In 1924, the poet
Henry Newbolt wrote of Owen:

■ He [Siegfried Sassoon] has sent me Wilfred Owen's Poems, with an
Introduction by himself. The best of them I know already – they are terribly
good, but of course limited, almost all on one note. I like better Sassoon's
two-sided collection, there are more than two sides to this business of war,
and a man is hardly normal any longer if he comes down to one. S. S. says
that Owen pitied others but never himself: I'm afraid that isn't quite true –
or at any rate quite fair. To be a man one must be willing that others as well
as yourself should bear the burden that must be borne. When I looked into
Douglas Haig [1861–1928, Commander-in-Chief of the British army during
the First World War] I saw what is really great – perfect acceptance, which
means perfect faith. Owen and the rest of the broken men rail at the Old
Men [the term is capitalized because it was used to refer specifically to
the older generation of men in power during the First World War] who sent the
young to die: they suffered cruelly, but in the nerves and not the heart – they

haven't the experience or the imagination to know the extreme human agony ... .[64] □

Here, although Newbolt describes Owen's poetry as 'terribly good', he sees Owen's representation of the war as highly problematic. He is also slightly dismissive of Owen's suffering as of 'the nerves and not the heart'. Despite Sassoon's arguments to the contrary, he sees Owen as self-pitying. As we will examine in more detail in the next chapter, it was not until the late 1920s and early 1930s that Owen's readership increased and his reputation as the definitively compassionate war poet began to build up. In the next two subsections, however, we will concentrate on the way in which poets were received and understood by their contemporaries.

MENTORS AND CRITICS

There are many diaries, letters and memoirs by First World War poets that display keen interest in the work of their contemporaries. These show the extent to which poets influenced each other's work, and occasionally inspired intense admiration.

Sassoon met Owen in 1917 at Craiglockhart War Hospital and acted as mentor and friend to Owen at a crucial point in the latter's poetic development. In *Anthem for Doomed Youth: Twelve Soldier Poets of the First World War* (2002), Jon Stallworthy points out that a surviving manuscript of Owen's poem 'Anthem for Doomed Youth' clearly shows the amendments and suggestions that Sassoon made, including the title itself. Stallworthy writes:

■ Some indication of the nature of Sassoon's contribution to Owen's poetic development can be gained from the fact that the final manuscript draft of this poem contains nine words and several cancellations in the handwriting of the older poet, whose own work would never equal the rich density of meaning and music in those lines.[65] □

As we saw earlier, Sassoon had also talked to Henry Newbolt of Owen's qualities as a poet, in particular his capacity for compassion. Among Owen's paeans of praise for his mentor was the comment: 'if I had the choice of making friends with Tennyson or with Sassoon, I should go to Sassoon ...'.[66]

Owen and Sassoon were also aware of the different strains of war poetry being published, including work by jingoistic and militarist poets who continued to urge support for the war. Having witnessed and taken part in trench warfare, and knowing something of the sheer scale of casualties in what by 1917 Sassoon was calling a 'war of aggression', pro-war poetry by non-combatants was especially offensive to them. Both Owen and Sassoon were aware of the 'white feather' women, who gave the feathers as symbols of cowardice to any man they judged to be avoiding military service, and both wrote poems aimed at what they saw as women's pernicious role.

Sassoon's bitter poem 'Glory of Women' describes women as romantic hypocrites: keen for men to be sent to the battlefront, but reluctant to understand the nature of the fighting or register the horrific nature of the injuries sustained: 'You love us when we're heroes, home on leave,/ Or wounded in a mentionable place.'[67] The type of attitude Sassoon satirizes here was exemplified by the work of Jessie Pope, whose poem 'The Call' we considered briefly earlier in this chapter. Owen made his own response to the militant, non-combatant female poets by dedicating the poem 'Dulce et Decorum Est' to Pope herself. The following short quotation from this poem illustrates Owen's determination to represent the very visceral and unromantic nature of his comrades' suffering:

■ If you could hear, at every jolt, the blood
Come gargling from the froth-corrupted lungs,
Obscene as cancer, bitter as the cud
Of vile, incurable sores on innocent tongues,–
My friend, you would not tell with such high zest
To children ardent for some desperate glory,
The old Lie: Dulce et decorum est
Pro patria mori.[68] □

Both Owen's and Sassoon's poems have been the source of considerable debate, with some feminist critics arguing that they express the fundamentally misogynistic thinking of their day. Further examples of feminist and cultural–historical approaches to poems such as these will be considered in Chapter Five.

One of the poets most frequently mentioned by his peers as a point of reference or subject of poetic interest, is Rupert Brooke. Brooke is discussed from a range of perspectives: sometimes admiring, but often with a degree of caution, critical distance or even wry humour. These comments are interesting not only for the observations they make about Brooke and the prevalence of his famous war sonnets, but also for the thoughts they offer more widely on the poetic representation of the war and on the poet's own literary contexts and antecedents. In a letter to his friend the composer Herbert Howells in May 1916, the poet and composer Ivor Gurney incorporates a partial quotation from Brooke's sonnet 'The Soldier':

■ What have you been writing this term? Something clear and English I hope. Does the war still obsess you? If so, you are, perhaps, less fortunate than your comrades in the Army, whose mind is full of pack and rifle, buttons and boots.

When you get back to London, ask Miss Scott for the two books of poems I lent her; you will probably find something to suit you. How I envy you the chance of seeing Shakespeare, a desire that is very strong in me. O to see Antony and to be thrilled once again by Antony's passion and the proud defiances of the great queen. If I must die think only this of me, that I sincerely wish that what rag of a mantle I possess should descend on you, and inspire you someday to turn your thoughts to an Antony symphony.[69] □

In this extract, Gurney makes an important and interesting reference to contrasting perceptions of the war. For those at home, he implies, war is a grandiose and ultimately abstract concept, whereas for soldiers the day-to-day details and necessities of military life are all-consuming, leaving little room to consider any larger idea of war.

Gurney's contrast between remote, abstract perceptions of war and the activities and ideas that 'matter' is also carried through into his next point. Drawing on a quote from one of Rupert Brooke's war sonnets, 'The Soldier', 'If I should die, think only this of me', Gurney implies a sense of being compelled to sacrifice himself, by changing 'should' to 'must'. He also expresses a wish that Howells might take Gurney's creative 'mantle' upon himself. Here, Gurney seems to be anticipating the likelihood of his death in battle, and asking for his musical legacy to be continued by Howells by means of a symphony on the story of Anthony and Cleopatra. Gurney refers to Brooke's work in variety of ways in his letters, sharing, to some extent, his passion for Englishness. He is at times clearly admiring of Brooke's poetry. In this instance, however, the way in which a line from Brooke's sonnet is used creates an ironic overtone. The quotation is incorporated abruptly into the paragraph and juxtaposed with the anti-heroic attitude to army life that Gurney has already displayed. As we will consider in the final subsection, it is important to remember that Brooke's war sonnets were not only popular, they had also become closely intertwined with the official discourses of heroic sacrifice. For many of those who had experienced the war, phrases such as Brooke's 'If I should die ...' had already become synonymous with the superficial romanticization of war, and were, quite simply, overused.

For Isaac Rosenberg, too, the heightened emotion of Brooke's sonnets was unsatisfactory. As the following quotation from a letter written during the war shows, Rosenberg was interested in the development of fresh modes of expression and a more careful direction of the emotional content of a poem:

> ■ The Poetry Review you sent is good – the articles are too breathless and want more packing, I think. The poems by the soldiers are vigorous [sic] but, I feel a bit commonplace. I did not like Rupert Brookes begloried sonnets for the same reason. What I mean is second hand phrases 'lambent fires' etc takes from its reality and strength. It should be approached in a colder way, more abstract, with less of the million feelings everybody feels; or all these should be concentrated in one distinguished emotion.[70] □

Rosenberg sees Brooke's language as rather artificially grand ('beglo-ried'), unoriginal ('second hand') and too commonplace in the emotions expressed. Rosenberg had a very different social and cultural background to Brooke, coming from a family of poor, Russian Jewish émigrés and, as Michael Schmidt points out in his *Lives of the Poets* (1998), Rosenberg also had a very different relationship to poetic language and image:

> ■ What are received diction and form for his Georgian contemporaries are simply inexpressive for him. Language remains dynamic, resistant. Paying little attention to punctuation, concentrating on cadence and image, he never shies away from mixed metaphor or questionable and archaic usage. When he had a war image to convey he did so with resolute objectivity, nei-ther blurring nor heightening the literal.[71] □

According to Schmidt, Rosenberg's thinking about poetry emanates from a specific context, one imbued with biblical imagery and a rhythm and tone quite distinct from that of the Georgians.

We have already touched on the wartime debates about the desir-ability of a poet's closeness to action, not only in a literal, physical sense but also in terms of an immersion in the details and emotions of combat experience, and the impact of this on their poetry. At the end of the sub-section on protest and pacifism, we noted that some critics saw a lack of aesthetic distance in Sassoon's war poetry, proposing that his anger and indignation were symptoms of his suffering rather than reasoned or jus-tifiable responses. The issue of objectivity or distance from one's subject was also of interest to other war poets. Charles Sorley, again discussing Brooke, argues that Brooke's fixation with the idea of his own sacrifice focuses attention obsessively and self-indulgently on the poet himself:

> ■ … I saw Rupert Brooke's death in *The Morning Post*. *The Morning Post*, which has always hitherto disapproved of him, is now loud in his praises because he has conformed to their stupid axiom of literary criticism that

the only stuff of poetry is violent physical experience, by dying on active service. I think Brooke's earlier poems – especially notably 'The Fish' and 'Grantchester', which you can find in *Georgian Poetry* – are his best. That last sonnet-sequence of his, of which you sent me the review in the *Times Lit. Supp.*, [*The Times Literary Supplement*] and which has been so praised, I find (with the exception of that ['The Dead'] beginning 'These hearts were woven of human joys and cares, Washed marvellously with sorrow' which is not about himself) overpraised. He is far too obsessed with his own sacrifice, regarding the going to war of himself (and others) as a highly intense, remarkable and sacrificial exploit, whereas it is merely the conduct demanded of him (and others) by the turn of circumstances, where non-compliance with this demand would have made life intolerable. [72] □

Sorley holds to a determinedly functional view of soldierly duty, by asserting that the individual's military role in wartime is a matter of compliance with 'the turn of circumstance'. Brooke, he argues, overlays this with a largely self-serving ideology of sacrificial dedication.

POETRY AND HISTORY

Later in this Guide, we will examine some of the key literary critical models developed to represent and understand the poetry of the First World War, including those based on the primacy of the individual soldier's experience and others which focus on the literary and mythological nature of the war. It is also important, however, to consider the close relationship between the historical and poetic representations of war, and the role of this in the development of the genre.

For example, in J. C. King's historical account *The First World War* (1972), one section is entitled 'Trench Life'.[73] This, amidst the various sections describing and analysing wartime policies and conditions, consists almost entirely of literary extracts or whole texts. A large passage is quoted from Graves's *Goodbye To All That*, followed by 16 complete poems, including work by Sassoon, Owen and Yeats.[74] Very little analysis is given of the content or status of these texts within the overall historical narrative; the poems are printed consecutively, as in an anthology. The inference is that these samples of war literature can illustrate history, perhaps even in a small way be a substitute for a prosaically academic account of combat conditions.

Commentators have, in the second half of the twentieth century, begun to explore what it means to use war poetry as a historical tool: to question how far war poems can give a special insight into the individual experiences behind the grand historical narratives of war. As we discussed in Chapter One, however, the association between war poetry and war history continues to thrive. In this subsection, we will consider briefly the ways in which this association began to take shape during the First World War, by looking at two contrasting extracts from wartime texts. Both extracts refer to or imply the view that war poetry offers a means of telling different kinds of history.

When the death of Rupert Brooke was announced in 1915, an obituary notice written by Winston Churchill, then the First Lord of the Admiralty, was printed in *The Times,* illustrating how useful poetry and poets had become to those who were involved in prosecuting and sustaining the war:

> ■ Rupert Brooke is dead. A telegram from the Admiral at Lemnos tells us that his life has closed at the moment when it seemed to have reached its springtime. A voice had become audible, a note had been struck, more true, more thrilling, more able to do justice to the nobility of our youth in arms engaged in this present war than any other, more able to express their thoughts of self-surrender, and with a power to carry comfort to those who watch them so intensely from afar. The voice has been softly stilled. Only the echoes and memory remain; but they will linger. ...
>
> The thoughts to which he gave expression in the very few incomparable war sonnets which he has left behind will be shared by the many thousands of young men moving resolutely and blithely forward into this, the hardest, the cruellest, and the least-rewarded of all the wars that men have fought. They are a whole history and revelation of Rupert Brooke himself. Joyous, fearless, versatile, deeply instructed, with classic symmetry of mind and body, ruled by high undoubting purpose, he was all that one could wish England's noblest sons to be in days when no sacrifice but the most precious is acceptable, and the most precious is that which is most freely proffered.[75] ▯

The terms in which Churchill represents Brooke bear some similarities with the description in the *Times Literary Supplement* review discussed earlier. Brooke's youth and artistic promise are referred to, his poetry is described as doing 'justice' to the nobility of the young soldiers fighting for Britain and he is 'all that one could wish England's noblest sons to be'. Following the discussions in the subsection on propaganda, we can see that the language used to describe Brooke is carefully tailored to support the recruitment drive, referring to the high esteem in which an honourable military death is held. Churchill's portrayal was important in reinforcing a glorified idea of Brooke as soldier and aesthete, despite Brooke's very limited combat experience. This image was eagerly reinforced by other public and literary figures, including the poet Frances Cornford (1886–1960), whose ode written on Brooke's death included the description of him as a 'young Apollo, golden-haired'.[76]

Churchill's depiction of Brooke is also, crucially, one in which his war sonnets stand as a 'history and revelation' of Brooke himself. On one level, this description is a reflection of the iconic status being ascribed to Brooke, suggesting that his reputation is significant and will endure. Yet in the context of the obituary as a whole, the phrase 'history and revelation' is suggestive of both an internal and external dimension. Clearly Brooke's sonnets are not constructed around narratives of battle in the sense that Tennyson's 'Charge of the Light Brigade' is. Yet Churchill does imply that the poetry reveals the heroic nature of Brooke as a soldier-poet, and that it records some of the larger issues and events in which he played a part. As a major public figure and author writing an official obituary, Churchill has the capacity to interpolate Brooke into the governmental history of the war as the war itself is still under way.

There are other, far less romantic instances of the tendency to interweave the war poetry genre and historical representations of the war. In the periodical *The New Age* (1907–22) the initial response to war was often to turn a mocking face to the jingoistic excesses of pro-war poets, and many parodic verses were printed in its pages. As early as 17 December 1914, the 'pastiche' column of *The New Age* included a poem by 'Attila', called 'William Watson, War-Eater'. Watson, to whom *The Times* reader's letter discussed earlier in this chapter refers, was one of the most prolific and popular pro-war poets of the day, yet as the following extract from the 'Attila' poem shows, he was viewed by some as an absurd and vicious figure:

■ And granny Bridges got the Laureate's crown.
Watson was dumb, we knew his shot was sped,
But Watson barren is not Watson dead.
Once more he clamours loudly from his hearse
And makes war viler with his verse and worse,
Once more our blatant, beefy bard explodes
In sonnets, jingo jingles and in odes.
This apoplectic patrio, fierce and hot,
Plasters the saffron press with smoking rot;
He buries (rigged with pseudo-Shakespeare rhymes)
The Kaiser, and he barks from out the 'Times' –
(So much per bark), or snorting through the nose,
Follows the odorous breeze that Harmsworth* blows.[77] □

* Alfred Harmsworth became Lord Northcliffe, the newspaper proprietor mentioned earlier in this chapter.

Watson is parodied here as an excessively bellicose voice, piqued at Robert Bridges' appointment to the position of Poet Laureate and escalating anti-German feeling. The quality of the poetry is mocked as 'jingo jingles' and 'smoking rot', and the unsophisticated technique associated with Watson's work is mimicked within the poem itself through the use of clumsy, emphatically rhyming couplets. At the heart of this poem, though, is not only its parody of a particular poetic style but also its caricature of historically 'real' and dominant public figures and of the claustrophobic interdependence of poetry and pro-war fever. It is not only Watson's jingoism that is condemned, for instance: repugnance is also expressed towards the stance adopted by the daily press: 'the odorous breeze that Harmsworth blows'. This particular replaying and subverting of Watson's verse illustrates the extent to which war poetry was understood to be a highly effective political and historiographic form.

Over the course of the twentieth century, war poetry has continued to be treated by many critics and readers as offering historical accounts of war. As we discussed in Chapter One, this has attracted many objections, for example on the grounds that the poetic domain should not be defined by its ability to reflect the past in any literal or factual sense, being shaped to a large extent by the metaphorical, by imaginative projections and reinterpretations, and by complex, elusive, codified language. Yet war poetry has retained a strong historical undertow, derived in large part from developments in the First World War. In particular the rise of soldier poetry and the growth of interest in the romantic image of the soldier-poet helped reinforce contemporary thinking about the fundamental nobility of military duty. In the next chapter, we will examine how readers with very different ideas about the peaks of human achievement, and a profound antipathy to war, placed the figure of the soldier-poet under new scrutiny.

CHAPTER THREE

The Interwar Years

INTRODUCTION

Why should we consider the 1930s a significant period for the war poetry genre? In what way were attitudes to war developed during a decade in which the main historical issues might be thought to be economic, social and political, rather than military? In fact, the 1930s proved to be a time of critical change for the genre: not only was the aftermath of the First World War still being felt, but existing attitudes and representations of it were being challenged, particularly through literature. In many ways, the legacy of the 1930s, especially the interest in finding new types of heroic war poets, is still with us today.

This chapter, then, examines some of the key developments in war poetry during the period between the two world wars. It was during this period, and from the late 1920s to the late 1930s in particular, that a combination of historical and political circumstances and theoretical and literary contributions helped shape a newly anti-war conception of war poetry that has endured across many decades.

The first section of the chapter explores some of the divergent yet overlapping contexts in which war poetry was anthologized and read during the period. Whilst increasing interest in pacifist thought during the early 1930s created fertile ground for the appreciation of poets such as Owen, proudly patriotic anthologies of First World War poetry continued to be published. This section also discusses the role of the 'war books' of the late 1920s and early 1930s in stimulating biographical and literary interest in both war poetry and the figure of the war poet. The second section goes on to trace important changes in the reputations of two key war poets during this period, and considers how a more intense focus on the ideas of integrity, authenticity and the experiential basis of war poetry contributed to the cultural construction of the 'war poet'.

The third section looks more broadly at specialist interpretations of war poetry, beginning with the influence of post-First World War theoretical developments in literary criticism. This section examines views on the distinctive nature of poetry about war and whether it should be considered as somehow outside the poetry canon; it also discusses responses to more experimental representations of war within poetry.

The final section includes a selection of critical responses to Spanish Civil War poetry, many of which consider the themes of experience and authenticity in a different light. In this section the extracts examine the tendency towards ideological polarization in the Spanish conflict, leading to concerns with the relationship between war poetry and political orthodoxy, the role of poetry in conveying propaganda and the sincerity of political diction.

KEY CONTEXTS

PATRIOTISM IN WAR POETRY

The period between the two wars is important in understanding the way that values and images have accreted around the term 'war poet'. In earlier chapters we have seen how key figures in public life such as Winston Churchill had a role to play in this process, and how in particular the figure of Rupert Brooke was posthumously enshrined as an idealized son of England. In the decade following the war, verse collections in the heroic, patriotic vein, such as Rupert Brooke's *Sonnets*, sold extremely well: later examples in this vein include the 1918 anthology *For remembrance: Soldier Poets who have Fallen in the War* edited by A. St John Adcock[1] and the 1924 *Patriotism in Literature* edited by the poet and playwright John Drinkwater (1882–1937).

In Drinkwater's text, the selected poetry is inscribed within a passionately patriotic extended commentary: indeed Drinkwater asserts that it is more an essay on patriotism which has been illustrated by poems, than an anthology. In this, one of the central ideas espoused is that of 'The devotion of the individual citizen to the State, the consent of the free man in subjection to the prevailing interest of the whole body politic.'[2] The poems discussed are drawn from several hundred years and most are in the heroic or romantic mould, including an excerpt from Shakespeare's *Henry V* and Drayton's 'A Ballad of Agincourt'. Yet also included are poems by Sassoon, a poet known at this point (as discussed in Chapter Two) for his protest about the First World War. Drinkwater comments on Sassoon's oeuvre in the following terms:

■ As is well known, when the emotion of action itself, during the Great War, was more poetically, if not more pointedly expressed, it was generally in terms of almost ferocious denial, as in the war poems of Mr. Siegfried Sassoon and others.[3] □

Drinkwater here addresses the apparently contradictory conjunction of his patriotic ethos and Sassoon's poetic critique of military authority: he situates Sassoon within a wider grouping of First World War poets whose experiences resulted in 'ferocious denial'. By framing poetry critical of the war as 'denial', Drinkwater is able to sustain his overarching emphasis on the supreme importance of personal sacrifice for country. Also, as Sassoon was a decorated officer who returned to his military post after his period of protest, he can be incorporated as a rebellious figure redeemed by his heroism and sense of comradely duty. The decision to include him in *Patriotism in Literature* suggests considerable confidence in the text's ideological and literary principles. Drinkwater operates from within a heroic and militaristic literary tradition. He assumes a readership of proud patriots, able to reconcile some of the more visceral details of warfare with a continuing satisfaction and gratitude in the war's outcome. The individuals selected are described as 'soldier poets', part of a victorious historical enterprise both martial and artistic in nature.[4] The patriotic soldier-poet tradition continued well into the 1930s in parallel with the newer anti-war interest in the figures of Owen and Sassoon, examined later in this chapter: *An Anthology of War Poems* by F. Brereton was published in 1930[5] and F. W. Ziv's anthology, *The Valiant Muse: An Anthology of Poems by Poets Killed in the World War* appeared in 1936, the year the Spanish Civil War began.[6] Indeed, elements of this tradition, in adapted and updated forms, have continued to be in evidence throughout the twentieth and into the twenty-first century, as we will examine further in Chapter Five.

PACIFIST THOUGHT

While the patriotic type of anthology continued to be popular during the 1918–39 period, the conception of war poetry as primarily heroic and noble was to be challenged and extended. One of the challenges was raised by an upsurge of sympathy with pacifist ideas, particularly amongst intellectuals, a phenomenon that the historian Angus Calder refers to as a 'great revulsion of feeling against war in the early 1930s'.[7] There had, as mentioned in Chapter Two, been Conscientious Objectors in the First World War, who had protested on a variety of grounds, including religious beliefs (for Quakers, pacifism was a basic tenet of faith), and the conviction that the war was being conducted by rival imperialist powers, with little regard to ordinary lives. In the main, First World War Conscientious Objectors were making individual stands of conscience in the face of the specific war that was under way.[8] The anti-war views of the late 1920s and early 1930s, however, grew from the desire to prevent future conflicts and for many on the Left, this formed part of a more general desire for radical change to the existing social and political order.

Many writers and poets of the 1930s were preoccupied with perceived failures in the political system, including the prominent figures of W. H. Auden (1907–73), Stephen Spender, Cecil Day Lewis and Louis MacNeice (1907–63). When Stephen Spender later came to review the decade in *The Thirties and After* (1978), he described the prevailing mood as a 'left-wing orthodoxy' that had been in place amongst his generation since the First World War, founded on a deep antipathy to the older generation, the officer class and the British Empire.[9] He also emphasized that many literary figures of the 1930s were convinced of the need for the writer to engage with social and political issues, rather than producing art primarily for its own sake or keeping to subjects previous generations had thought suitable for poetry. Within the left-wing orthodoxy that Spender describes, war was often a target of opprobrium, symbolic of the corruption of the ruling class and the failure of the system.

This type of thinking is evident in the anthologies *New Signatures* (1932)[10] and *New Country* (1933).[11] In these, the editor, Michael Roberts (1902–48) argues for the overthrow of democratic capitalist liberalism, criticizing in particular the rampant commercialization and social and cultural impoverishment of everyday life and calling for the way to be prepared for 'an English Lenin'. A key issue for Roberts was the prospect of war as the ultimate destructive expression of what he saw as the 'anticultural capitalist system'.[12] In the following quotations, Roberts argues that the writing and poetry in *New Country* has a role or a function beyond the purely aesthetic; that the contributors are attempting to have a wider impact upon the external world:

> ■ I think, and the writers in this book obviously agree, that there is only one way of life for us: to renounce that system now and to live by fighting against it. And that not because we would sacrifice the present to the future, nor because we imagine that the world which we shall help to make will be in any absolute sense 'better' than the present, but because there is no other decent way of life for us, no other way of living at our best. [...][13]
>
> The writers in this book are trying to make something, to say something as clearly as may be, to express an attitude which this preface can only adumbrate. They are no more concerned with making 'literature' than Plato [428–348 BC, Greek philosopher] was, or Villon [about 1431–1463, French poet] or Wilfred Owen: 'The poetry is in the pity.'[14] □

Here, it is possible to see Roberts' tendency to draw his contributors together, to imply a sense of unity or joint identity, a characteristic that has been commented on by many critics. For example, the poet, critic and editor Geoffrey Grigson (1905–85) reviewing *New Country* in the

1933 edition of his literary periodical *New Verse*, comments acerbically on the way that 'Roberts in a long preface "uses" and "ours"'.[15] The degree of consistency among the political views of the *New Country* contributors was, however, far less than Roberts at times suggested. The leftish orthodoxy amongst writers and intellectuals of the 1930s was a loose conglomeration of broadly left-wing views rather than a coherent movement towards a specific ideology. As Spender points out, the four individuals often viewed as the literary heart of this orthodoxy, Auden, Lewis, MacNeice and himself, held substantively different political beliefs and did not meet as a group.[16]

Despite the slightly misleading preoccupation with a unified identity, however, Roberts's editorial emphasis on 'making' and 'saying' something through literary texts was shared by many writers and poets of the 1930s, and his use of Owen and the First World War as key points of reference was indicative of a broader phenomenon. Owen was becoming a poetic and pacifist role model for those of Spender's generation, a development examined in more detail later in this chapter. Perhaps more surprisingly, Roberts refers to First World War experiences in explaining his radical proposals for social and political change: at one point he argues that many men had experiences of working together for some common purpose in the First World War in a way that 'almost seemed to justify the filth and inhumanity of war'.[17] This comment illustrates how profoundly the First World War affected the 1930s generation but also gives some indication of the complexity of the war's place in personal and cultural memory. Images of the war could be drawn upon selectively and to very different effect: even those who condemned the overall conduct and purpose of the war could filter out and cherish an image of communal cooperation and mutual support. The tensions between pacifist ideals, radical socialist aspirations and admiration for what might be described as Owenesque heroic humanitarianism[18] were to have an enormous impact on the production and reception of war poetry during the decade, particularly when the commencement of the Spanish Civil War in 1936 caused a large number of pacifists from different traditions to support a military struggle against Fascism.[19] Some of the literary developments and debates that were stimulated by these events are examined later in this chapter.

MEMOIRS OF WAR

One of the factors that encouraged the growth of pacifist opinion was, as Martin Ceadel describes in *Pacifism in Britain, 1914–1945*, 'an increased sensitivity to the suffering any war would involve – induced not only by the flood of books about the Great War which had appeared in 1928–30, but more especially by the horrific visions of a future air gas war depicted in the pro-Disarmament Conference propaganda of 1931–2.'[20] Along with the fear of new methods of warfare, a number of texts appeared that began to have a significant impact on the historiography and popular representations of the First World War. These books were notable for reviewing the events of the First World War with critical, sometimes caustic voices, exploring in detail the level of human degradation involved in trench warfare. Perhaps even more importantly, some of these books revealed the varying levels of competence among senior officers and the anti-heroic methods and habits to which many men were reduced in order to cope physically and mentally with combat. In the play *Journey's End* by R. C. Sherriff (1896–1975), first performed in 1928, the protagonist Stanhope's flawed heroic leadership is shown to be bolstered by petty cruelties and dipsomania. The other key characters, Raleigh, the innocent, hero-worshipping youth, and Osbourne, the loyal professional, are killed in action. The play focuses upon a new officer's misguided reliance upon a romantic view of war and a public school code of conduct, and notably avoids any redeeming moral conclusion. The script went through ten impressions during the following year. Another influential text that revealed a new view of the war was *All Quiet on the Western Front* (1929) by the German novelist Erich Maria Remarque (1898–1970).[21] Both Remarque and Sherriff had been soldiers in the First World War.

During broadly the same period, poets of the First World War began to give accounts of their combat experiences in prose. Siegfried Sassoon touched upon elements of his life as an infantry officer in his first three volumes of memoirs, published between 1928 and 1936;[22] Edmund Blunden's *Undertones of War* came out in 1928 and Robert Graves's *Goodbye to all That* appeared in 1929. In 1933 the writer, pacifist and feminist Vera Brittain (1893–1970), who had served as a VAD (Voluntary Aid Detachment) nurse in the conflict, produced her first volume of autobiography, *Testament of Youth*, which made extensive references to the poetry of the war and the poetic practice of 'ordinary' soldiers. In addition, the book-length prose poem *In Parenthesis*, written over a period of approximately ten years by the poet and artist David Jones, was published in 1936 (the next section of this chapter examines Jones's work in more detail). *In Parenthesis*, which used a number of Modernist techniques such as a constantly shifting centre of consciousness and fluid treatment of time, also invoked elements of the memoir; the author announces at the beginning of his preface: 'This writing has to do with some things I saw, felt & was part of', identifying several of the poem's key subjects and events with his own experiences during the war.[23]

The various war books and memoirs had a role in altering public perceptions of how the First World War had been fought, at what price, and whether, subsequently, it had been accurately represented. They also offered new perspectives on the war poets themselves, affirming the place of the war poet as a subject in his or her own right. Unlike much of the attention that had been directed towards Brooke, however, the poets' self-reflexive accounts of the war included more subtle investigations of the motivations and methods of the combatants, the successes and failings of the military hierarchy and the impact of extensive periods of trench warfare on the individual. As memoirists, the poets tended towards a pared down, observational writing style that appears, at times, intentionally anti-heroic. Yet, they also wrote extensively about contemporary formulations of heroism and bravery and the way in which class, regional and regimental identity and personal value systems shaped the principles of honourable and dishonourable behaviour in combat. Despite extensive critical coverage of bungled operations and inadequacies in supplies, training and preparation for combat, there is little doubt for Graves, Blunden or, ultimately, Sassoon that it is an officer's duty to lead his men effectively. Observations about the inefficacy of many field operations and graphic descriptions of the war wounded or dead run in parallel with tacit or explicit acknowledgements of courage and bravery. In *Goodbye to All That*, for example, Robert Graves gives the following description of the aftermath of the disastrous push at Cambrin (1915):

■ No order came at dawn, and no more attacks were promised us after this. From the morning of September 24th to the night of October 3rd, I had in all eight hours of sleep. I kept myself awake and alive by drinking about a bottle of whisky a day. I had never drunk it before, and have seldom drunk it since; it certainly helped me then. We had no blankets, greatcoats, or waterproof sheets, nor any time or material to build new shelters. The rain poured down. Every night we went out to fetch in the dead of the other battalions. The Germans continued indulgent and we had few casualties. After the first day or two the corpses swelled and stank. I vomited more than once while superintending the carrying. Those we could not get in from the German wire continued to swell until the wall of the stomach collapsed, either naturally or when punctured by a bullet; a disgusting smell would float across. The colour of the dead faces changed from white to yellow-grey, to red, to purple, to green, to black, to slimy.[24] □

The passage culminates in an account of a particularly courageous rescue by a fellow officer whom Graves recommended for the Victoria Cross; yet the authorities, notes Graves, thought this worth no more than the lower status Distinguished Conduct Medal. This disturbing episode is used to represent an instance of comradely bravery, yet Graves makes it quite clear that this is entirely distinct from the abstract idea of patriotism, which is considered too remote from the trenches to be relevant to the soldiers.

These memoirs provided descriptions of other soldier-poets, commented on the relationship between combat experience and poetry, and even offered alternative perspectives upon elements of specific war poems. In *Goodbye to All That* the following description of an incident in Mametz wood appears:

■ Not a single tree in the wood remained unbroken. I collected my over-coats, and came away as quickly as I could, climbing through the wreckage of green branches. Going and coming, by the only possible route, I passed by the bloated and stinking corpse of a German with his back propped against a tree. He had a green face, spectacles, close-shaven hair; black blood was dripping from his nose and beard. [25] □

Compare this passage with Graves's 1916 poem, 'A Dead Boche':

■ To you who'd read my songs of War
And only hear of blood and fame,
I'll say (you've heard it said before)
'War's Hell!' and if you doubt the same,
To-day I found in Mametz Wood
A certain cure for lust of blood:

Where, propped against a shattered trunk,
In a great mess of things unclean,
Sat a dead Boche; he scowled and stunk
With clothes and face a sodden green,
Big-bellied, spectacled, crop-haired,
Dribbling black blood from nose and beard. [26] □

The two representations seem to be based around the same image, yet viewing them together in this way shows the contrast between the laconic, factual emphasis of the memoir description and the more sarcastic use of language, strong rhythm and emphatic message of the poem. The war books reinforced the growing biographical interest in the figure of the war poet as a point of fusion between experience and art; an embodiment of the idea that extremity of experience is conducive to artistic expression.

The growing interest in preventing war, the keenness of writers to become involved in the social and political struggle, and the publication of war memoirs all contributed to a new receptiveness towards critical and protest poetry of the First World War. The fear of another war and greater insight into the conditions of the recent war began to cast heroic patriotism in a more problematic light. In the next section, case studies examining the changing fortunes of two poets of the First World War show how these factors began to influence biographical and literary readings.

THE WAR POETS EMERGE

THE RISE OF OWEN

Prior to 1928, very few outside a small, specialist circle of poets and poetry critics were aware of Wilfred Owen; a collection of his poems had been published in 1920 but had failed to reach a wider audience.[27] In his introduction to the 1997 Everyman edition of *Rupert Brooke & Wilfred Owen*, George Walter compares the muted initial response to Owen's work with the success of Brooke's *1914 and Other Poems*:

■ *Poems by Wilfred Owen* was, in commercial terms at least, much less successful. Despite an enthusiastic reception from reviewers, it failed to sell particularly well and a second, slightly enlarged edition published in 1921 suffered a similar fate. However, it did succeed in its aims of arousing some interest in both Owen's poetry and his personality. Edith Sitwell's selection of poems, carefully made and arranged so as to emphasize Owen's compassion and moral indignation, presented the picture of a tragic, selfless, talented young man whose humanism in the face of wartime atrocity spoke out from every poem. The inclusion of Owen's perplexing Preface, with its stress on 'Poetry' and 'pity', and Sassoon's measured introduction, which spoke of allowing Owen's poems 'backed by the authority of his experience as an infantry soldier' to speak for him, reinforced the picture. Nothing was included that would disrupt this image and it is, to a large extent, Sitwell's and Sassoon's construction of Owen and his work that has survived to this day.[28] □

As Walter goes on to argue, the Churchillian view of the war that had held sway in the 1920s began to show cracks in the more critical climate of the early 1930s. These were more favourable conditions for the appreciation of Owen's poetry and by the time Edmund Blunden published an edition of his work in 1931, a new generation of readers and poets was becoming interested in Owen's poetic style and content.[29] This change is illustrated well by the analysis in Cecil Day Lewis' *A Hope for Poetry* (1934), in which Day Lewis situates the poet Gerard Manley Hopkins (1844–89), Owen and T. S. Eliot as the trinity of poetic ancestors of, or key influences on, his post-First World War generation. In the following long extract, Day Lewis examines Owen's contribution to English poetry in a way that illustrates clearly the centrality of his biography and personal connection with the war:

■ Gerard Manley Hopkins died young in the year 1889. His poems were not published till 1918, the year in which Wilfred Owen was killed. Hopkins would have been a poet under any circumstances: Owen, I am inclined to think, was made a poet by the war. The notes which he set down for a preface to his poems give the clue to his identity.

This book is not about heroes. English poetry is not yet fit to speak of them. Nor is it about deeds or lands, nor anything about glory, honour, dominion or power,

> Except War.
> Above all, this book is not concerned with Poetry.
> The subject of it is War, and the pity of War.
> The Poetry is in the pity.
> Yet these elegies are not to this generation,
>   This is in no sense consolatory.
> They may be to the next.
> All the poet can do to-day is to warn.
> That is why the true Poets must be truthful.

This noble, fragmentary message reached the next generation, as he hoped, and meant more to them than perhaps he ever had expected. We must be careful not to misunderstand him, though. When he says that his book 'is not concerned with Poetry', he is not simply expressing what most artists feel at times, particularly at times of great external crisis – a sense of the ineffectiveness and isolation of their own form of life. Nor does he imply that poetry can ever be concerned with itself to any advantage. He is saying, I think, that there are times when the poet's allegiance must be divided: when his duty towards his neighbour ceases to be necessarily identical with his duty towards his god, Poetry, the former acquiring temporarily a relatively enlarged significance in his mind. In other words, circumstances may force the poet unwillingly to take up the position of a prophet – 'all the poet can do to-day is warn'. Again, when he says, 'That is why the true Poets must be truthful', he is not suggesting that there are times when true Poets are allowed to tell lies. There is poetical truth, and there is common honesty; they are very distant relations: Owen's plea was that the crisis should bring them together, that the greater – poetical truth – should temporarily put itself under the command of the lesser. Owen commends himself to post-war poets largely because they feel themselves to be in the same predicament; they feel the same lack of a stable background against which the dance of words may stand out plainly, the same distrust and horror of the unnatural forms into which life for the majority of people is being forced. They know in their hearts exactly what Owen meant when he said 'the poetry is in the pity'.

> Move him into the sun–
> Gently its touch awoke him once,
> At home, whispering of fields unsown.
> Always it woke him, even in France,
> Until this morning and this snow.
> If anything might rouse him now
> The kind old sun will know.

Think how it wakes the seeds –
Woke, once, the clays of a cold star.
Are limbs so dear-achieved, are sides
Full-nerved – still warm – too hard to stir?
Was it for this the clay grew tall?
O what made fatuous sunbeams toil
To break earth's sleep at all?
['Futility']

It is difficult to call this anything but a perfect poem. Poetical truth becoming here, as in almost all his poems, the servant of common honesty – of Owen's determination to tell the factual, un-'poetical' truth, so far from being cramped and degraded, is enlarged and glorified. Owen had mastered that easy, almost conversational kind of verse at which many of the Georgian poets were aiming, in their reaction away from the laborious magniloquence of the 'Nineties': unlike them, he never seems to lose dignity in the process; he speaks as one having authority, never condescending to language or adopting the hail-fellow-well-met tones of the poet who has a craving to be 'understood'. The first verse of the poem quoted above is an object lesson in the simplicity that never was paucity: in the second, engined with pity and indignation, the poetry leaves the ground and ascends into heaven, culminating on a line, 'Was it for this the clay grew tall?' which would stand out from the work of any but the greatest poets.

One of the traditional tests of a poet is the number of outstanding, memorable lines he has written: this test Owen passes triumphantly. The lines of his which stick most in our memory can be divided into two types. The first of these is highly 'poetical', in the grand manner, reminding us of Keats [1795–1821] – a poet with whom Owen had a great deal more in common than an early death. It is exemplified in such lines as –

... Whatever shares
The eternal reciprocity of tears.
['Insensibility']

... Whose world is but the trembling of a flare,
And heaven but as the highway for a shell. ...
['Apologia pro Poemate Meo' ('A Defence of My Poem')]

... Mine ancient scars shall not be glorified
Nor my titanic tears the seas be dried.
['The End'][30]

The second type is restrained, often witty in the seventeenth-century sense, always ironical: it works through a kind of under-statement which recalls to us at once the grim and conscious irony of those who knew that 'their feet had come to the end of the world'. We find it perpetually recurring in his work. He is writing of a draft entraining for the front –

> Dull porters watched them, and a casual tramp
> Stood staring hard,
> *Sorry to miss them from the upland camp.* ...
> ['The Send-Off'. Day Lewis's italics.]

Of a disabled soldier ('there was an artist silly for his face'), helpless in a wheeled chair –

> ... Now he is old; his back will never brace;
> *He's lost his colour very far from here,*
> Poured it down shell-holes till the veins ran dry ...
> ['Disabled'. Day Lewis's italics.][31]

Or, in his poem 'Greater Love,' the lines –

> Heart, you were never hot
> Nor large, nor full like hearts made great with shot; ...[32]

These deliberate, intense under-statements – the brave man's only answer to a hell which no epic words could express – affect me as being both more poignant and more rich with poetic promise than anything else that has been done during this century. Owen was not a technical revolutionary: his one innovation is the constant use of the alliterative assonance as an end rhyme – (mystery, mastery; killed, cold). But he was a true revolutionary poet, opening up new fields of sensitiveness for his successors. If he had lived there is no knowing what his promise might have achieved; he would have found, active in different guises, the cant, the oppression, the sufferings and courage which had challenged his powers during the war. As it is, his unsentimental pity, his savage and sacred indignation are the best of our inheritance, and it is for his heirs to see that they are not wasted.[33] □

Day Lewis's portrayal of Owen has many elements in common with the image of him that is often perpetuated today. He is figured as noble, prophetic, a writer of 'perfect' and memorable war poetry but above all 'intense' and 'sensitive'. These adjectives have adhered to the legend of Owen, supported by his dutiful and pensive photographic presence in many anthologies. The Owen constructed by Day Lewis appears to be beyond reproach, emblematic of the best humanitarian impulses, and categorized firmly within the canonical space reserved for the greatest poets.

REINTERPRETATIONS OF BROOKE

What, then, of Rupert Brooke's reputation during this interwar period? As discussed in Chapter Two, the projection of Brooke as an iconic, soldier-poet figure, in whom patriotic feeling, poetic ability and physical beauty were combined, had been well under way during the First World War. The construction of Brooke as the 'young Apollo, golden-haired', evident within the Churchill obituary and Frances Cornford's ode, drew on Edwardian public discourses of passionate patriotism. It was this image of Brooke that dominated the *Collected Poems of Rupert Brooke, with a Memoir* published in 1918 and edited by Edward Marsh, the *Georgian Poetry* anthologist and friend and mentor to Brooke. As the book itself makes clear, the interest in further detail about the poet's life was considerable. The memoir begins with an introductory note written by Rupert Brooke's mother, in which she states: 'I feel that an apology is due to those who have been looking for some time for a Memoir of my son.'[34] In the lengthy memoir, which takes up approximately half of the total volume, Marsh intersperses excerpts from Brooke's diaries with quotations from the letters of a range of admiring friends. The hagiographic tenor of this is illustrated by the following quotation, from a letter by one of Brooke's school friends, Hugh Russell-Smith:

> ■ Rupert had an extraordinary vitality at school, which showed itself in a glorious enthusiasm and an almost boisterous sense of fun – qualities that are only too rare in combination. Of his enthusiasm it is hard to speak; we knew less about it, although we felt it.[35] □

There is a strong emphasis throughout the memoir on Brooke's boyish energy and charm, not only in the letters of his contemporaries, but also in comments such as the following, from Marsh, on Brooke's involvement in amateur dramatics when he was an undergraduate at King's College, Cambridge:

> ■ It turned out that he was one of the successes of the evening. His radiant, youthful figure in gold and vivid red and blue, like a Page in the Riccardi Chapel, stood strangely out against the stuffy decorations and dresses which pervaded those somewhat palmy days of the Cambridge Theatre. After eleven years, the impression has not faded.[36] □

The Rupert Brooke figured in this memoir signifies ardent and talented youth: he is admired as much for his reputed impulsiveness, generosity and sensitivity as a man as he is for his poetry. He is constructed as a heroic figure according to a model of idealized upper-class Englishness of the Edwardian period, and it is precisely this model that begins to be viewed with increasing suspicion and criticism in the 1930s.

In the memoirs by Sassoon, Graves and others considered earlier in this chapter, First World War combat is no longer represented as an uncomplicatedly heroic enterprise; yet Brooke's reputation was built around an idea of purity of motive and action in war. For poets and writers exploring their literary and cultural identity in the early 1930s, many of whom felt far less affiliated to the values of the ruling class than the previous generation, the Brooke legend seemed to signify elements of the ignorant bellicosity of his era rather than gallant adventurousness. The next section will further examine how new forms of literary criticism also began to register changes in perceptions of Brooke's oeuvre. While there continued to be a steady popular readership for Brooke's poetry throughout the 1930s, a number of poets and critics were increasingly ready to articulate their disapprobation of Brooke's idealism. The Cambridge-based literary critic Q. D. Leavis (1906–81) was able, at the end of the 1930s, to employ Brooke's name as an emblem of the complacency of Georgian poets and the upper-class metropolitan literary establishment. In the following passage from a review that appeared in the periodical *Scrutiny* in 1939 Leavis is commenting on Edward Marsh:

■ A Classic at Westminster, he passed second in the Civil Service examination, and thereafter, mixing as intensively as possible with the best people, he became an innocent blotting-paper to all literary aspirants he met in the right company, particularly good-looking young men with fetching manners. He was overwhelmed by Rupert Brooke, and after meeting Ivor Novello he became so impressed with the talents of the author of *Keep the Home Fires Burning* that he even took a passionate interest in musical comedy.[37] [...] He still believes that 'Rupert Brooke is destined to remain as a considerable figure in English Literature', [and] that Georgian poetry will soon be rehabilitated ...[38] □

Leavis goes on to press her imputed associations between Brooke and literary pretentiousness and effeminacy further in this review. In doing so, she shows that Brooke's fame is seen as resting on poetry for which the ideological basis has become less acceptable. Leavis's comment also shows the extent to which Brooke is associated with Georgianism, seen here as a conservative and sentimental movement. Marsh's belief that Brooke will remain a considerable literary figure is intended, therefore, to speak for itself: both Marsh and Brooke have become symbols of dubious politics, poor taste and, as Leavis makes clear, a kind of upper-class elitism and protectionism. Furthermore Marsh and Brooke have become, along with Ivor Novello, symbols of sexual ambiguity.

It was not only the figure of the war poet or the fluctuations in individual poetic reputations that became increasingly significant during the interwar period. As a literary category, war poetry was also subject to analysis and reinterpretation from specialist perspectives, including those of academics, anthologists and poets. The next section describes how interwar developments in English studies impacted on the genre, and examines ways in which war poetry was positioned (and sometimes excluded) as special or different – a category apart.

THE DEVELOPING GENRE

ENGLISH STUDIES

As the extracts from Day Lewis and Q. D. Leavis in the previous section show, the interwar debate about who the true 'war poets' were and what exactly they stood for, became significant in expressing a range of literary, cultural and political values, particularly in relation to the First World War and the Establishment figures most closely associated with it. It was a debate that was stimulated and influenced by the growing interest in anti-war opinions and movements. Yet the interwar period was also a period of great change for English Literature as a university subject and this, too, formed an important part of the context for the gradual development of a liberal and pacifist model of war poetry.

The nineteenth-century interest in using English literature as education had largely been, as Terry Eagleton recounts in *Literary Theory: An Introduction* (1983), a 'liberal, "humanizing" pursuit' aimed at working people and at women, to encourage pride in national culture and achievement and to raise sights above their immediate material conditions and complaints to the universal values and higher truths.[39] Eagleton writes from a Marxist perspective, seeing this as part of a bourgeois political project for pre-empting class strife: English literature, he argues, is figured as a means of engaging with the emotions and experiences of the working classes in the face of dwindling religious faith, being a more convenient and accessible medium for doing so than the Classics. According to this argument, the First World War challenged the conception of English as a feminine and insubstantial subject through the creation of a more assertively nationalistic sense of identity:

■ It is no accident that the author of one of the most influential Government reports in this area, *The Teaching of English in England* (1921), was none other than Sir Henry Newbolt, minor jingoist poet and perpetrator of the immortal line 'Play up! play up! and play the game!' Chris Baldick has pointed to the importance of the admission of English literature to the Civil Service examinations in the Victorian period: armed with this conveniently packaged version of their own cultural treasures, the servants of British imperialism could sally forth overseas secure in a sense of their national identity, and able to display that cultural superiority to their envying colonial peoples.[40] □

Prior to the First World War, English was only reluctantly and gradually taken into the university realm, tending not to be regarded by established professors as a valid academic subject of study. During the war, large numbers of men volunteered or were called up for active service, causing wholesale disruption to the ordinary business of universities. This also, according to Eagleton, created a new perspective from which English was to be viewed:

■ One of the most strenuous antagonists of English – philology – was closely bound up with Germanic influence; and since England happened to be passing through a major war with Germany, it was possible to smear classical philology as a form of ponderous Teutonic nonsense with which no self-respecting Englishman should be caught associating. England's victory over Germany meant a renewal of national pride, an upsurge of patriotism which could only aid English's cause; but at the same time the deep trauma of war, its almost intolerable questioning of every previously held cultural assumption, gave rise to a 'spiritual hungering', as one contemporary commentator described it, for which poetry seemed to provide an answer. It is a chastening thought that we owe the University study of English, in part at least, to a meaningless massacre. The Great War, with its carnage of ruling class rhetoric, put paid to some of the more strident forms of chauvinism on which English had previously thrived: there could be few more Walter Raleighs [1861–1922, a critic and the first Professor of English Literature at Oxford] after Wilfred Owen. English Literature rode to power on the back of wartime nationalism; but it also represented a search for spiritual solutions on the part of an English ruling class whose sense of identity had been profoundly shaken, whose psyche was ineradicably scarred by the horrors it had endured. Literature would be at once solace and reaffirmation, a familiar ground on which Englishmen could regroup both to explore, and to find some alternative to, the nightmare of history.[41] □

As we have seen earlier in this chapter, forms of chauvinism (used here to refer to bellicose patriotism) 'on which English had previously thrived' did in fact survive and sustain themselves, for example, in the continuation of a robust tradition of patriotic poetry anthologies throughout the 1920s and beyond. Yet at the same time, the war had brought about substantial change. For those demobilized students returning to their studies after 1918, there was the awareness that many older teachers (who had not fought in the war) respected them as soldiers and, symbolically, protectors of the nation.[42] Those involved in the study of English in the academy were indeed registering and digesting the sense of a profound questioning of a number of 'previously held cultural assumptions'.

I. A. RICHARDS AND F. R. LEAVIS

Two academics in particular, I. A. Richards and F. R. Leavis, emerged from this environment of uncertainty that followed the war to interrogate the purpose and value of the study of English in radical new ways. Richards rejected much of the established approach to literature, and set himself apart from the critics who saw their first duty to 'be moving, to excite in the mind emotions appropriate to their august subject-matter'.[43] He placed an emphasis on the importance of maintaining a critical distance from literature whilst paying close attention to the text, and asserted the need for a more detailed understanding of human psychology and its relationship to literature:

■ Criticism, as I understand it, is the endeavour to discriminate between experiences and to evaluate them. We cannot do this without some understanding of the nature of experience, or without theories of valuation and communication. Such principles as apply in criticism must be taken from these more fundamental studies. All other critical principles are arbitrary, and the history of the subject is a record of their obstructive influence.[44] □

Richards's method, developed and elaborated further in his *Practical Criticism: A Study of Literary Judgement* (1929), was to influence generations of teachers and students.

Two of Richards's students, who became highly influential in their own right, were F. R. Leavis and Q. D. Roth, who were married in 1929. Drawing on the central 'practical criticism' method of the close reading of texts, the Leavises developed a distinctive stance based on a profound belief in the moral seriousness of literary study and a severe attitude towards elitism in literary and academic milieus. (A flavour of this approach is evident in Q. D. Leavis's comment on Edward Marsh and Rupert Brooke in the previous section.) In the quarterly review *Scrutiny*, set up in 1932 by the Leavises and other like-minded critics, literature tended to be discussed with a strong awareness of social context, although without any particularly formulated social agenda.[45] The latent intent of a piece of literature, whether it was, for example, sincere and authentic, was also a highly significant issue in much Leavisite criticism. An illustrative application of 'Leavisite' concerns to war poetry can be seen in the following extract from a 1932 *Scrutiny* article by H. L. Elvin (a Fellow of Trinity Hall, Cambridge):

■ Rupert Brooke is the only one of the early war poets still generally read by the public. He did more than merely express the current mood of idealism: his expression of it was so influential that he helped to form and perpetuate it in others. And, as has often been said, his death set the seal on his reputation.

He was concerned with war more personally than were Wordsworth and Tennyson, and yet it must be said that in inspiration his war poems are curiously derivative. So much is this so, that one is forced to question their ultimate authenticity. They are unquestionably sincere at a certain level, but they seem to lack an achieved integrity of spirit. The most fitting criticism is undoubtedly that of Charles Sorley, another soldier-poet (I take it from Mr Middleton Murry's essay, 'The Lost Legions' in his *Aspects of Literature [1920]*):

'He is far too obsessed with his own sacrifice ... It was not that "they" gave up anything of that list he gives in one sonnet: but that the essence of these things had been endangered by circumstances over which he had no control, and he must fight to recapture them. He has clothed his attitude in fine words: but he has taken the sentimental attitude.'

If one examines these sonnets one finds that they were written in a way which would inevitably evoke the 'stock responses'. Their vogue was due to that, and to their author's technical ability. The first sonnet,

Now God be thanked who has matched us with his hour
And caught our youth and wakened us from sleeping [46]

sounds that same note we heard in Tennyson and Wordsworth. The nation is to arouse itself from sloth and throw itself with God-given strength into the struggle. And Brooke finds a relief not unlike that of the hero of [Tennyson's] *Maud* [1855] in leaving 'all the little emptiness of love' and abandoning himself to war enthusiasm. Again, in his third sonnet, there is the old quaint feeling that in peace there was something dishonourable, and that the war has somehow brought back 'Holiness' (what a ghastly notion!):

Honour has come back, as a king, to earth,
    And paid his subjects with a royal wage;
And Nobleness walks in our ways again;
    And we have come into our heritage.

It would have been interesting to have seen, if Brooke had lived, whether in 1917 he would have written as Sassoon did. By then most of the poets, except the stay-at-home ones, were disillusioned. [...]

If one looks back, then, at some of the typical war poetry of the last hundred years, one may make certain generalizations. The poetry that has been popular has been that which has told the public in accents of sincerity, if not of the completest intellectual integrity, that the war was a righteous war and one of God's own choosing. With the aid of any idealist elements they could find in the struggle, the poets have 'liberalised' the war for the verse-reading public and for those influenced by the verse-readers. They have suggested that the peace preceding the war had been sordid, and that this war would be in the cause of Honour because it demanded sacrifices from those who had been prosperous previously. The services of the poets have been especially important in rallying the middle classes: somehow the working classes, though they may have responded to calls, have preserved a not uncritical sense of humour, and quite literally, have 'made less of a song about it.' In looking at the history of mankind one's final feeling may be disgust at our incompetence in permitting the continuance of war as an institution, but in reading the war poetry of the last century one is above all impressed by the way in which the surface stirring of generous impulses has assisted in the perpetration of barbarity.[47] □

Although the early 1930s revulsion against war is certainly in evidence here, the main target is Brooke's 'surface' manipulation of rhetoric and imagery in order to produce a 'stock response' or sentimental attitude. Elvin identifies Brooke's work as perpetuating war idealism in others and he questions the *authenticity* of the war poems. In the context of fuller knowledge of First World War combat experiences, careful attention to the use of poetic language and a morally charged approach to reading literature, Brooke's concern with 'self-sacrifice' is seen by Elvin as slipping out of the heroic patriot mould and into the self-indulgently romantic. Implicit in this analysis is the idea that war poets should have 'intellectual integrity', an ability to reach beyond the official or public discourses, a theme that recurs throughout twentieth-century war poetry criticism. One of the primary concerns here is how poets relate their understanding or appreciation of war's purpose to their own experience, and whether they have an ability to balance their individual perspective with the wider context. These critical concerns with the place of experience and integrity in poetic representations of war came to prominence during the 1930s, not only in relation to Brooke and Owen, but also in relation to the polemical poetry of the Spanish Civil War, as discussed later in this chapter.

WAR POETRY AS 'DIFFERENT'

One of Elvin's premises in his critique of Brooke is that poetry is influential within non-artistic spheres: if inauthentic and idealistic war poetry has 'assisted in the perpetration of barbarity', then there is at least a theoretical space in which war poetry might be judged as authentic, and a force for good. Yet even while Brooke's poetry was being analysed increasingly critically and interest in the pacifist-humanist figure of Owen was burgeoning, challenges were being raised about the suitability of war as a subject for poetry. When W. B. Yeats (by then an established and widely admired poet entering his seventies) edited *The Oxford Book of Modern Verse 1892–1935* in 1936 it included few poems that dealt with war, and no poetry by Wilfred Owen. The surprise and displeasure that followed this omission was partly a sign of the consensus building up around Owen's literary stature. Yet the exclusion of Owen and other First World War poets was a considered decision on the part of Yeats. In the anthology introduction, he describes his opinion of poetry about war in the following terms:

> ■ I have a distaste for certain poems written in the midst of the great war; they are in all anthologies, but I have substituted Herbert Read's *End of a War* written long after. The writers of these poems were invariably officers of exceptional courage and capacity, one a man constantly selected for dangerous work, all, I think, had the Military Cross; their letters are vivid and humorous, they were not without joy – for all skill is joyful – but felt bound, in the words of the best known, to plead the suffering of their men. In poems that had for a time considerable fame, written in the first person, they made that suffering their own. I have rejected these poems for the same reason that made Arnold [Matthew Arnold, 1822–88] withdraw his *Empedocles on Etna* [1852] from circulation; passive suffering is not a theme for poetry. In all the great tragedies, tragedy is a joy to the man who dies; in Greece the tragic chorus danced. When man has drawn into the quicksilver at the back of the mirror no great event becomes luminous in his mind; it is no longer possible to write *The Persians* [by Aeschylus], *Agincourt* [by Drayton], *Chevy Chase* [one of the oldest English ballads]: some blunderer has driven his car on to the wrong side of the road – that is all.
>
> If war is necessary, or necessary in our time and place, it is best to forget its suffering as we do the discomfort of fever, remembering our comfort at midnight when our temperature fell, or as we forget the worst moments of more painful disease.[48] □

In this much-quoted passage, Yeats honours the military actions of poets, their 'courage and capacity', but argues that the 'passive suffering' born of war is inconsistent with poetry. Yeats suggests that the poetry of war exists in a separate category to poetry 'proper'; that it is, or should be, distinct from the poetry canon. Yeats's statement of 'distaste' for war poetry reflects his injunction that the most unpleasant details of war, and the individual's reflexive concern with his experience – being drawn to 'the back of the mirror' – should be forgotten. The experiential basis of First World War poetry is precisely the reason for its *unsuitability*: the criticism is not that it is inauthentic, but that concentration on passive suffering detracts from the edifying function of poetry. Yeats's comments relate to a romantic and mystical notion of poetry as raising human emotion and experience to a different level, infusing the ordinary with luminosity, investing it with extraordinary significance and power. In excluding Owen and others from his anthology, Yeats constructs and, indeed, cordons off war poetry as a distinct, unique (but perhaps subordinate) category of literature.

MODERNISM

David Jones's approach to the distinctiveness of war as an experience is quite different from Yeats's relegation of war poetry to outsider status. In the preface to his extended prose-poem, *In Parenthesis*, published in 1937, Jones wrote:

■ This writing is called 'In Parenthesis' because I have written it in a kind of space between – I don't know between quite what – but as you turn aside to do something; and because for us amateur soldiers (and especially for the writer, who was not only amateur, but grotesquely incompetent, a knocker-over of piles, a parade's despair) the war itself was a parenthesis – how glad we thought we were to step outside its brackets at the end of '18 – and also because our curious type of existence here is altogether in parenthesis.[49] □

The mixture of slightly fraught, hesitant observation, critical self-reflection and confident assertion relates to a number of contexts: Jones writes as a committed Roman Catholic, reminding readers of the theological implications of his work's title (the brevity of mortal life), but also as a First World War 'veteran' and a self-critical experimental artist and poet. At a literal level, the *In Parenthesis* title suggests that the text belongs to the category of reminiscence and memoir, given a brief existence through the author's desire to recollect. The tone of Jones's comments in the quotation above, however, suggests that a purely literal reading is not intended: if the 'war itself was a parenthesis', the effect of the war has clearly not evaporated given the book-length work Jones has produced. Nor does it seem that the soldier's post-war life is as different or as promising as hoped: 'how glad we *thought* we were to step outside its brackets' [my italics]. For Jones, the parentheses highlight the complexity of representing the phenomenon of war.

T. S. Eliot, who helped ensure the work's publication, wrote a note of introduction to the second edition of *In Parenthesis*, published in 1963; we have already quoted part of this in Chapter One. Eliot was writing in a decade that saw, as will be discussed in Chapter Five, another pacifist-oriented resurgence of interest in war poetry; he was writing about a work still not well known and about a poet whose approach to poetic language and form can still be considered relatively challenging. In the following extract, Eliot covers issues such as the range of themes in the work and the way he believes the poetry is best appreciated:

■ *In Parenthesis* was first published in London in 1937. I am proud to share the responsibility for that first publication. On reading the book in typescript I was deeply moved. I then regarded it, and I still regard it, as a work of genius.

A work of literary art which uses the language in a new way or for a new purpose, does not call for many words from the introducer. All that one can say amounts only to pointing towards the book, and affirming its importance and permanence as a work of art. The aim of the introducer should be to arouse the curiosity of a possible new reader. To attempt to explain, in such a note as this, is futile. Here is a book about the experiences of one soldier in the War of 1914–18. It is also a book about War, and about many other things also, such as Roman Britain, the Arthurian Legend, and diverse matters which are given association by the mind of the writer. And as for the writer himself, he is a Londoner of Welsh and English descent. He is decidedly a Briton. He is also a Roman Catholic, and he is a painter who has painted some beautiful pictures and designed some beautiful lettering. All these facts about him are important. Some of them appear in his own Preface to this book; some the reader may discover in the course of reading.

When *In Parenthesis* is widely enough known – as it will be in time – it will no doubt undergo the same sort of detective analysis and exegesis as the later work of James Joyce [1882–1941] and the *Cantos* of Ezra Pound. It is true that *In Parenthesis* and David Jones's later and equally remarkable work *The Anathemata* [1952], are provided by the author with notes; but author's notes (as illustrated by *The Waste Land* [Eliot's own famous Modernist poem, published in 1922]) are not prophylactic against interpretation and dissection: they merely provide the serious researcher with more material to interpret and dissect. The work of David Jones has some affinity with that of James Joyce (both men seem to me to have the Celtic ear for the music of words) and with the later work of Ezra Pound, and with my own. I stress the affinity, as any possible influence seems to me slight and of no importance. David Jones is a representative of the same literary generation as Joyce, Pound and myself, if four men born between 1882 and 1895 can be regarded as of the same literary generation. David Jones is the youngest, and the tardiest to publish. The lives of all of us were altered by that War, but David Jones is the only one to have fought in it.

Those who read *In Parenthesis* for the first time, need to know nothing more than this and what the author tells us in his own Preface, except that *In Parenthesis* and *The Anathemata* have been greatly admired by a number of writers whose opinions usually command attention. The commentaries, as I have said, will follow in time. Good commentaries can be very helpful: but to study even the best commentary on a work of literary art is likely to be a waste of time unless we have first read and been excited by the text commented upon without understanding it. For that thrill of excitement from our first reading of a work of creative literature which we do not understand is itself the beginning of understanding, and if *In Parenthesis* does not excite us before we have understood it, no commentary will reveal to us its secret. And the second step is to get used to the book, to live with it and make it familiar to us. Understanding begins in the sensibility: we must have the experience before we attempt to explore the sources of the work beyond itself.[50] ☐

In this passage, Eliot identifies the way in which he and others of his generation were 'altered' by the war and describes *In Parenthesis* as about 'the experiences of one soldier in the War of 1914–18' and as a 'book about war'. Jones is also presented as having a special status in being, of the generational group referred to by Eliot, the 'only one to have fought in it'.

While these comments bear superficial similarities to critical discussions elsewhere on the combat credentials of war poets, Eliot's brief account of Jones and his work is more concerned with other issues. He points out first of all that the poem's themes are not limited to war but reach out into the historical and mythic past, into 'Roman Britain' and 'Arthurian legend'. He then goes on to stress the importance of allowing instinctive responses to the poem to emerge before developing a more consciously intellectual analysis; he suggests that there is a subconscious level of access to poetic understanding that is too often neglected. This appears to relate to allegations concerning the difficulty of Modernist texts: as Eliot also notes, there are affinities of technique between Jones and a number of other writers, including Eliot himself, who now tend to be grouped together as 'Modernists' (due to the extensive use of a stream of consciousness, the multiplicity of poetic voices, and so on). Here, then, Eliot implies that the onus is on the reader to engage with the complexity of subject, language and form. However, as the introduction indicates, the text was still not widely known despite a lapse of nearly 30 years since its first publication. The war poetry that had begun to be celebrated during the 1930s and favoured by anthologists not only tended to be shorter in length, but also often used single, coherent poetic voices and gave relatively realistic accounts of combat or injury. During the interwar period, assumptions about the war experiences of poets had led to a decided preference for poetry that readers might easily identify with, and more experimental approaches to the representation of war were to continue to meet with a mixed reception, as will be discussed in Chapter Four.

The next section will consider the impact of a new conflict, the Spanish Civil War, on the developing genre. This section will discuss the tendency for poets of the war to move in the opposite direction to Jones's formal experimentation with multiplicity of subject, voice and meaning, and towards a greater concern that war poetry should deliver the 'right' message. It will also examine how the conflict in Spain disrupted pacifist formulations of war poetry and simplistic perceptions of war poets as anti-war figures.

THE SPANISH CIVIL WAR

TAKING SIDES

By the time the Spanish Civil War began in 1936, collections of war poetry had long been available in Britain, many of which concentrated on the poetry of the First World War. The poetry and poets of that war had been the subjects of numerous critical investigations, some examples of which have been touched on earlier in this chapter. The cultural stature of Owen was growing into that of a legendary literary figure, a symbol of 'savage and sacred indignation'.[51] Yet, as discussed in previous sections, Owen was not without his detractors, and idealistic and jingoistic representations of war poetry were still being produced and read. Brooke's poetry continued to sell, and Ziv's *The Valiant Muse* anthology was published in 1936. While the terms 'war poetry' and 'war poet' were in evidence during the 1930s, the combat-oriented term 'soldier poet' was also commonly used in interwar anthologies and some texts referred more explicitly, and with heroic overtones, to 'poets who had fallen/died in the war'.[52]

For the poets of what Spender described as the left-wing orthodoxy, the Spanish Civil War was a decision point. It no longer seemed possible to be of the Left and to continue to be part of the move towards pacifism and international disarmament; the uprising of Fascist forces opposed to the Republican Government of Spain was seen as requiring an unequivocal and proactive response. The demand for clear ideological commitment on the part of writers was made perhaps most famously in the 1937 pamphlet, whose signatories included W. H. Auden, Stephen Spender, the Chilean poet and diplomat Pablo Neruda (1904–73), the German novelist Heinrich Mann (1871–1950), and the pamphlet's organizer, poet and editor Nancy Cunard (1896–1965):

■ *Are you for, or against, the legal Government and the People of Republican Spain? Are you for, or against, Franco and Fascism?* For it is impossible any longer to take no side.[53] □

The responses to this question were printed in *Left Review* under the headings 'FOR the Government' (149), 'AGAINST the Government' (5) and 'NEUTRAL?' (16). This survey has often been treated as emblematic of the cultural and political atmosphere of the period and has been referred to in much subsequent literary history and criticism: in Murray Sperber's *And I Remember Spain: A Spanish Civil War anthology* (1974), for example, a selection of the responses to the survey are reproduced.[54] This includes strongly worded affirmations for Republicanism from C. Day Lewis and Hugh MacDiarmid (1892–1978), both poets and, at this time, active Communist Party members, and a clear vote for Franco's cause by novelist Arthur Machen (1863-1947). Yet in his contribution to *Class, Culture and Social Change: A New View of the 1930s* (1980), 'Neutral?: 1930s Writers and Taking Sides', Valentine Cunningham takes issue with what he refers to as the 1930s orthodoxy of the 'red decade', using this survey as a case study. While accepting that the 'broad picture' given by the survey was convincing, Cunningham criticizes the methods of the survey's compilers, commenting on the writers who were omitted and the categorization of doubtful and cautious responses as unequivocally 'for' the Government. In the following extract, Cunningham examines the implications of George Orwell's response to the survey, and its absence from the summary of responses:

■ We know for certain that the survey's organizers were capable of acts of suppression that seem scarcely unpolitical. James Joyce replied by phone, but only to tell Nancy Cunard 'I am James Joyce. I have received your questionnaire': too unquotable an indifference it would seem. Orwell's response was angrier. In April 1938 he told Spender how he'd responded to 'that bloody rot which was afterwards published in book form (called *Authors Take Sides*)' and 'that damned rubbish of signing manifestos to say how wicked it all is': 'I sent back a very angry reply in which I'm afraid I mentioned you uncomplimentarily, not knowing you personally at that time'. The sort of rough handling *Homage to Catalonia* (1938) was to receive from the Communists and their publishing and reviewing sympathizers within the British Left is a measure of how dangerous Orwell's disillusioned Republicanism was felt to be. And the *Left Review* clique was evidently not going to allow Orwell to upset the pamphlet's orthodox pretences about seamless unity to its cause, to expose rifts within socialism. That the Spanish situation might be complicated and that honourably wounded Republican sympathizers like Orwell might have developed unsimple opinions unsettled the desired myth. If only in the case of Orwell the pamphlet's Publisher's Note was misleadingly reassuring: 'It has proved impossible to include all the answers received ... in no instance has an Answer been omitted on grounds of "policy" ... all the answers omitted fell under the ... head of "FOR".'[55] □

Cunningham argues here that the *Authors Take Sides* episode reveals more than simply a desire on the part of many writers to support Spanish Republicanism. Indeed, in pointing to the possibility that the manifesto's organizers were selective in the presentation of responses, Cunningham suggests that for Cunard and others, there was an effort to eliminate fractions and ambivalences within left-wing thinking. We will consider further this desire to simplify the ideological debate between Left and Right in the next subsection.

LEFT AND RIGHT

Left-wing periodicals such as the *New Statesman and Nation* and *Left Review* were explicitly supportive of the Republican cause. In 1937 the *Left Review* also printed a Manifesto which stated that 'in the actual war that Fascism has begun against culture, democracy, peace and the happiness and well-being of mankind in general, no neutrality is possible or to be thought of'.[56] The issue of 'taking sides' on the war, however, was clearly not confined to such surveys or editorial positions. As discussed under 'Key Contexts', many writers of the 1930s had already been experimenting with incorporating social and political issues into their work, or taking up ideological stances with persuasive, sometimes propagandist intent. For some poets, the Spanish Civil War appeared to provide a new and dynamic opportunity for polemical verse; Spain became the literal and symbolic arena in which the class struggle would be played out and the forces of Fascism defeated. Poets who died in combat tended to be viewed by Republican sympathizers as heroic martyr figures: the potent combination of war experience, political commitment and poetic output resulted in the lionization of writers such as Ralph Fox (1900–36) and John Cornford (1915–36). It is possible to see some similarities here with the intense admiration directed towards Brooke in the First World War.

In the *Left Review* of March 1937, for example, following the death of John Cornford, the editorial by Edgell Rickword (1898–1982) illustrates how the construction of the noble soldier-poet figure of the First World War could be taken up and adapted to function within Communist discourse. Here, the poet's biography, political views and poetry are presented as correlatives of one another:

■ At London, and during his first term at Cambridge, his articles on art and the class struggle in the *Student Vanguard*, which he edited, showed how deep his understanding was. Even at sixteen he had written to his mother of her own poetry: 'Are the poems that you write really your most important experiences? ... it always seems to me that you have a great deal that needs to be said more urgently but can't be, because of the limitations of your view of poetry ... because I should guess that until recently you would have denied that every subject is equally poetical ... I believe in a much stricter vocabulary and a much wider range of subject.' His own poetry at the time was powerful and highly imaginative. At Cambridge, however, his energy and his genius for organization made him joint organizer of the Communist Party in his second term, and his creative ability took the form of intense political activity. Only in Spain did he begin to write poetry again, and then, the two fine poems he wrote came as a complete confirmation of the prophecy he had made five years before. Take the poem printed here ['Full Moon at Tierz: Before the Storming of the Huesca']. He writes quite naturally and in simple language of Maurice Thorez [French Communist Party leader, 1900–64] and the Seventh Congress. And when he writes of himself,

'though Communism was my waking time,'

the writing is purely objective and lacks the romantic attitude in which poets have seen themselves in the past.[57] □

Here Rickword puts great emphasis on Cornford as an active and disciplined party member, whose aesthetic concerns are profoundly informed by his communism, and whose talents as Communist Party organizer are in themselves 'creative'. Rickword also includes a quotation from Cornford's letter to his mother: as we have seen, Frances Cornford was a poet during the First World War, and the writer of the ode to Rupert Brooke, in which the reference to him as a 'golden-haired Apollo' was coined. Rickword's description contrasts the dedicated son, advocate of 'strict' vocabulary and the 'most important' experience, with the romanticizing mother. At the same time it suggests a contrast between the generation that led the country into the First World War and the radical post-war generation, of whom John Cornford was a symbol.

In his autobiography *Light on a Dark Horse* (1951), the poet Roy Campbell (1902–57) situates his views on the Spanish Civil War within a very different tradition. As a South African who had lived in Britain, Spain and France, Campbell was dismissive of British left-wing intellectuals whose support for the Republican Government was not based on knowledge of the country or its people. In *Light on a Dark Horse*, Campbell describes the orthodoxy of left-wing approaches to the war in highly critical terms:

■ Anyone who was not pro-Red in the Spanish War automatically became a 'fascist'. I owed my independence in taking sides to being able to earn my living independently of my vocation as an artist. Had I depended for my living on writing or painting, as I do now, since I have been crippled, I should not have so much as dared to think which side I would take, since one's bread and butter depended on thinking pro-Red.[58] □

Later in the same book, Campbell states his own analysis of Spain's needs:

■ From the very beginning my wife and I understood the real issues in Spain. There could be no compromise in this war between the East and West, between Credulity and Faith, between irresponsible innovation (which catches all 'intellectuals' once they have been hereditarily derailed) and tradition, between the emotions (disguised as Reason) and the intelligence.[59] □

Campbell represents the 'pro-Red' interests as powerfully influential, operating a kind of intellectual closed shop, yet in the second extract his own views are asserted in similarly indisputable terms. He and his wife, Campbell asserts, 'understood the real issues' in Spain and one of the most important of these was the Catholic Church: the Campbells converted to Catholicism just prior to the war. Campbell is one of the few poets of the period to become publicly associated with the Right. In 1939, he published his long poem on the Spanish war, *Flowering Rifle: A Poem from the Battlefield of Spain*, in which the introductory note exhorted 'VIVA FRANCO! ARRIBA ESPANA!'.[60] In this poem, sections are dedicated to colourful and strident denunciations of the Left:

■ A Hundred years of strife with warring vans
Had winnowed Spain in two distinctive clans
Upon the left, inflammable, the chaff,
Corn to the right, the vulnerable half,
And thus in Spanish history began
The war between the Wowser and the Man –[61] □

Campbell's use of derogatory nicknames is a characteristic element of his prose, as well as his poetic style. In the quotation above, he expresses his political perspective through a metaphorical link between the worthless 'chaff' of the corn and the left-wing faction in Spain, reinforcing his point with the dismissive term 'wowser'. In Campbell's terms, 'wowser' is usually used in antithesis to the construction of 'man' as strong, brave and loyal; it thus bolsters the image of the Francoist supporter by impugning the masculinity of those on the opposing political flank. The question of how far poetry about the Spanish Civil War is concerned with the articulation of political views and political persuasion is considered further in the next subsection.

POLITICAL POETRY

As the Spanish Civil War was generally viewed as an ideological conflict, the relationship of poetry about the war to the propagation of specific political beliefs was a key debate. C. Day Lewis had argued that there was no reason why poetry should not be a vehicle for propaganda, providing the aesthetic value of the poem was not degraded.[62] Yet this political-aesthetic harmony was a difficult issue to judge, and not everyone saw it as such a desirable goal. Rickword's obituary of Cornford honours his political dedication first and foremost; there is no reference to the Cornford who wrote 'To Margot Heinemann', in which the Republican cause is poetically subordinated to the intimate fears and attachment of the poetic subject:

> ■ On the last mile to Huesca,
> The last fence for our pride,
> Think so kindly, dear, that I
> Sense you at my side.
>
> And if bad luck should lay my strength
> Into the shallow grave,
> Remember all the good you can;
> Don't forget my love.[63] □

Auden's occasional poem *Spain*, first published in 1937, further exemplifies some of the tensions provoked by the war both for poets and political fellow travellers. The poem, in a contemporary review by Stephen Spender, was seen as an 'abstracted view' of the Spanish situation 'in which the element of personal experience and direct emotional response is rigorously excluded ... a remarkable interpretation of the issues and implications of the struggle'.[64] Auden, however, became increasingly critical of his poem, first producing a modified version of it with elements of the original deleted, and eventually rejecting it wholesale. Having travelled to Spain intending to work as an ambulance driver, Auden had been shocked by some of the sights he had witnessed, particularly the desecration of churches. By 1939, in his article 'The Public vs. The Late Mr W. B. Yeats', Auden seems to be moving towards the importance of religious ideas and away from any notion of poetry as political practice:

> ■ A purely religious solution may be unworkable, but the search for it is, at least, the result of a true perception of a social evil. Again, the virtues that the deceased [Yeats] praised in the peasantry and the aristocracy, and the vices he blamed in the commercial classes were real virtues and vices. To create a united and just society where the former are fostered and the latter cured is the task of the politician, not the poet.
>
> For art is a product of history, not a cause. Unlike some other products, technical inventions for example, it does not re-enter history as an effective agent, so that the question whether art should or should not be propaganda is unreal. The case for the prosecution rests on the fallacious belief that art ever makes anything happen, whereas the honest truth, gentleman, is that, if not a poem had been written, not a picture painted nor a bar of music composed, the history of man would be materially unchanged.[65] □

Yeats himself, who, as described in the previous section, had already set out his 'distaste' for 'certain poets of the last war', gave new emphasis to his views in one of his last poems, 'Politics': 'How can I, that girl standing there,/ My attention fix/ On Roman or on Russian/ Or on Spanish politics?'.[66]

As Michael Roberts had indicated in his introduction to *New Country*, Wilfred Owen was very much the icon of First World War poetry for writers of the pacifist left. However, Owen's signification as a pacifist figure presented inevitable tensions for those who came to believe in the importance of armed intervention in Spain and, subsequently, in war against Germany. Spender was later to describe how Auden, Day Lewis, MacNeice and himself:

> ■ … who had sneered at Rupert Brooke and whose feelings about war had been absorbed from the poetry from the Western Front written by Wilfred Owen and Siegfried Sassoon – and from Robert Graves's *Goodbye to All That* – were rather embarrassed to find themselves in one respect like Rupert Brooke: that is to say, writing poetry in support of war against Germans – although these Germans were not Kaiser Wilhem's spike-helmeted Prussians but the Nazi SS. They remained, of course, repelled by the manner and matter of Rupert Brooke's famous war sonnets. In the event, what they wrote was anti-fascist poetry which was profoundly influenced by the diction and attitudes of Wilfred Owen – a kind of anti-fascist pacifist poetry.[67] □

Their poetry might, Spender says here, be classified as 'a kind of war poetry'. This comment usefully illustrates the process of continual fluctuation and negotiation around genre boundaries: a consensual understanding of a particular genre influences and informs artistic practice, yet poems written in new contexts may modify or cast fresh light upon the genre itself, even alter the 'consensus' definition of the genre. In the quotation above, Spender tacitly acknowledges that the war poetry to which he is referring had moved away from the genre examples that inspired it.

For George Orwell, who volunteered and fought on the Republican side, experience of the Spanish Civil War led to a profound anger and disillusionment with the intellectual and cultural climate of the period. In his 1940 essay 'Inside the Whale', he bitterly attacked what he saw as the destructive and blinkered ideological positions that had been taken up:

> ■ By 1937 the whole of the intelligentsia was mentally at war. Left-wing thought had narrowed down to 'anti-Fascism', i.e. to a negative, and a torrent of hate-literature directed against Germany and the politicians supposedly friendly to Germany was pouring from the Press. The thing that, to me, was truly frightening about the war in Spain was not such violence as I witnessed, nor even the party feuds behind the lines, but the immediate reappearance in left-wing circles of the mental atmosphere of the Great War. The very people who for twenty years had sniggered over their own superiority to war hysteria were the ones who rushed straight back into the mental slum of 1915. All the familiar wartime idiocies, spy-hunting,

orthodoxy-sniffing (Sniff, sniff. Are you a good anti-Fascist?), the retailing of atrocity stories, came back into vogue as though the intervening years had never happened. Before the end of the Spanish war, and even before Munich, some of the better of the left-wing writers were beginning to squirm. Neither Auden nor, on the whole, Spender wrote about the Spanish war in quite the vein that was expected of them. Since then there has been a change of feeling and much dismay and confusion, because the actual course of events has made nonsense of the left-wing orthodoxy of the last few years. But then it did not need very great acuteness to see that much of it was nonsense from the start. There is no certainty, therefore, that the next orthodoxy to emerge will be any better than the last.[68] □

In much later criticism of Spanish Civil War poetry there has also been a preoccupation with the 'mental atmosphere' to which many poets seemed to cling. In particular, there has been a concern with the extent to which combatant poets failed to accommodate their orthodox political beliefs with their lived experiences. In *The Last Great Cause* (1968) by Stanley Weintraub, the work of several of the Spanish Civil War poets is discussed. Few were established as poets prior to their volunteering, and, Weintraub argues: 'The reaction to battle often froze experienced writers into mannered, insincere language. It also sometimes made poets of men who had never written verse before, and would never do so again.'[69] Here, response to experience is central to the conception of war poetry; it is seen as a reactive phenomenon. The measure of good war poetry is again that of sincerity, authenticity and, as illustrated in Weintraub's comment on Charles Donnelly (1914–37), objectivity: 'His few weeks of war had generated in him an objectivity which had freed him, in his best verse, from dated political diction.'[70]

This dichotomy between mannered political rhetoric and the 'objective' poetry stimulated by experience can be seen as an extension of critical constructions of First World War poetry (where idealistic patriotism was contrasted with Owenesque empathy and freshness of diction and perspective). In the First World War many volunteers were motivated by a deeply inculcated belief in patriotism and the importance of personal sacrifice for one's country, yet they were forced to redefine, accommodate or discard these beliefs within the 'lived experience' of the trenches. For many critics from the early 1930s onwards, the best First World War poems, and subsequently Spanish Civil War poems, gave voice to new perspectives that resulted from the disruption or collapse of such assumptions and value systems.

In this chapter, we have seen how different conceptions of war poetry – as heroic, pacifist or political – developed alongside one another during the interwar period. While anti-war feeling helped to raise poets seen as pacifist, primarily Wilfred Owen, to far greater prominence, the appetite for the heroic continued and even found new forms. For example, some of the poetry written during the Spanish Civil War, under the auspices of socialist or Communist ideology, had distinctly heroic overtones. Some of the Spanish Civil War poets, as we have seen, were uncomfortably aware of their connection to the legacy of Rupert Brooke and his war sonnets, with their ethos of righteous and just sacrifice for a greater good. By the start of the Second World War in 1939, expectations about the war poetry to come were high. In the next chapter, we will consider the critical responses to the huge outpouring of poetry in this war, and examine how far they were conditioned by the images and discourses that had developed around the soldier-poets of the Great War.

CHAPTER FOUR

The Second World War

INTRODUCTION

If the First World War tends to be represented in terms of the tragedy of the 'lost generation' on the battlefields of the Western Front, the Second World War has often, by contrast, been portrayed as the 'just' war. Like the First World War, however, it has been intensively analyzed, investigated and imaginatively reconstructed: the Second World War has played a very significant role in the way that British nationality has been formulated and represented in the second half of the twentieth century. It has also become a frequent subject for films, perhaps in part due to the many different national, cultural and geographical contrasts suggested by the main theatres of war. Yet the war is as often remembered in terms of the supposed national characteristics it brought out: the 'Dunkirk spirit' of calm bravery in the face of adversity, or the civilian 'Home Front' stoicism of the 'Blitz'.

As we have seen already in the first two chapters of this Guide, First World War poetry had begun, by the 1930s, to be positioned as a means of remembering the war's losses, and, gradually, of implying distaste for the idea of war in the abstract. How, then, was it possible that 'war poetry' could be written about a new, global conflict arising from the expansionist aggression of a country led by a Fascist dictator? Were poets inspired, as so many were with the Spanish Civil War, to express themselves politically, or did they rather turn away from poetry, in the belief that it could no longer provide a useful vehicle for ideas about the purpose of war? In this chapter we will consider the many different views among poets and critics of the significance of the war, and the emphasis that poetry might have in wartime, from propagandist to visionary and personal.

The start of a second major war only two decades after the First World War had a profound impact on a range of cultural activities, including poetry. The first section of this chapter considers contemporary views about the social and cultural role of poetry in wartime. The section goes on to examine expectations that there would be 'war poets' in the mould of famous First World War poet figures, representing patriotic aspirations and providing hope and comfort to the nation. These views are then contextualized with extracts from contemporary critical discussions of left-wing intellectual bankruptcy, Englishness and a 'common' national culture.

In the second section we consider issues relating to the quantity of poetry that was published during the Second World War, including wartime readers' demands for new literary offerings, critics' fears about diminishing poetic quality and the continuing debate about the relationship between war and art. A number of wartime literary groupings and contexts are surveyed, including the networks of economic and cultural connections in London, and the role and variety of wartime anthology publications are examined.

The final section of this chapter explores the culture and preoccupations of poets serving in the armed forces, looking at the transition from civilian to soldier and perceptions of battle as the 'central' experience of war. The involvement of large numbers of women in different types of war work is also considered, leading into a discussion of some examples of war poetry by female poets. Finally, the significance of two overarching themes in Second World War poetry, unity and dissonance, is explored.

CULTURAL AND CRITICAL POSITIONING

HISTORY REPEATS ITSELF

During the early phase of the Second World War, anxiety was expressed in the press that British poetry was proving unable to engage with the new hostilities.[1] This anxiety, and the precise nature of the lack of war poetry, needs to be understood in relation to the existence of a body of First World War poetry, widely read and variously associated with celebrating victory, commemorating and mourning casualties, or expressing in general 'the pity of war'.[2] With the Second World War under way, expectations were voiced that contemporary poets should write about the new conflict in order to represent wartime experiences, aims and ideals and to help the nation endure the dangers and privations of war. In this subsection we will consider two extracts that put forward contrasting views of war poetry in the light of the new socio-historical and cultural conditions.

Many poets and critics addressing the condition of British poetry in the Second World War were haunted by the war of 1914–18. For these individuals, the First World War was not simply a set of unhappy memories but a pivotal event, a disastrous eruption of evil that had never been fully quelled. This perspective is evident, for example, in a 1939

Times Literary Supplement leading article by the journalist Philip Tomlinson, in which a sense of historical repetition is prominent. Here, the Second World War is figured as a type of potential new Dark Age, in the face of which Tomlinson calls on contemporary poets to express a degree of optimism:

■ We review in this issue some collected poetry of 1939. What can the poets do with the year 1940, when the world seems to be threatened with a new Dark Age? Of one thing we can be certain: if, shocked by the suffering inflicted by nations in tumult, they fall into resignation or despair, and yearn only for the nothingness where lost man may find 'what changeless vague of peace he can,' then the Dark Age is assured. And that is true too if they try to make harmonies from hatreds or seek the salvation of man in political formulas labelled Left or Right.

This war has followed so close on the heels of the other that it conveys no sense of novelty to awaken the creative spirit. It has the forbidding aspect of an old foe. Consciousness has been struggling vainly to free itself from the mark of the last calamity, but our poetry continued to be permeated, in varying forms and degrees, with the memory and often with the mood of 1914–18. A quarter of a century of moral disquietude and revolt has not been accompanied by any clear conception of what new order should replace the old. Deliberately heedless, even defiant of ancient values, poetry receded and, but for some faithful hands, might have lost itself. It can no longer be argued that these were symptoms of an age of transition; there never was any other kind of age. Here we are faced with an undeniable repetition of history, with nothing original, nothing unique about it. What can the poets make of it in their explorations of reality? Is it possible to find in this convulsion not the cloud of a Dark Age but the dawn of another Renaissance?

The prospects are precarious, but not hopeless. The first shock of the war produced a paralysis of the poetical intelligence. Verses turned to tears. But already those who are concerned to keep poetry alive are adding their comment on where the world stands.[3] □

Several of the key themes raised in Tomlinson's comments can be seen to permeate poetry and poetry criticism throughout the war. Apart from the sense of history repeating itself, there is a related concern that there is nothing 'original' to be expressed in war poetry, and a fear for the future of poetry in general. Some of these concerns increased as the war progressed and large quantities of poetry began to be published, a situation discussed further in the section 'Anthologies and the poetry boom'. Tomlinson's comments, written only three months into the war, highlight a fundamental assumption that poetry should be written to serve a special purpose in wartime. War poetry is situated by Tomlinson within several potentially conflicting injunctions: it must be original and creative; it must 'explore reality'; and it must not 'fall into resignation and despair'. Indeed, the war poet's work here seems at least as defined by the demands of social duty as by those of aesthetic expression.

In fact, relatively little poetry was published in the first few months of war, and only a small number of poems were written that attempted to represent emotions and ideas arising from the new conflict. There was considerable uncertainty about how events would unfold, and for many individuals there was a delay before the war had a substantial impact on their way of life. There were sometimes, for example, long waits before call-up papers arrived or war-work was allocated. This was combined with the failure of the anticipated bombing raids on Britain to take place until the summer of 1940. During this period, known as the 'Phoney War', many poets experienced a sense of creative near-paralysis; even once mobilized, many established and aspiring poets had difficulty in finding the time and satisfactory conditions in which to write.[4] In the following passage from the essay 'Growing up in wartime' (1946), the poet and critic Henry Treece (1911–66) offers his own analysis of this period of poetic paucity and the reasons for the indignant media demands:

■ The very fact that one was left completely free to decide whether or not to join the International Brigade made the Spanish War into something privately Quixotic [idealistic, lofty or visionary], a symbol of free action, and a stimulus to free thought.

But in 1939 the present war had all the terror and the inevitability of cancer; the nightmare had to proceed, however much the patient screamed, protested his innocence, his frightened inability to bear the pain.

Nevertheless, from the start, although I was too close to the war to derive from it any poetic material – a process which even now has not begun to show itself – I made up for the lack of fresh stimulus by getting completed all the work which had been started or projected before the war came. I imagine that many other writers, and especially poets, were doing the same thing at this time, and I expect that this is one of the reasons why so little poetry, directly concerned with war and its impedimenta, is being written; which in its turn is answer enough to the occasional bleats from the daily press, which ask when the poets are going to immortalize the Battle of Britain, to bring further honour to the heroes of Dunkirk. And because no such poems are forthcoming, the popular inference is that poetry is dead! Whereas, from my own observation, there has been as much poetry written during this war as there was before it. It just doesn't happen to be what the public calls 'War Poetry'. And this is not because the poets are shut away from war; on the contrary, most of the poets I know, and certainly all the poets I respect, unless they are over military age at present, are involved in the war in one or other of the services. It is rather, as I have suggested, that the poets have until now, or at least for a considerable time after the beginning of the war, been occupied in recording the impulses that were a part of the texture of their lives before ever war started.[5] □

Treece uses the Spanish Civil War as a point of comparison, suggesting that for the British, the freedom to choose whether or not to participate infused that war with a romantic sense of opportunity. By contrast, as discussed in the section 'Civilisation and its discontents' later in this chapter, the Second World War seemed to affect everyone; there was no safety or immunity from its effects. In the next extract, Treece highlights this sense of 'universality' as one of the key obstacles to the type of war poetry that the public and press want:

■ *Time-lag* and *imminence* are I believe two interdependent factors which may account for the comparative lack of distinguishable 'war poetry'. Another factor, I think, is war's *universality*. What everyone knows about, few honestly wish to talk about. And this applies even to love, a process – at the worst, a mechanism – which is discussed publicly and frequently only by prisoners, commercials [travelling sales representatives] and adolescents, or by such as are forced to live similar lives to prisoners, commercials and adolescents. The last war, despite its name, did not implicate at first hand more than a minority in this country; a minority which was, in consequence, eager to read of war's peculiar situations – as eager as the poets and novelists were to write them up. These poets and novelists, sensing the communication expected of them, and feeling, moreover, the singularity of their position, satisfied both the public and themselves. Now, however, the experience is not restrictive. Every British subject has a knowledge of this war and its implications, often at first hand. The pain and pity of war are no more news than is man's ability to walk on two legs. It is no more a subject for poetry than is a journey in a train.[6] □

Here, Treece suggests that Owen's famous emphasis on the 'pity of war' has been superseded: poetic representations of war's 'pain' have lost their power to shock, because war is a part of everybody's experience.

The above extracts from Treece's essay echo Tomlinson's earlier point, that the Second World War conveyed 'no sense of novelty to awaken the creative spirit'. Unlike Tomlinson, however, Treece perceives that there are other dimensions to the apparent lack of war poets. The public, he observes, wants war poetry to depict celebratory or heroic images of the war, and is unable to understand or appreciate a different approach to the genre. Contemporary poets, however, were often still preoccupied with pre-war conditions and concerns as much as with the details of the war itself; they could not be expected to react immediately to war, nor to produce stock reactions. Behind Treece's interest in 'time-lag' and 'imminence' is his belief that experience needs to be gradually assimilated into the subconscious before it can inform or inspire poetry. He argues, therefore, that the conditions of the new war made it difficult to gain the intellectual and emotional distance necessary for poetry. Yet Treece also sees positive poetic outcomes from wartime: war has, he concedes, produced in him a greater religious awareness, and 'a degree of maturity which a decade of peace might not have brought'.[7] War can result in poets experimenting with language and developing their capacity for 'sincerity' and 'sympathy'. Whilst resisting some of the conventional heroic expectations of the genre, Treece sees poetry in wartime as offering the possibility of both literary renewal and personal salvation.

WAR POETS REVISITED

Amidst the debate about where the war poetry was in the Second World War, and how it could be defined and understood, a related question emerged: who would the new war poets be? As poetry publishing began to increase after the 'Phoney War' period, it became evident that there was a considerable range of individual poets representing distinct aspects of war experience, and a diversity of opinion about the meaning and value of the 'war poet' label. In Chapters Two and Three, we have seen how two different models of the 'war poet' became established, the idealistic patriot and the pacifist protester, both of which were associated with forms of wartime heroism. Although the popularity of the idealistic patriot model had waned in the 1930s, particuarly with the left-wing intelligentsia, it had not lost its hold in the public imagination. (This is affirmed in the comment by Treece above, when he notes that there is a public search for poets who would 'immortalize the Battle of Britain' and 'bring further honour to the heroes of Dunkirk'.) The popularity of Owen also remained strong, yet the influence of the intellectuals and social realist poets who had championed him was subject to considerable criticism during the war years. This is examined further in the next subsection, in relation to 1940s debates about Englishness, class and the possibility of a 'national culture'.

By 1939, contemporary poets and writers were generally familiar with aspects of the lives and work of the most famous First World War poets. The frequently anthologized Second World War poet Keith Douglas, for example, was known to have admired Wilfred Owen,[8] another widely recognized Second World War poet, Alun Lewis, was inspired by the work of Edward Thomas,[9] and the lesser-known poet Patric Dickinson (1914–94) wrote in his memoir of a lifelong, deep attachment to Owen as a poetic father figure.[10] However, the poetic legacy of the First World War was not experienced purely through the work and reputations of specific individuals: as we have already seen, the term 'war poet', like 'war poetry', had acquired a wider potency as a cultural signifier. In the poem 'Where are the War Poets?', Cecil Day Lewis expresses resentment at the pressure to fulfil a particular role:

■ They who in folly or mere greed
Enslaved religion, markets, laws,
Borrow our language now and bid
Us to speak up in freedom's cause.

It is the logic of our times,
No subject for immortal verse –
That we who lived by honest dreams
Defend the bad against the worse.[11] □

In this poem, Day Lewis comments on the hypocrisy of those who, whilst fully implicated in the war, demand that 'war poets' produce poems of freedom. His idea of 'defending the bad against the worse' crops up in many other poets' work during the Second World War. The poet Sidney Keyes also articulates a sense of conflict arising from the literary and cultural expectations that abounded. In 'War Poet', Keyes suggests that the possibility of poetry is undermined by the violence imposed by war:

■ I am the man who looked for peace and found
My own eyes barbed.
I am the man who groped for words and found
An arrow in my hand.[12] □

There was, then, a contradiction between public perceptions of the 'war poet' as self-sacrificial, heroic and noble, and a war that many poets viewed as a necessary evil, but an evil nevertheless.

In this context, poets of the Second World War can be seen distancing themselves from or implicitly questioning the 'war poet' label. In his memoir of the period, *The Strange and the Good* (1989), for example, the poet and novelist Roy Fuller (1912–91) reflects on the implications of being both poet and serviceman in the war:

■ Undoubtedly, the verse I wrote between the outbreak of war and my call-up is a better record of the world than what had gone before, not that that is claiming a great deal. The rhetoric is ballasted to some extent by observation and an occasional generalization of reasonable insight. But the sum total is meagre of those that could be allowed to be seen by other eyes. The period covered was quite extensive in a sense, and even bombed out and benighted I welcomed the passage of the days as meaning fewer eventually in the disagreeable role of serviceman. No patriotic or even anti-fascist feeling tempered the urging on of time and the war while in moderate control of one's fate. Sometimes, moving well into 1941, a reassuring proportion of the months the war could last seemed already to have gone by; and then, considering German triumphs, British disasters, the weary laps ahead seemed unfairly numerous. There was still ample time in which to be scared, mutilated and killed.[13] □

This account of the impact of the early stage of the war upon a poet is quite different to that of Treece, discussed earlier. For Fuller, concerned with a predominately realistic approach to poetry, and influenced by Auden and the politically aware 'social realists', the wait for call-up presented an opportunity to observe, and, perhaps, to draw out a 'reasonably' insightful generalization. As he accustomed himself to service life, however, Fuller struggled to apply his poetic principles of simplicity and verisimilitude to his new routine and fellow servicemen:

■ It will seem curious to poets now, as it does to me, that I did not exploit more thoroughly the material life then unfolded, having found one reasonably satisfactory way to do it in the poem referred to, called 'Saturday Night in a Sailors' Home'. This was a simple sonnet in octosyllabics [lines of eight syllables], further democratized by the introduction of a couple of phrases of what was intended as verisimilitudinous speech, e.g. 'Please shake me at five' – 'shake' being the Navy word for rouse from sleep, therefore in frequent use because of the perpetual business of going on watch. John Lehmann [1907–87] was at that time choosing the poetry for *Tribune* [a Left-wing weekly journal], and I well recall him objecting to the original two phrases as being insufficiently colloquial. I changed and, however unlikely it may seem, improved them: the superfluous 'please' had to be kept because it was a rhyme word – no bold Yeatsian changing of rhyme schemes for me in those days, nor for donkeys' years subsequently. What one was after was a Sassoon-like directness, which lack of skill in my case made difficult to combine with the traditional forms that Auden had, after the experimentalism of the Twenties, rendered pretty well obligatory once more. All the same, I am glad *vers libre* [free verse, irregular, syllabic or unrhymed verse, in which the ordinary rules of prosody are disregarded] was out of fashion, for the task of being a 'war poet' (by no means a conscious aim: rather the problem of continuing, in the role of serviceman, to write verse at all) might then have been too easily, superficially achieved. I could say, indeed, that one aspect of a whole lifetime's poetry has been the effort of trying to make strict forms 'natural', using that last word to beg a number of more or less complex questions.[14] □

Fuller invokes Siegfried Sassoon as an influence, yet describes the 'task of being a "war poet" ' as 'by no means a conscious aim'. He writes with a tone of self-consciousness and gentle self-mockery, suggesting that there is both uncertainty and contrivance involved in any poet's efforts to shape a poetic persona and style. Fuller also sees the fashion for traditional verse forms as a useful constraint or discipline, one that prevented him from slotting into a poetic role which might have been too 'superficially achieved'. The wariness about categorizations evident in Fuller's comments is also manifest in the poetry and memoirs of other poets of the Second World War, and is discussed again in the subsection on anthologies.

ENGLISHNESS

As observed by Roy Fuller in the passage above, the influence of Auden's poetry upon some of the younger poets was still considerable, but by the 1940s his reputation had undergone a significant change. Auden and his friend, the writer Christopher Isherwood (1904–86), had emigrated to America early in 1939, an act construed by many previous admirers of their work as one of abandonment, even betrayal. Auden had often been viewed as speaking on behalf of an entire body of left-wing and literary-minded younger people about the need for social and political criticism and change and for a poetry committed to such criticism. In departing for America just before war was declared, it appeared that he was disavowing his responsibilities or duties as a 'social poet'.[15] Some of Auden's contemporaries, and subsequent critics, have sought to defend him, arguing that it is unfair and aesthetically counterproductive for poets to live under such public obligations. Auden himself, however, did not attempt an overt defence of his emigration and as discussed in the previous chapter, he had been gradually moving away from a treatment of poetry as political. This can be seen in his poem 'September 1, 1939', which places substantial emphasis on personal responsibility, religious faith and love.[16]

Apart from the specific issue of Auden and Isherwood's emigration, the work and views of the Auden group of poets were being subjected to criticism from a number of quarters. For example, the novelist Virginia Woolf (1882–1941), in a lecture delivered to the Workers Educational Association in 1940, emphasizes that these poets shared the advantages, indeed privileges, that middle- and upper-class writers had enjoyed for decades. Woolf, herself from a highly intellectual upper-middle-class background, had become a substantial literary figure through her development of impressionistic and indirect narrative technique in the 1920s and the 1930s. Moving on from a discussion of the secure identities of young male writers prior to the beginning of the

First World War in 1914, Woolf observes:

■ From that group let us pass to the next – to the group which began to write about 1925 and, it may be, came to an end as a group in 1939. If you read current literary journalism you will be able to rattle off a string of names – Day Lewis, Auden, Spender, Isherwood, Louis MacNeice and so on. They adhere much more closely than the names of their predecessors. But at first sight there seems little difference, in station, in education. Mr Auden in a poem written to Mr Isherwood says:[17] Behind us we have stucco suburbs and expensive educations. They are tower dwellers like their predecessors, the sons of well-to-do parents, who could afford to send them to public schools and universities. But what a difference in the tower itself, in what they saw from the tower! When they looked at human life what did they see? Everywhere change; everywhere revolution. In Germany, in Russia, in Italy, in Spain,[18] all the old hedges were being rooted up; all the old towers were being thrown to the ground. Other hedges were being planted; other towers were being raised. There was communism in one country; in another fascism. The whole of civilization, of society, was changing. There was, it is true, neither war nor revolution in England itself. All those writers had time to write many books before 1939. But even in England towers that were built of gold and stucco were no longer steady towers. They were leaning towers. The books were written under the influence of change, under the threat of war.[19] ☐

Woolf describes Auden and others as holding to the 'ivory tower' privileges of a middle-class income and a sense of superiority achieved through education, whilst highly conscious of the need for dramatic social and political change. In Woolf's analysis, this group of writers has failed to resolve the contradiction in its position, and is outmoded: she clearly identifies the group as having 'come to an end' in 1939, with the first year of the war. In the conclusion to the essay, Woolf declares that writing should no longer be left to 'a small class of well-to-do young men who have only a pinch, a thimbleful of experience to give us', and calls for literature to be seen as 'common ground'.[20]

Other writers similarly explored the significance of the war not just in physical terms of survival, but in relation to national identity, class and the ownership of, or access to, culture. These explorations revealed concerns not only with whether the English way of life would survive, but also with latent questions of what, in fact, it meant to be 'English'. What did the English culture that was being defended actually consist of? For George Orwell, as for Virginia Woolf, a key theme in this debate was the stance of middle-class intellectuals such as Auden, Spender and Day Lewis; and from Orwell's point of view, as we observed in the previous chapter, the negative aspect of that stance had become all too apparent during the Spanish Civil War. Orwell saw this episode as having revealed a carping, self-destructive tendency within the 'left-wing intelligentsia' and from this he drew a number of wider conclusions in his essay, 'England Your England' (in *The Lion and the Unicorn: Socialism and the English Genius* (1941)):

■ The mentality of the English left-wing intelligentsia can be studied in half a dozen weekly and monthly papers. The immediately striking things about all these papers is their generally negative, querulous attitude, their complete lack at all times of any constructive suggestion. There is little in them except the irresponsible carping of people who have never been and never expect to be in a position of power. Another marked characteristic is the emotional shallowness of people who live in a world of ideas and have little contact with physical reality. Many intellectuals of the Left were flabbily pacifist up to 1935, shrieked for war against Germany in the years 1935–9, and then promptly cooled off when the war started. It is broadly though not precisely true that the people who were most 'Anti-Fascist' during the Spanish civil war are most defeatist now. And underlying this is the really important fact about so many of the English intelligentsia – their severance from the common culture of the country.[21] □

Many left-wing intellectuals are, according to Orwell, completely detached from the common culture on which the future of England depends.

Orwell is arguing in this essay for an understanding of Englishness as defined not according to social class, but by national and cultural characteristics. Indeed, he portrays all nations as differentiated by fundamental 'differences of outlook', seen as vital and intrinsic to individual, as well as national, identity. The English are described by Orwell as 'not gifted artistically', hypocritical, snobbish and disinclined towards abstract thought; yet at the same time as highly independent, moral, humorous and above all gentle. This gentleness of outlook, Orwell claims, imbues British literary achievements too, and translates into a tendency to dwell on defeats and losses, rather than pride and victory:

■ In England all the boasting and flag-waving, the 'Rule Britannia' stuff, is done by small minorities. The patriotism of the common people is not vocal or even conscious. They do not retain among their historical memories the name of a single military victory. English literature, like other literatures, is full of battle-poems, but it is worth noticing that the ones that have won for themselves a kind of popularity are always a tale of disasters and retreats. There is no popular poems about Trafalgar or Waterloo, for instance. Sir John Moore's army at Corunna, fighting a desperate rearguard action before escaping overseas (just like Dunkirk!) has more appeal than a brilliant victory. The most stirring battle-poem in English is about a brigade of cavalry which charged in the wrong direction. And of the last war, the four names which have really engraved themselves on the popular memory are Mons, Ypres, Gallipoli and Passchendaele, every time a disaster. The names of the great battles that finally broke the German armies are simply unknown to the general public.[22] □

Orwell is writing about the Left from a disaffected stance, as a volunteer who had, as discussed in the previous chapter, become disillusioned about the Republican cause in the Spanish Civil War. His language in describing the English 'left-wing intelligentsia' is thus antagonistic: he sees them as privileged individuals who espouse causes, yet who are uninformed by relevant and necessary practical experience. This critique is used as a point of contrast, as a means of highlighting the overall tolerance and worthiness of the mass of English society and culture. The 'battle' poems Orwell refers to are used as evidence for his belief in the gentle, unconscious patriotism of the common people. There is no mention of, or explanation for the popularity of patriotic or jingoistic poetry, such as that of the First World War, for example. Orwell's essay illustrates the way in which poetry can be interpolated within an ideological position through careful selection and discussion; it further illustrates a specific tendency to use patriotism as a framework for giving significance to war poetry. These issues will be considered further in the anthology subsection.

A different perspective is evident from the poet, critic and editor Edgell Rickword, whose account of John Cornford was quoted in the previous chapter, and who wrote three important articles relating to war poetry during the Second World War.[23] Rickword shares to some extent Orwell's interest in the idea of a common culture, but as part of an overarching Communist conviction that in pre-capitalist society oral poetry was a part of everyday life, and that this condition could once again be achieved. In 'Notes on Culture and the War' (1940), Rickword discusses the politically and culturally transformational potential of wartime:

■ A century of industrialism has broken the roots of our tradition and left us dependent on imported song, the anaemic product of commercialized inspiration (except for what we have lifted from the Negroes). But there is plenty of evidence – the popularity of Unity Theatre [a left-wing workers' drama group, founded in 1936], the circulation of this paper – that the blood is beginning to flow again in the numbed limb. Everything now depends on the development of democratic initiative, on whether the people are really roused and not merely shepherded ...[24] □

The scenario envisaged by Rickword here is of an authentic, popular tradition emerging from within 'the people', rather than one in which popular cultural forms are designed and foisted on the people by the ruling class. He is aware, however, of the dangers of associating war with the possibility of cultural renewal. In a subsequent article, 'Poetry and Two Wars' (1941) he warns against the tendency of contemporary critics to glorify the impact of war upon poetry:

■ 'In the stress of a nation's peril some of its greatest songs are born', claimed the Preface to an anthology of patriotic verse published in 1914. 'The fact is', asserts a leader in The Times Literary Supplement in 1941, 'the war may mean a renaissance of English literature, which for years has threatened to pass away in fatuous experiments.' 'Thank God this has burnt up the aesthetes', a literary friend wrote to me in 1915. And in January this year Sir Hugh Walpole [1884–1941, novelist] proclaims, 'After Dunkirk, new poets were born'.

The parallelism between these utterances at the outset of two wars could be illustrated by many other examples. Though emotional rather than intellectual, they expose the bankruptcy of middle-class literary theory, which can prescribe no other remedy for the rejuvenation of our literature than a periodical blood-bath in which a large proportion of its potential creators must be destroyed.

Granted that a close contact with reality is the essential for a healthy literature, it is precisely those forces which have a practical monopoly of the means of expression whose pressure has all the time been exercised in keeping the intellectuals from participation in the vitalizing social struggle, and who now endeavour to represent mutual massacre as the divinely-ordained opportunity for genius to fulfil itself. But the parallels with the First World War are less interesting than the disparity which the lapse of time reveals as this much-prophesied parturition [birth] is once again dangerously delayed.

Whenever history repeats itself, or is about to, on a higher level, it has its farcical or sentimental reflection on a lower one. And as, after Brooke's sonnets, no heroic literature did in fact develop, but instead the damning veracity of Barbusse [Henri Barbusse (1873–1935), French writer and First World War soldier, author of the novel Le Feu [Under Fire] (1916)] Sassoon, Owen – so we can expect that the terrible logic of experience will prove stronger than the wishfulness of The Times. 'This book is not about heroes. English poetry is not yet fit to speak of them', wrote Owen of his own poems in 1918. Nor has poetry employed the interval in qualifying to do so.[25] □

Again it is the middle-class intelligentsia that is the target. Rickword pinpoints in particular the literary journalists, who welcome an event as violent and destructive as war on the grounds that it rejuvenates poetry. The notion that Rickword takes issue with here, that war poetry emerges from a vital engagement with experience, is one that persists throughout the twentieth century. In this essay, Rickword refers to it as an example of how social and political interests and power relations shape cultural values. Rickword argues, in essence, that in this case, the representation of war as having beneficial aesthetic effects is a disguise; it is in the ruling class interest to defend war, as it is this class that will benefit the most from a victory. Later in this chapter we will consider other comments on the political and social significance of poetry in wartime, particularly in the discussion of the editorial role in war poetry anthologies.

THE POETRY 'BOOM'

POETRY PUBLISHING

Despite the initial slow start, more poets were writing about war in the Second World War than in the First: according to Catherine Reilly's bibliography *English Poetry of the Second World War*, there were 2679 poets compared with 2225.[26] Reilly accounts for this increase with three observations: first, that there was a greater number of people who were routinely in danger in the Second World War; second, that the publishing industry had grown substantially during the interwar period; and third, that there was an increase in reading during wartime, including the reading of poetry.[27] As Reilly also points out, the interest in writing poetry about war was not confined to those directly involved in combat, or even to those in the uniformed services (by which Reilly refers to the armed forces, the auxiliary forces and the various branches of civil defence): only 831 of the poets that she lists were in the services, with the remainder covering a vast range of wartime roles and occupations.

Reilly's mapping of the Second World War poetry corpus provided a foundation for many subsequent investigations of the field, and in establishing her bibliographical framework she usefully identified a number of practical considerations in working with the genre. For example, she points out the need to take into account the 'delayed nature' of poetry publishing, not only because of the length of the publication process itself, but also because poets often accumulated their work over months or years before submitting it for publication. She also observes that anthologies of Second World War poetry have an overlapping, sometimes repetitive quality, drawing frequently on poetry selections made by other texts, whether periodicals, editions of individual poets' works or anthologies. A fuller discussion of the cultural and literary standing of Second World War anthologies, of which Reilly lists 87, is included later in this section.

Reilly's bibliographical work was carried out from a late twentieth-century perspective, and will be considered again in Chapter Five, as part of a period in which several scholars focused upon the place of 'war poetry' in the literary and cultural history of wartime. It is worth noting here, however, the way in which Reilly perceives war poetry as a genre with a clear function and role:

■ Literature, especially poetry, that most sensitive of instruments, mirrors the society from which it springs. Even in the more pedestrian verse the social and military historian will find a rich harvest of comment on the war which, as time passes, will assume greater importance as a record of history. An account of a wartime incident in verse with careful choice of words and language can be more graphic than a longer prose account of the same incident. However, apparent autobiographical clues in the poems must be regarded with a great deal of caution. Poetic licence often results in the transferred voice – poets writing in the imagined role of perhaps a Battle of Britain pilot or a concentration camp victim.[28] □

According to this thinking, wartime incidents are 'accounted for' more graphically in 'verse' than in prose, and the implication is that war poets are primarily interested in veracity. The genre is seen as built around poets' 'honest responses' to war:

■ The incidents of war did not make the poetry; the poetry was made by the poets' honest responses. The work of the major poets is characterized by a cool control and economy of language which suggests that the poets of the Second World War were more wordly-wise, sophisticated and far less idealistic than their counterparts in that earlier war.[29] □

Here, then, scholarly interest in the quantity of wartime poetry is underpinned by a belief that it offers a kind of special access to, or witness account of, war. The perceived affinity between war and poetry is a theme much in evidence during the Second World War, and is referred to again later in this section.

The market for reading material grew quickly during the war, as fear of attack and restricted movements increased the amount of time civilians spent inside the home or shelter, particularly during blackout and bombing raids. Reading was a common leisure pursuit among the forces, too, during prolonged periods of waiting for orders or transport. Yet for the publishing industry, especially for companies established prior to the war, meeting the demand for reading matter was problematic. As contemporary novelist and biographer Arthur Calder-Marshall (born 1908) succinctly described it, 'Large numbers of books were destroyed in the blitzes, and before the War's end pre-War stocks were exhausted.'[30] Substantial quantities of paper were diverted into War Office use for official publications and the government reduced publishers' paper allocations to only a small proportion of pre-war supplies.

Some publishers, aware of the imminent restrictions, had stockpiled paper prior to rationing, whilst new publishing houses (which were not governed by the same principle of pre-war usage), together with a number of 'mushroom' companies, set up using any paper supplies available. In 1942, the Publishers Association negotiated among its members a Book Production War Economy Agreement to encourage optimal use of paper during wartime, and printed statements of conformity were included in many books.

After the slow start of the 'Phoney War' period, and despite the practical difficulties of paper supply and stock damage, an abundance of poetry was published. There were, as already mentioned, fears for the likely future direction of poetry and there were widely differing judgements on the quantity and quality of the poetry produced. The poet, novelist, biographer and editor Julian Symons (1912–94), whose own literary periodical *Twentieth Century Verse* closed in the summer of 1939, predicted a general change of mood and attitude towards poetry with the onset of war. In his memoir *Notes from Another Country* (1972), Symons describes this anticipated change in the following terms:

> ■ The *New Verse Anthology*, published at the end of August, now reads like a valediction: the end of *New Verse* is the end, for this time, of the movement towards commonsense standards in English letters. It is axiomatic that 'commonsense' has little chance in a war: and it is obvious too that inflation of language and sentiment in literature is as certain in wartime as inflation of prices .... It is not difficult to see what will happen in the near future. The emotional temperature will go up, poetry and prose will become more 'poetic', Eliot's just remark that 'poetry is nearer to "verse" than it is to prose poetry' will be forgotten ....[31] □

The poet Keith Douglas noted the increasing quantities of poetry publications with the cool observation: '... no paper shortage stems the production of hundreds of slim volumes and earnestly compiled anthologies of wartime poetry, *Poems from the Forces, &c*';[32] while Stephen Spender commented that the first impression of the 'enormous quantities of poems' that have been produced is one of 'disintegration'.[33]

Cyril Connolly (1903–74), critic and editor of the literary periodical *Horizon* (1939–50), also commented on the apparent increase in poetry being published. Connolly harboured frequent anxieties concerning the negative impact of war upon art, at one stage announcing that war was the 'enemy of creative activity'.[34] In a response to this printed in *Horizon* (July 1940), the journalist, editor and poet Goronwy Rees (1909–79) argued that Connolly had misunderstood the nature of war:

> ■ The war is not some obscene intruder on an idyllic scene in which the artist once happily flourished; it is the continuation of social processes in

new and more violent forms and, as Proust once showed, contains and develops all those elements which have made it inevitable.[35] □

As can be seen from Rees's assertion, not everyone was prepared to accept that war was an extreme but temporary aberration in civilized existence, or that it was necessarily an obstacle to art. The implication of Rees's argument is rather that art should address the 'new and violent forms' of social processes that war brings about. The burgeoning of poetry in wartime raised questions, familiar from debates in the early 1930s, about the relationship between war, art and society; it also divided opinion about the quality of the poetry that was being published. Did an increase in quantity, and an apparent rush to publish, inevitably imply poorer quality work? Perhaps poetry, as Symons put it, would suffer from an 'inflation of language and emotion' by attempting to address the conditions of wartime. Was it possible to put war at arm's length, and treat art as too precious to be tainted by its destructive presence, or was engaging with war central to understanding the society and culture poets lived and worked in?

LITERARY GROUPINGS

As discussed at the beginning of this chapter, the tendency in war poetry criticism following the early fame of Brooke, and the celebration of Owen in the 1930s, was to place a very strong emphasis on the role of individual poet figures. The question springing most readily to commentators' lips in the first two years of the war was not 'where is the war poetry?', but 'where are the war poets?'. Certainly, a discussion of the Second World War poetry corpus needs to take account of the individuals who rose to prominence as 'war poets', and to consider the cultural conditions and critical responses that contributed to this status. In the next subsection of this chapter, and in Chapter Five, we will consider the way in which poets such as Keith Douglas, Sidney Keyes and others have been incorporated into the war poetry canon, and deployed as standard bearers for a combat-oriented construction of Second World War poetry. However, it is also important for an understanding of the genre to consider some of the ways in which poets have been categorized and grouped. This section will examine some of the factors that united or distinguished wartime literary groupings, both in terms of geographical and social contexts, and approaches to poetic theory, technique and subject. It will also consider how poets have been categorized in relation to the war as a historical and cultural period.

Stephen Spender's brief survey of the poetry of the war period, *Poetry Since 1939*, is particularly useful from a literary historical point of view. It was published in 1946, allowing Spender to see the war with an element of distance, whilst drawing on poetry and events that would have been still fresh in impact and memory. In his survey, Spender delivers a fairly negative judgement on the poetry of the war, citing in particular a lack of coherent literary movements:

■ Enormous quantities of poems have been produced in war-time Britain, for there has been a boom in poetry and several publishers have been glad to use much of their paper in printing books of it. At first the general impression produced by this poetry has been one of disintegration. If one compares anthologies such as *Poems from the Forces* and *The White Horseman* with the collection produced by imagists or any other advanced movement since 1918, one notices at once the lack of rhythmic tension, the confused imagery, the over-literary fashions of thought, the uncritical writing which stakes all its ambition on a vague faith in inspiration or on some preconceived if chaotic attitude towards life.

It is not to the 'movements' that I would look for any promising signs in English poetry today but to poets and to poems.[36] □

Spender in fact states that it is *not* his intention to give any particular significance to poetry written in wartime; he explains that his concentration on the war period is due to the widespread ignorance of wartime literary developments. The poets are grouped according to shared characteristics: generational, aesthetic, political and social; underlying these is a clear distinction between those poets with established literary reputations prior to the war, and those who have only become known 'since 1939'. At times, however, despite Spender's disclaimer, the focus on the period of war appears to have a more than purely pragmatic or educational function.

For Spender, then, there is firstly a grouping of poets 'of an elder generation'. This includes Edmund Blunden, Walter De la Mare, Siegfried Sassoon, Herbert Read, John Masefield and Laurence Binyon, with Spender identifying the foremost elder generation poets as T. S. Eliot and Edith Sitwell, and giving them chapters to themselves. Most of these individuals wrote poetry in the First World War, and this leads Spender to consider how the poetry of the two wars might be compared:

■ Blunden and Sassoon, these poets of the last war, are always interesting but their experience seems circumscribed, perhaps indeed by the influence of the war itself. One wonders whether the poets of this war will show similar qualities and similar limitations. Probably their development will be different because this war, with all its terrors, has been adventurous and expansive, more likely to produce agoraphobia than the claustrophobia of the war of 1914–1918.[37] □

In this quotation, Spender suggests a link between the scale and scope of a particular war, a poet's personal experience of it and the nature and quality of their poetry. Elsewhere, it is the lack of a poet's war experience that appears to inform categorizations. For example, Spender dedicates a chapter to 'W. H. Auden and the poets of the Thirties', describing them as a group of friends linked through experience of university life, an intellectual approach to poetry and a common feeling of malaise with the world. Spender writes admiringly of Auden as the outstanding poet of his generation. There is, however, a separate chapter given to Day Lewis, MacNeice and Spender, a decision that partly acknowledges Auden's literary difference and superiority, and partly indicates his distance from his contemporaries, through his emigration to America. The significance of the war as a period is also evident in the construction of one of the final poetic groupings: a section on the poets who have become known since 1939. This includes: Vernon Watkins (1906–67), Laurie Lee (1914–97), F. T. Prince (1912–2003), Henry Reed, Sidney Keyes, G. S. Fraser, Terence Tiller (1916–87) and Roy Fuller. In discussing the work of this cluster of poets, Spender gives particular praise to a number of 'soldier poems', including Prince's 'Soldiers Bathing', which is quoted in full, and Reed's 'Naming of Parts'.[38]

In one of his final chapters, Spender notes the number of poets from the regions, and declares that 'regionalism' is set to become a 'cultural movement'.[39] Many wartime poets were born and brought up in the regions: for example, Alun Lewis and Dylan Thomas (1914–53) from Wales, Robert Greacen (born 1920) from Northern Ireland, Hamish Henderson (1919–2002) and Edwin Muir (1887–1959) from Scotland and Roy Fuller and Nicholas Nicholson (1914–87) from North-West England. These poets diverged greatly in the extent to which their poetry or literary careers were shaped by a sense of regional identity. Nicholson included topographical references and place names in his poetry, and some of the Scottish poets wrote in dialect. There were also attempts to sustain regionally based and regionally oriented poetry publishing, including the Welsh Nationalist Druid Press and the periodical *Wales*, run by the poet and editor Keidrych Rhys (1915–87). But regional identity was rarely a theme for the majority of poets and it was in London that they chose, or were obliged, to seek publishers.

Many established and influential pre-war literary figures lived or worked in the capital, including T. S. Eliot and Herbert Read.[40] In addition to major publishing houses such as Faber and Faber and Routledge & Kegan Paul, Ltd., many literary periodicals and magazines had their offices in London, including *Poetry Quarterly*, *Poetry London*, the popular *Penguin New Writing* and, as mentioned above, *Horizon*.[41] Individual writers and poets were often involved in several different London-based literary enterprises simultaneously, such as anthology or periodical editing: for example, the poet Wrey Gardiner (1901–81) ran the Grey Walls Press and edited *Poetry Quarterly*.[42] Several poets who were not in active service worked in the Ministry of Information, in radio broadcasting, film production or the print media.[43] The writing and publication of poetry in wartime London was, therefore, concentrated in a network of individuals with a variety of personal, political and professional affiliations.

In addition to critical surveys such as Spender's, there are a number of memoir sources that add to the understanding of literary groupings during the war period. These sometimes refer to contemporary debates about poetic form, subject and the treatment of poetic 'voice', revealing that these issues were experienced as more than individual aesthetic choices: they could be perceived as part of a wider system of thought or outlook, and passionately adhered to. In his memoir *Inside the Forties* (1977), for example, the poet and critic Derek Stanford (born 1918) writes of his attempts to win over others to the 'Neo-Romantic colours', a phrase suggestive of a distinctly formulated position to which he belonged. As can be seen in the following quotation, it was defined partly in opposition to other poetic approaches, publications and institutions. Here Stanford is commenting on one of the most popular literary journals of the period:

■ Of all periodical publications of the 1940s, none was so commercially successful as *Penguin New Writing*. But among the younger generation of Neo-Romantic writers, it was not all that welcome. The reasons for this were twofold: first, it was associated with the Social Realist movement of the thirties; secondly, and more to the point, it did not often print their work when they were most in need of publication.[44] □

John Lehmann, editor of *Penguin New Writing*, whose editorial policy allegedly excluded those of a Neo-Romantic tendency, defended himself from such accusations in the following terms:

■ It seemed to me that the spirit of *New Writing* was in fact very far from confined to the association of left-wing politics and literature, whatever might be said by the detractors and those who, silent in their hostility before, [i.e. before the war] were now eagerly gathering round the burial ground they had marked out for it. The belief in literature as part of life, the belief in the power of the creative imagination to give meaning to life; these were surely going to be as important as ever in the times we were about to enter. The reviews and the letters and messages that were coming in hinted that once one had taken on a responsibility towards young writers, it was not so easy to put it down again without looking a little selfish, a little cowardly (though I was aware of the ambuscade [ambush] of vanity in this argument). If *New Writing* was to go on, it must avoid the political, yes, but emphasize the human, be committed to the human scene even more completely; it could be a laboratory, an experimental ground for the development of a new consciousness; it would probably find itself moving towards something more lyrical and individual, burlesque and satire too of a kind that represented the revolt of the free human spirit against the prisons that the war with its imperatives and its bureaucratic impersonality threatened to build up round us ...[45] □

In Lehmann's vision for the future of *New Writing*, art is an expression of personal freedom in the face of the anonymity and relentless demands of war.

Equally passionate beliefs were held by other poetic groups, such as the Apocalyptics, who are discussed in the final section of this chapter. Yet it is important to note that while some poets identified unequivocally with a particular view of, or approach to poetry, most poets continually evolved and modified their outlook and values during the course of their lives. Many poets could not be satisfactorily placed against any single descriptive term as they overlap the boundaries of several categories. Additionally, as we will examine further in Chapter Five, movements and groupings are sometimes reconfigured or reinterpreted in the light of subsequent critical work.

WARTIME ANTHOLOGIES

In a 1945 article called 'The Price of Books', the poet Sean Jennett (born 1910) describes a key trend in wartime reading tastes, when he comments: '[books] that would have been sold out within a few days if they had appeared now, remain on stock with the publisher only, it seems, because they were published before the war'.[46]

As Jennett emphasizes here, the 'new' was being sought over and above the established and the traditional. Among the various wartime poetry publications, ranging from pamphlets to periodicals, the poetry anthology occupied a popular place. Anthologies offered the reader a variety of poetic voices and styles, and although (as pointed out by Reilly) it was common for poems in anthologies to be reprinted from other sources, they were perceived as offering new work to many readers. Derek Stanford believed that the poetry anthology had a particular allure because it was seen as an indicator of new directions in literature: 'As much perhaps as these magazines, anthologies which ran to one or more numbers helped to define the climate of the time. The appearance of each one seemed to indicate fresh paths opening in the literary landscape'.[47] Stanford suggests that along with the periodicals, anthologies had an important role in divining new developments and mapping the literary terrain in wartime.

As we saw in Chapter One, anthologies are highly mediated and constructed texts. The edited anthologies published during the Second World War engage with the war in a number of different ways, as can be seen from an analysis of editorial discourse and poetic contents. It is worth noting here that the use of 'wartime' as a descriptor for these anthologies is problematic. The most common usage of 'wartime' is as a reference to the period of war itself, 1939–45. This does not, however, indicate the extent to which the editor or selected poems are influenced by the war, or address it as a conscious theme. There are, for example, several anthologies published during the Second World War that allude only very indirectly or marginally to the contemporary experience of war. Both the popular 1944 anthology edited by Field Marshal Viscount Wavell (1883–1950), *Other Men's Flowers* (as we noted in Chapter One, the etymology of 'anthology' is from the Greek for *anthos*, flower, and – *logia*, collection), and the English Association's *England: An Anthology* (also published in 1944), consist largely of pre-Second World War poems on a wide variety of subjects. In both anthologies, poetry is represented as a pleasure and solace in difficult times: Wavell asks 'indulgence for the conditions in which this anthology has been compiled'[48] and in *England: An Anthology*, a prologue by General Smuts (1870–1950), Prime Minster of South Africa in the Second World War, stresses that although the blitz has destroyed much, the 'splendour of the spirit' and the soul of the English people has not been lost.[49] Although the contemporary war is in the background, the anthologies are, through their contents and through the main emphasis of the editorial introductions, designed to lead the reader away from war into more abstract and reassuring preoccupations.

In the introduction to *England: An Anthology*, writer, diplomat and politician Harold Nicolson (1886–1968) represents the poems as expressions of the national character, and as sources of patriotic inspiration:

■ The present collection, which has been compiled by a Committee of the English Association, has been chosen with a definite purpose in mind; it is an attempt (and in my judgment a successful attempt) to indicate how diverse and yet how similar have been the impressions which English poets of many centuries have derived from English life and character. It is an example, on the one hand, of the continuity of English literature, and on the other of its variety. For, although the instruments which form the vast orchestra of English poetry are diverse both in strength and form, the main themes are strangely recurrent and one can detect throughout the centuries a resonant continuity of tone.[50] □

In some cases, the 'continuity of English literature' is even depicted by Nicolson through flattering comparison with foreign poets, as in the following comment: 'But the love of Nature which for so many centuries has inspired and fortified our English poets has a quality more intimate and more natural than that which marks the nervous reactions of foreign writers.'[51] In the war section of this anthology, alongside militaristic poems such as Michael Drayton's 'A Ballad of Agincourt', 'Trafalgar Day' by George Meredith (1828–1909) and Thomas Hardy's 'Men Who March Away', a small number of Second World War poems are included. These, including 'The other little boats' by Edward Shanks (1892–1953) celebrating the military operation at Dunkirk, are also in harmony with the patriotic tone of the introduction. For both Wavell and Nicolson, the anthology's primary task is to represent the stability and confidence of the national character, through the image of a consistent, heroic and robust literary tradition.

In a number of other anthologies, the editors represent the war far more directly as a key theme, or as an essential condition of their production. Often this is indicated in the title, as can be seen in Patricia Ledward (born 1920) and Colin Strang, *Poems of this War, by Younger Poets* (1942); M. J. Tambimuttu, (1915–83), *Poetry in Wartime* (1942); and William Bell, (1924–48), *Poetry from Oxford in Wartime* (1945). Some variations on this type of title formulation can be found. For example, the 1944 anthology edited by Nancy Cunard, *Poems for France*, makes a more pointed reference to the fate of a particular nation, and echoes the title of the famous 1939 *Poems for Spain*, edited by Stephen Spender and John Lehmann. Yet even in these anthologies, with their clear references to war, editors are often circumspect about their aims and, in particular, their relationship to the 'war poetry' genre or the 'war poet' label. As discussed in the first chapter, these terms still carried strong connotations of heroism, self-sacrifice and the First World War. Tambimuttu, for example, made the following equivocal comment in the introduction to his anthology *Poetry in Wartime*: 'I suppose they may be called our "war poets", and this anthology is chiefly meant as an introduction to their work.'[52] Editors such as Tambimuttu would have been aware that war poets were often seen either as idealistic martyrs or heroic protest figures; in 1942 when the *Poetry in Wartime* anthology was published, neither sentiment quite seemed appropriate.

A second cluster of anthologies can be distinguished by the military constituency of the contributors, as well as the military preoccupations of their editors. In these texts, most or all of the poets are serving members of the armed forces or uniformed services. These anthologies tended to fit the popular perception of war poetry most neatly, with their references to army life and combat experience. For example, in his introduction to *New Poems 1944: An Anthology of American and British Verse, with a Selection of Poems from the Armed Forces*, the American poet and editor Oscar Williams (1900–64) describes the value of poetry by active servicemen in the following terms:

■ The experience of active participation in the jeopardy of war does enhance the validity of well-written verse. Sometimes the living reality of the poet's experience biases our judgement in his favor and we may perhaps over-rate his place in literature.[53] □

Such bias can, however, be justified, Williams argues, on the grounds that: 'poets who are physically engaged in war bring us more vital news than can the headlines.'[54] This is an instance of the belief in poetry's special role in the direct and 'vital' representation of war, a position referred to earlier in this section in relation to Catherine Reilly, and evident in much post-Second World War criticism. As Williams shows, war poetry by 'active participants' was seen as particularly authentic, and there was a tendency during the Second World War for anthologies to play up their 'forces' status through their titles. Other examples of forces anthologies include the twin anthologies *Poems from the Forces* (1941) and *More Poems from the Forces* (1943) edited by Keidrych Rhys, the 1944 Eighth Army anthology *Poems from the Desert*, the result of a poetry competition in the Western Desert following the El Alamein victory of 1942, and Len Jackson's *Muse in Exile: An Anthology from Fighting Men of South East Asia* (1945). As these examples demonstrate, this type of anthology proclaims a clear military identity, usually by reference to specific branches of the forces or theatres of war, although not all contributors necessarily saw combat.

Rhys's 1941 *Poems from the Forces* anthology was one of the first to be presented to the Second World War reading public as the exclusive product of the forces. In his introduction, Rhys describes his editorial motivations at length: particularly evident is his desire to answer the voices indignantly bemoaning the lack of war poets that we discussed earlier in this chapter. He argues for a new definition of the war poetry genre, to accommodate the 'realism and violence' being expressed by younger poets. Rhys is preoccupied with a desire to move beyond what he sees as the clichés of war poetry and to recognize newer poetic approaches to war, but also to resist the imprecations of older generation Establishment figures:

■ Only the wagging, accusing tongue of politician and publicist alike, so fond of humiliating my generation, which, as always, has borne the brunt of wars, now bids mailed poets to spring up like dragon's teeth in all areas without any sort of creative encouragement.[55] □

For Rhys the writing and publishing of war poetry is fraught with power relations, and more specifically with inter-generational, class and cultural tensions. Following on from the discussion of Orwell's and Rickword's interests in class and common culture, this is a useful example of the way in which, for many who lived and served in the war, social and political issues informed both the writing and publishing of poetry.

CIVILIZATION AND ITS DISCONTENTS

FORCES POETRY

Mass-Observation, a voluntary organization established in 1937 to observe and record British life, produced a book called *War Begins at Home* in 1940 that described one of the distinguishing features of the Second World War in comparison with the First in the following terms: 'The [Second World] war is potentially total. Neither danger nor endurance is limited to the front line.'[56] Participation in the war was demanded of the majority of the population in a way quite different from the First World War, with its concentration on trench warfare on the Western Front and its relatively protected civilians. This factor is important to the understanding of military identities in the Second World War, as the shared vulnerability to attack profoundly challenged the conception of wartime heroism. No longer was this seen as the sole preserve of soldiers in front line positions; indeed Robert Graves, writing in his 1942 essay 'The Poets of World War II', commented that deliberate heroism was 'so far outmoded as to seem vulgar or quaint'.[57]

The war presented other new dimensions that marked it out from the previous war. Again, in the words of Mass-Observation:

■ The generation most concerned in fighting this war is perhaps the first generation in European history which has been brought up to expect that there will not be another war. It has been brought up in the atmosphere of an international idealism, the League of Nations and the Peace Ballot, disarmament.

Conscription is accepted as a military necessity in Britain from the beginning of the war. The voluntary system is not tried.

A new civilian army, A.R.P [Air Raid Precautions], W.L.S., A.F.S. [Auxiliary Fire Service], etc., including every rank of society. They are the outward symbols of what has now become known as the Home Front.

In this war, women are, for the first time here, citizens, enfranchised, extensively organized.[58] □

As this extract shows, there had been a number of crucial changes in the approach to war and in the recruitment and organization of the army. Since the First World War women had gained the vote; in the Second World War they were, as the extract describes, 'extensively organised', for example, within the auxiliary services and in agriculture and industry. Elsewhere in the Guide we have considered how women's poetry has sometimes been judged as ineligible for entry into the genre of war poetry, or elided from critical studies. In Chapter Five, we will give further consideration to the debate about the quality of women's war poetry and the relationship of this debate to critics' assumptions about 'active participation' in war. In the next subsection of this chapter, however, we will concentrate on examining a sample of the poetic approaches and war-related preoccupations of female poets in the Second World War.

As the reference to the 'new civilian army' in the above extract suggests, the auxiliary services, with their socially diverse membership, were sometimes seen as prime instances of democratic participation in the war. To some extent they also represented a challenge to the First World War soldier/civilian dichotomy, when the experiences of each group tended to be quite separate and distinct. In the last subsection we will consider some of the important themes and concerns that are expressed in Second World War poetry from poets across a variety of wartime roles.

This subsection, however, will examine some of the specific themes arising from Second World War forces' experience and culture. As mentioned above, there was in 1939 no option for a 'voluntary' approach to war. In some cases, individuals who had fought in the First World War were facing combat in a major conflict for the second time in 25 years, and a younger generation reared on expectations of peace was being co-opted into what was soon being referred to as 'total war'. For both younger and older members of the forces, the First World War was a meaningful recent event, whether as part of living memory, or absorbed through shared cultural consciousness and historical narrative.

Contemporary perceptions of the First World War are explored in the 1943 *Anthology of War Poetry 1914–18* edited by Robert Nichols. The poems in this anthology are drawn exclusively from the First World War, yet the first 82 pages are given over to a 'Preface' presented as the transcript of a conversation between Nichols, a poet and veteran of the First World War, and Julian Tennyson (1915–45), a young poet about to depart for duty in the Second World War. One of the main themes is the contrast between newly enlisted soldiers' expectations at the beginning of the respective world wars. When, for example, Tennyson proposes that Nichols and his comrades of 1914: '…did not expect death. You only rather fancied it. To entertain the notion of death was in your own eyes a rather gallant gesture'.[59] Nichols takes great exception to the implications of contrivance or posturing inherent in the use of the word 'gesture':

■ Nothing could make us reflect. We simply felt. And what we felt was exaltation. Beyond that was a blank. How can a boy consider what he can't imagine? And the only alternative to the unimaginable was something decisive – an event resembling the sudden descent of a great beam of light. It was with a sensation of being gathered up and lifted that we submitted to being swept forward whither that light might fall. About that beam of light there was something mysterious, as there is something mysterious about such a beam in a cathedral, since, passing within its clustered shafts, the individual becomes invisible.[60] □

Nichols's depiction of the 1914 military volunteer culture, of 'being gathered up and lifted' into a mysterious and spiritual place, contrasts starkly with the muted, anxious or matter-of-fact recollections of poets who had been conscripts in 1940.[61]

The transformation from civilian into military personnel was a critical moment, and there were many different responses to it. For the young poet Sidney Keyes, for example, still an undergraduate at Oxford University and deeply immersed in the Romantic poets, war seemed remote and abstract until he joined the army in 1942. According to the brief summary of Keyes's life by his friend, Michael Meyer, this was a decisive point in Keyes's poetic development:

■ For the first time, the poet in him came into immediate contact with the material world. Love and Death, inextricably entwined, became vital problems instead of subjects for laboratory analysis. The world of his imagination blended with the world of reality. He lost his duality. He found his imaginary fears shared by thousands, and became the spokesman for a generation. Inevitably, he abandoned the Apollonian conception [of 'supreme detachment' and 'active contemplation'], and moved gradually towards the Dionysiac, 'the dolphin's mire and blood.' ['Dionysiac' relates to the Greek god Dionysius, associated with orgiastic excess and savagery.] Death is not a problem that the soldier can solve through 'active contemplation'. A belligerent generation must discover a new solution in the ruck and chaos of battle.[62] □

To some extent, this transformation follows a similar trajectory to that described by Nichols: the poet's starting point is a world of romantic abstractions and it is only through entry into the 'ruck and chaos of battle' that poetic talent can come to fruition. Yet, according to Meyer, there is a type of foreknowledge, a conscious, fatalistic acceptance of the 'mire and blood', which accompanies Keyes's transition from civilian poet into soldier and poet of war. This element of acquiescence in or even eagerness for the 'Dionysiac' dimension of war is quite different from the images of purity, light and cleanness prevalent in early First World War poets' work.

For Keith Douglas, the prospect of battle was to be embraced. Douglas, like Keyes, had written poems prior to the war and during the

war he wrote both poetry and prose, including accounts of his battle
experiences in *Alamein to Zem Zem*, posthumously published in 1946. In
the following extract he describes his attitude to war:

> ■ I had to wait until 1942 to go into action. I enlisted in September 1939,
> and during two years or so of hanging about I never lost the certainty that the
> experience of battle was something I must have. Whatever changes in the
> nature of warfare, the battlefield is the simple, central stage of the war: it is
> there that the interesting things happen. We talk in the evening, after fight-
> ing, about the great and rich men who cause and conduct wars. They have so
> many reasons of their own that they can afford to lend us some of them.
> There is nothing odd about their attitude. They are out for something they
> want, or their Governments want, and they are using us to get it for them.
> Anyone can understand that: there is nothing unusual or humanly exciting at
> that end of the war. I mean there may be things to excite financiers and par-
> liamentarians – but not to excite a poet or a painter or a doctor.[63] □

Douglas writes about war in determinedly unsentimental terms: he
refers to it as a natural phenomenon and to the attitude of those who
cause war as 'nothing odd'. This relates, in part, to Douglas's identity as
a professional soldier, with a fundamental acceptance of war. In the passage above, Douglas also seems to consider the rationale for war as a
formality, rather than resulting from a passionately held principle or just
cause. The more pressing issue is how to acquire, as speedily as possible,
the 'central' experience of battle. In this thirst for military experience,
Douglas is different from many other forces poets of the Second World
War: R. N. Currey (1907–2001), Herbert Corby (born 1911) and Gavin
Ewart (1916–95), for example, all expressed far less enthusiasm for
army life.[64] Post-war criticism has tended to position Douglas as one of
the most admired and emblematic war poets of the Second World War.
It is a tradition in which biographical and autobiographical narratives of
his 'soldierliness' have played a prominent part.

Many of the forces poets, then, did not share Douglas's view that
battle was the central experience of war; indeed, many saw little, if any,
active combat. If Douglas's air of knowingness and detached observation
was characteristic of one poetic approach to the Second World War, and
Keyes's romantic abandonment to the mess and pain of war another,
there was a plethora of other perspectives from the forces, and an
enormously wide range of responses. As with the First World War, the
diversity of the corpus has tended to be obscured as dominant critical
preferences repeatedly identify the same few poets or poems for attention. In Chapter Five we will consider criticism that has consciously
attempted to redress the balance in a variety of ways.

Simon Featherstone's *War Poetry: An Introductory Reader* examines how for Scottish poets Sorley MacLean (1911–96) and Hamish Henderson (1919–2002) a very different set of ideas and associations was triggered by the war. Here, using the Welsh poet David Jones (see Chapter Three) as a point of comparison, Featherstone argues that MacLean articulates his specific cultural identity in the context of war:

■ For Jones the idea of a British national identity had nearly disappeared, and in *In Parenthesis* he reinvents the idea of Britain using the fragments of a largely forgotten past. [...] MacLean's Gaelic identity, on the other hand, is never in doubt, nor is the traditional means of asserting it. In 'Dol an Iar/Going Westwards' [...] he resolves a poem of self-questioning with the lines:

I am of the big men of Braes
of the heroic Raasay MacLeods,
of the sharp-sword Mathesons of Lochalsh;
and the men of my name – who were braver
when their ruinous pride was kindled?

Here the heroic traditions of caste identity are freshly available to a soldier in the Second World War without any of the jingoist or imperialist connotations such allegiances would evoke in an English context. In MacLean's work the Gaelic heroic tradition is in opposition to imperialism, and becomes a flexible instrument for the interpretation of contemporary political and personal experience. This is demonstrated in the poems 'Alasdair MacLeoid/Alasdair MacLeod' and 'Curaidhean/ Heroes'.[65] □

Featherstone points out here that 'heroic' war poetry in the English context has strong suggestions of 'jingoism'. For writers such as MacLean, however, the frame of reference is not the history of English imperialism but a confident assertion of Gaelic identity. Featherstone demonstrates the importance of careful contextualisation: of considering the relationship between genre and the regional or 'caste' identities of the poet, as well as poets' views on, or experiences of, the war.

WOMEN'S WARTIME POETRY

The Second World War was a challenging period for war poetry as a genre. 'War poetry', and 'war-' or 'soldier-poets' had become familiar terms in the way we have already examined in the first two chapters of this Guide, yet the nature of the 1939–45 conflict itself was, in many ways, new and strange. The rationale, techniques and machinery of war and governmental approaches to the management and control of civil society were very different to those of the First World War.

As already indicated, women were more widely involved in the Second World War in a wide variety of occupations, including the auxiliary services, civil defence and 'essential' industrial employment. When the Government began to approach the issue of women's war work, there was resistance from both sexes to the idea of women in combat; the eventual introduction of conscription was accompanied by reassurances that no woman would be *obliged* to take up combat duties.[66] Yet if not in this sense 'combatant', the work carried out by women could be extremely arduous and dangerous. There is a large quantity of poetry written by women about experiences of the 'auxiliary services' and of a variety of other roles on the home front during the war: as Catherine Reilly points out in her anthology of women's poetry of the Second World War, little of this poetry is well known.[67] For Reilly, this neglect is the result of the prominently combatant orientation of many post-1945 war poetry anthologies, an argument that will be considered further in the next chapter.

In a 1944 *Times Literary Supplement* review of the anthology *Poems by Contemporary Women* (1944), compiled by Theodora Roscoe and Mary Winter Were, it is possible to see the way in which contemporary attitudes to poetry, and specifically to poetry about war, were gendered:

■ An anthology of verse by contemporary women which contains no example of the work of Kathleen Raine [1908–2003], to cite an obvious omission, is not fully representative. But if containing little that is compellingly original, this is an appealing collection and with V[ita] Sackville-West [1892–1962], Margaret L. Woods [born 1856], Ruth Pitter [1897–1992] and Dorothy Wellesley [1881–1956] among its older contributors cannot lack distinction. It certainly reveals the feminine gift for seeing the meaning and feeling the poignancy of small things, a ladybird in an A. R. P. bucket, for example, or the first bird that wakes to sing, or a bee trapped in a greenhouse, or a flycatcher beneath the eaves. From such 'trivial details', as V. H. Friedlander calls one of them, many of these poets evoke a sense of life that surrounds and encloses them. But only in a few of them, in Blanche Hardy's 'The Ghost,' for example, does imagination transform the familiar into the strange. War and the losses of war are reflected in many of the verses.[68] □

In this extract, the poetry is clearly identified as marked with a 'feminine gift', and the examples referred to suggest sanitized, almost infantile perspectives on the conditions of war ('a ladybird in an A. R. P. bucket'). Women did not restrict themselves to writing poetry about the more 'trivial' or 'detailed' aspects of wartime life, however.

Alternative perspectives upon women's concerns in wartime and their approach to poetry can be found in a range of anthologies and periodicals, and in personal journals. The wartime life of the writer Naomi Mitchison (1897–1999) is extensively documented in her memoirs for Mass-Observation, *Among You Taking Notes: The Wartime Diaries of Naomi Mitchison 1939–1945* (2000). The memoirs include commentary on key international political events such as the 'Russo-German treaty', expressions of anxiety concerning the likely involvement of family and friends in the war, and references to writing poetry. Mitchison's diary is a particularly useful source for exploring some of the complexities of female identity and role during this historical period. Here, for example, is an entry for 21 September 1939:

■ Then we heard the 6 o'clock news with the odd romantic bit about the Russians disarming and freeing the Polish soldiers. Denny M. said, it will all be over soon. I read them the poem, and got good praise from both; Denny M. said I was out there while you were reading: how was that? – meaning that I had really taken him out to the fishing in the poem. He said people will be remembering this long long after we are all dead; he said nothing like this was ever written. I think the poem is getting so technical that ordinary readers won't like it. Then he touched my shoulders and said Naomi Mitchison, this is the best you have done yet. He saw with extraordinary sensitiveness why I had changed the metres here and there and what I was after. They both did, really, but he, being a man, has to be most important to me as inspiration or whatever it is.[69] □

Mitchison was politically active and deeply involved in community affairs and her journal includes anecdotes of her determined efforts to overcome restrictive and conservative attitudes towards women's roles. In the quotation above, however, despite the radicalism of some of Mitchison's social and political attitudes, it is clear that her poetry is validated most powerfully by a man's literary judgement.

M. J. Tambimuttu's *Poetry in Wartime*, which was mentioned in the discussion of wartime anthologies, included poetry by Patricia Ledward (born 1920), Anne Ridler (1912–2001), Kathleen Raine and Lynette Roberts (1909–95). Several of the poems explore the impact of the war, not only as a personal experience of fear or loss but also in historical and philosophical contexts. Ridler's 'Now as Then', for example, places the current war in a long historical perspective, commenting on the moral complexities of modern wars, 'War is not simple: in more or less degree / All are guilty, though some will suffer unjustly.'[70] Ridler grapples with some of the most profound and troubling questions of war, concluding with the acceptance of a pragmatic moral position: '... since of two evils our victory would be the less' (a viewpoint similar to that expressed by

Day Lewis in 'Where are the War Poets', see the section 'War Poets Revisited' in Chapter Three of the Guide). In Raine's 'London Revisited', the poetic voice speaks of fragmentation and dissonance, not only in relation to the material wartime world with its bombed-out buildings and exposed interiors, but also in relation to the self:

■ Haunting these shattered walls, hung with our past,
that no electron and no sun can pierce,
we visit rooms in dreams
where we ourselves are ghosts.

There is no foothold for our solid world,
no hanging Babylon for the certain mind
in rooms tattered by wind, wept on by rain.

Wild as the tomb, wild as the mountainside,
a storm of hours has shaken the fine-spun world,
tearing away our palaces, our faces, and our days.[71] □

In this poem, Raine depicts a disintegration of many certainties. Here, it seems, it is only possible to access elements of personal identity through the world of the imagination and the subconscious: to visit 'ourselves' as 'ghosts'. The components of everyday reality are now seen in all their fragility, at the moment of their destruction.

There are a number of other anthologies that present distinctive versions of women's wartime poetry. Further examples include *Poems of the Land Army: An Anthology of Verse by Members of the Women's Land Army*, edited by Vita Sackville-West, and *Poems of This War by Younger Poets*, edited by Patricia Ledward and Colin Strang. The Ledward and Strang anthology is subdivided into sections, headed by quotations from the poems such as, 'We saw doom patterned in the ordinary sky', and 'Line after line, we wheel to enter battle'. These titles place great emphasis on a sense of collective fate and proximity to danger and death, and together with the juxtapositions of combatant and civilian poetry, they suggest a parity of experience between 'home front' and 'front line'. Ledward worked as an emergency nurse and subsequently as a driver with an anti-aircraft unit during the war, and three of her own poems are printed in the anthology, including 'Air-raid casualties: Ashridge Hospital'. In contrast to the poem by Raine, however, it is possible to see how Ledward's representation of suffering leans towards traditions of Georgian pastoral. Here the idealized and sanitized figure of the nurse is central, and references to the wounded soldiers' bodies are euphemistic:

■ Nurses with level eyes, and chaste
In long starched dresses, move
Amongst the maimed, giving love
To strengthen bodies gone to waste.[72] □

The post-war critical debate about the place and value of women's war poetry has addressed the dominance of traditionally masculine literary models, and this will be considered further in Chapter Five. The sample of poetry discussed here gives, however, an indication of the diversity of women's war poetry from 1939–45, showing how women's poetic responses to war ranged from representations of personal experiences to searching examinations of wider philosophical and ethical questions.

UNITY AND DISSONANCE

The Britain of the Second World War has sometimes been represented, in the post-war period, as a cooperative and spirited society, focused on the key democratic objective of defeating fascism.[73] This representative tradition draws on the idea that in times of extreme need, the capacity for national pride and solidarity comes easily to the British, illustrated by what have been portrayed as heroic triumphs of organized action, such as the evacuation of Dunkirk. We have already examined in this chapter a number of examples of how patriotic discourses of pride in country and unity of purpose were articulated during the Second World War, including Orwell's hope that victory would reap greater social and economic equality and the continuation of a vigorous national culture. In another instance, the poet John Pudney created an emblematic pilot figure, 'Johnny', to stand for the heroism and decency of the British forces. The RAF, in which Pudney served, recognized the propaganda potential of this poetry, requesting, in 1943, a poem to commemorate the RAF's 25th anniversary.[74] The film *The Way to the Stars* (1945) later used Pudney's poem 'For Johnny' to evoke wartime heroism.

Other poetic explorations of comradeship and solidarity during the Second World War are expressed in quite different terms. In his poem 'The Recruit', for example, the poet John Manifold (1915–85) portrays joining the army as a rite of passage, not in terms of a leap from the abstract conception of death into the real 'ruck and chaos' of battle, as with Keyes, but as a transition of a fundamentally social nature. Manifold represents the individual recruit as experiencing the revelation that national, regional, class and employment differences need not be an obstacle to a powerful sense of comradeship and connection:

■ Nation and region, class and craft and syndicate
Are only some; all attributes connect
Their owner with his kind, call him to vindicate
A common honour; and his self-respect
Starts from the moment when his senses indicate
'I' as a point where circles intersect.[75] □

In this scenario, the sense of 'common honour' is paramount; it is only through the acceptance of commonality with the other recruits, and the adoption of a group identity, that individual self-respect can develop. Whereas in the First World War, many poets wrote from an officer perspective, expressing their protective sense of pride, duty and sometimes love towards the men they were responsible for, Manifold's vision of comradeship is a profoundly levelling one, emerging from a revolution in the perception of self and social belonging.

Such preoccupations with unity are, however, only one aspect of the Second World War poetry corpus, and are far from being representative. Indeed in his cultural and psychological history, *Wartime: Understanding and Behaviour in the Second World War* (1989), Paul Fussell argues that few of the recruits of 1940 had a very clear idea of the war's meaning, or a distinct, patriotic sense of duty. In the following extract, Fussell describes how doubts and disillusionment characterized attitudes at the start of the Second World War; he begins by invoking the influence of two novels about the First World War, *A Farewell to Arms* (1929) by the American author Ernest Hemingway (1898–1961) and *Her Privates We* (1930) by the English writer Frederic Manning (1882–1935):

■ Many were familiar with Hemingway's understanding of military experience as vividly unfair and dishonorable in *A Farewell to Arms*, as well as with Frederic Manning's exposure of army life as not just pointlessly hazardous but bureaucratic, boring, and chickenshitty in *Her Privates We*. The result of this awareness was, as Robert E. Sherwood said, that the Second World War was 'the first war in American history [and of course even more so in British history] in which the general disillusionment preceded the firing of the first shot.'[76] Or as Rupert Croft-Cooke recalls the outbreak of the war, 'We were all conscientious objectors, and all in [the war].'[77] One of the actual COs, Edward Blishen, testifies that it was 'the literature of disgust' from the Great War that persuaded him to opt out, and indeed, when it was all over, he concluded that 'I think it was my father's war that I refused to fight.'[78] The egregious contrast between the credulity and even the enthusiasm of 1914 with the disillusion of 1940 is the specific point of Herbert Read's poem 'To a Conscript of 1940'. For over twenty years Read had meditated, in memoirs and poems, on the meaning of the Great War to himself and others caught up in it. In this poem he posits the ghost of a soldier from the former war who addresses a 'conscript' – the word seems carefully chosen – of this one. His message is one of disillusion bravely borne:

> We went where you are going, into the rain and the mud;
> We fought as you will fight
> death and darkness and despair;
> We gave what you will give – our brains and our blood.

We think we gave in vain. The world was not renewed.
There was hope in the homestead and anger in the streets
But the old world was restored and we returned
To the dreary field and workshops, and the immemorial feud

Of rich and poor. Our victory was our defeat ... .

Knowing that, the only wise course for the Second-War conscript is to fight without any hope that his labor and suffering will result in good. 'My brother and my ghost,' says the shade from the Great War,

> If you can go
Knowing that there is no reward, no certain use
In all your sacrifice, then honour is reprieved.

Indeed, the only appropriate awareness to bring to the new war is that

To fight without hope is to fight without grace.[79]

Asked in 1940 what he feels about the war, E. M. Forster replies, 'I don't want to lose it. I don't expect Victory (with a big V!), and I can't join in any build-a-new-world stuff. Once in a lifetime one can swallow that, but not twice.'[80] Virtually everyone agreed.[81] □

Fussell perhaps makes his point a little over-emphatically: there were a range of competing contemporary views about the purpose of the war, of which this disillusioned acceptance of war's necessity was only one. What he identifies, however, in the lack of enthusiasm for the 'big V Victory', is an important strain in Second World War poetry. Between 1939–45, many poets chose to depict the war by exposing the distance and dissonance between individual perception and public or official discourses about the aims and requirements of war.

Perceptions of disintegration and fragmentation were also central to the thinking of the poets of the Apocalyptic Movement. This revolved around the leading figures of J. F. Hendry and Henry Treece (whose observations on the poetry of the war have already been referred to earlier in this chapter) and a fluctuating group of poets and writers, several of whom later disowned or distanced themselves from their involvement.[82] The Apocalyptics, as they were often described, were part of a romantic reaction against the type of classical and cerebral poetry that Auden had become so well known for. They had similarities with the Surrealists in their approach to developing poetic images (through, for example, the conjunction of apparently unrelated objects), and were interested in the potential of myth and imagination as a means to reintegrate what they saw as the fragmentary elements of contemporary life. To the Apocalyptic poets, the war revealed the urgent need for a new understanding of language, thought and identity. In the following extract from J. F. Hendry's introductory essay to

The Crown and the Sickle, Hendry argues that the war holds a peverse attraction for society:

> ■ War, of course, has always been attractive because of its horror, the sense that 'anything might happen'. Its jargon has been extremely plausible. It talks its own language, and once we have learned that language we are involved in all its ridiculous assumptions. There is 'strategy'. There are 'tactics'. There are pieces to be moved about – pawns, who are always someone else's sons, or even our own – and all the time the colossal sense of some incalculable power actually moving, or even being moved by us. It satisfies our lamentable lack of living drama. It is the character and personality we lack, the projection of all the unsatisfied desires and strivings which we are incapable of resolving into a satisfactory personal drama, one of the great *external* stimuli of our time.[83] □

We are, Hendry argues, divided from ourselves, full of 'unsatisfied desires and strivings' and inclined to 'project on to society [our] inward restlessness': that is to say that war can only be addressed in relation to our own fragmented desires. The Apocalyptics were not presenting themselves explicitly under a 'war poetry' banner, yet war is the primary source used to illustrate their theoretical principles and inform their poetic imagery. The poetry is profoundly influenced by war, arguably a poetry 'of' war, yet not intended to be read as the aesthetic product of a historical witness, or an objective account. For the Apocalyptics, it is the very notion that war is an 'external' phenomenon that is being challenged, and for this reason, the work of the Apocalyptic poets provides an important and unusual instance of the war poetry genre.

In this chapter we have considered how poets of the Second World War were writing in the midst of well-established critical and cultural expectations about the role of poetry in wartime. Second World War poets were often unavoidably aware of their war poet forebears, some of whom were strong influences, yet they faced a war very different in nature from any other. In particular, the universal nature of risk, discomfort and danger in the war began to erode the distinction between soldier as active participant and civilian as passive observer. A large number of individual poets sought to represent aspects of wartime experience through poetry, including combatant poets keen to convey the intensity of battle. Many wartime poets, however, regarded the heroic overtones of the 'war poet' label with suspicion, and many registered a powerful sense of uncertainty about, and distance from, the wartime roles and conditions they found themselves in, regardless of the necessity of the war itself. As we will go on to see in the next chapter, some post-war critics have tended to view Second World War poetry through a lens designed for celebrating the martyred soldier-poets of the First World War, focusing on a small group of combatant male poets such as Douglas, Lewis and Keyes. For others, however, the variety of Second World War poetry, combatant and civilian, propagandist and philosophical, epitomizes both the complexity of responses to war and the very different uses that can be made of the war poetry genre.

CHAPTER FIVE

Post-1945 Critical Paths

INTRODUCTION

As we have seen in the previous three chapters, war poetry is a highly problematic genre to define and categorize. In each historical period we have considered, the notion of 'war poetry' has been undergoing a process of change: in the First World War, there was the gradual shift away from war poetry by home front patriots towards that of soldier-poets; in the interwar period there were debates about whether 'passive suffering' in war was a proper subject for poetry; and in the Second World War, there was the reluctance of many poets to be placed in a 'war poetry' category that was viewed as reductive and of another era. None of these issues was simply resolved, and all have continued to operate within critical studies of the genre as important methodological and conceptual questions.

Through extracts of critical material from the first half of the twentieth century we have seen how the genre has been shaped by political and historical assumptions about war and by different accounts of the relationship between war and literature. We have also, however, seen the powerful influence of critical selectivity upon the genre, through a focus on specific roles (such as the combatant poet), concepts (such as the authentic representation of suffering) and a canonical emphasis on a small number of individual poets. Examples of such selectivity in the post-war period will be considered further in this chapter, along with a range of approaches that have attempted to widen the theoretical basis for the study of war poetry, and to consider previously neglected or marginalized perspectives.

In this chapter, we will examine some of the views expressed within a range of post-1945 anthologies and critical works, looking at examples of the way in which war poetry has continued to be associated with very different sets of ideological beliefs, cultural traditions and even educational purposes. The main focus will be the two world wars: here, as elsewhere in the Guide and as discussed in Chapter One, the world wars provide the primary case studies for an examination of developments in the genre. However, rather than considering the post-war criticism purely in terms of different 'schools' or critical categories, or as a chronological survey, the chapter attempts to indicate the significant, but often overlapping, strains of thought that are expressed in these texts. Where an anthology or text is considered under a particular heading, this is not, therefore, an attempt to summarize or categorize it purely in these terms. Each section deals with a theme or setting that has been applied to war poetry, with reference to the post-1945 historical context where relevant, showing how the poetry has been cast and recast in different ways, and how it continues to be a potent and malleable genre in literary, cultural and political terms.

MILITARY AND NATIONAL IDENTITIES

THE SPIRIT OF THE SOLDIER

A large proportion of the anthologies and studies published in the post-1945 period are, as we shall examine later in this chapter, concerned with showing the destructive effects of war upon individuals, families and society. We have already explored a number of examples of this approach earlier in the Guide, such as the batch of controversial and critical 'war books' published during the 1920s and the 1930s, and the Auden group's initial adoption of Owen as an anti-war figure (see Chapter Three). Yet, as we also noted, there were anthologies such as Drinkwater's, steeped in patriotic rhetoric about the heroic soldier figure, which were published during the same period: the interest in war poetry as a source of humanitarian ideals or political protest coexisted with constructions of war poetry as a celebration of the heroic or nationalistic. This development of different traditions in tandem has continued since the end of the Second World War.

'Militarism' in its widest sense, as an expression of the spirit or tendencies of the professional soldier, has had considerable significance within the war poetry genre. As we discussed in Chapter One, there is still popular interest in, and a market for, militaristic war poetry; critics such as Featherstone have argued that this is an aspect of the genre frequently ignored by academic critics, many of whom focus disproportionately on anti-war voices.[1] Also often overlooked, however, is the fact that there is a great deal of interplay in the thinking of these two traditions: the notions of the 'professional' soldier and the soldierly and heroic spirit have not simply been allied to nationalistic or jingoistic beliefs, but have been of far wider interest. Whilst much of the poetry criticism discussed so far is concerned with poetry written by volunteers or conscripts rather than by 'professional' soldiers, the idea of proper or

professional conduct in war, or pride in being part of a military organization, has been a common and important theme, even from those
whose instincts are essentially keen to avoid war. This could be seen, for
example, in the conversation considered in Chapter Four between
Robert Nichols and Julian Tennyson, included as a preface to *An
Anthology of War Poetry 1914–18*, where an extended analysis is made of
First World War volunteer culture and paradigms of soldierly duty.[2]

Expressions and explorations of militarism, heroism and patriotism
in war poetry anthologies and critical studies take many forms. An
American volume produced just prior to the end of the Second World
War, *War and the Poet: An Anthology of Poetry Expressing Man's Attitudes to
War From Ancient Times to the Present* (1945) edited by the poet and critic
Richard Eberhart (born 1904) and the writer, poet and art critic Selden
Rodman (1909–2003) provides an interesting example of the way in
which the notion of war as 'natural' and the recognition of soldierly
enthusiasm for combat are incorporated within a fundamentally liberal
text. Although this anthology is not technically 'post-1945', it provides
a useful starting point for the consideration of trends that continued
long after the war had concluded.

In this text, Eberhart and Rodman's aim is to deliver a balanced
selection of poetry expressing 'attitudes about war' on the basis that the
'best war poems are about Man'.[3] This implies that one of the primary
values of a war poem resides in its revelatory capacity, in what it can dis-
close of the complexity of human nature, rather than simply its ability
to reflect the experience of fighting. This theoretical position enables the
editors to search widely amongst potential poetic candidates, and they
include several individuals not generally categorized as 'war poets',
such as Emily Dickinson (1830–86) and Robert Frost (1874–1963). In
the 'Preface: Attitudes to War', Eberhart discusses further how the
criteria for selection have been devised:

■ War poetry must be judged, like any other type of poetry, upon its essential excellence. The fact that men have written in all ages on war is as natural as that they have written on love, or on death. A time of war makes a
survey of work in the field timely, within limits constricted by exigencies of
the conflict. The implement of selection is, of course, taste, which in dual
editorship must be synthetic. The scope of a war book, being arbitrary,
could be any range of view, as large, or representative, or highly selective,
or given some critical bent, but in any case a selection of war poems cannot without immodesty, or even a raucous shout, be considered definitive.
Taste will change. Time will further define.[4] □

Eberhart's comment that writing about war is as natural as writing
about love or death figures war itself as an inevitability, an inescapable

fact of human existence: indeed, in a sense, as 'natural'. Furthermore, although Eberhart states that there is only one poet in the anthology, Friederich Adolf Axel Detlev von Liliencron (1844–1909), who actually 'boasts of loving war', this inclusion is essential to the multifaceted strategy of the text.[5] Eberhart highlights the difficulty of defining the scope of such an anthology, and the need to use editorial 'taste' as the main tool of selection. An anthology of war poems, he writes, cannot be considered definitive without 'immodesty, or even a raucous shout'.[6] This is to say that in order to do justice to the full spectrum of war poetry, editors must be prepared to make immodest or raucous claims; to assert their views and values.

A number of subsequent anthologies and critical works have focused more specifically, and sometimes more ideologically, on celebrating the soldier not only as a necessary figure, but also as representative of the highest virtues. In the introduction to *The Literature of War: Studies in Heroic Virtue* (1989), Andrew Rutherford (born 1929) contextualizes his focus upon the positive, heroic potential of war in the following terms:

■ The assumption that heroism, like saintliness, is obsolete as an ideal, and that the literature of heroism belongs to the childhood of the individual or of the race, seems typical of current intellectual opinion. Fortitude is out of fashion as a virtue. Indeed the portrayal of courage in the face of adversity, suffering or danger is now positively suspect in the eyes of many readers, whose unexamined ethical assumptions often predetermine their aesthetic judgments on the literature of war (leading them, for example, to see Falstaff's views on Honour as more normative than Hal's, or to discount war poetry when it is not anti-war). [Falstaff and Hal are characters in Shakespeare's *Henry IV* parts 1 and 2, in which Falstaff is renowned for unscrupulous cowardice and Hal for military courage.][7] □

The first edition of *The Literature of War: Studies in Heroic Virtue* was published in 1978, during the same period of anti-war and anti-nuclear activism that we noted as a context for Bold's anthology, *The Martial Muse*, in Chapter One. Unlike Bold, however, Rutherford adopts a polemical position in relation to what he sees as the anti-heroic emphasis in contemporary culture, which he interprets as an unthinking and superficial reversal of traditional values.

Rutherford objects to the way in which literary representations of ideal virtue and heroism, particularly in the military context, are treated as almost inevitably 'suspect'. This can be seen, he argues, through prevailing attitudes to different genres and 'modes' of art:

■ [The] reinterpretation of historical and psychological reality by art involves an opposition not only between high and low mimetic [imitative] modes (Victorian/Edwardian hagiography *versus* modern realism), but between the low mimetic, with its realistic characters much like ourselves, and the 'ironic', which in terms of Frye's [Northrop Frye, 1912–91, Canadian literary critic] useful definition portrays characters 'inferior in power or intelligence to ourselves, so that we have the sense of looking down on a scene of bondage, frustration, or absurdity'.[8] This, rather than the realistic, has become the dominant mode of literary vision in our time; and the implications for war literature, both past and present, are profound. Even when an historic reality, imitated realistically in art, can be shown to have existed, biographically or historically, readers may well feel uneasily that it affronts their expectations of both literature and life – that Richard Hillary's truth [Richard Hillary, 1919–43, Second World War fighter pilot and author, who became a heroic wartime figure], for example, is embarrassingly incompatible with Heller's fiction [Joseph Heller, born 1923, American novelist, who wrote *Catch-22* (1961), a satire on the absurdity of war], or that soldiers are more properly portrayed as victims, brutes or fools, or as a mixture of the three, than as conscious and effective moral agents.[9] □

Rutherford refers in this passage to Frye's theory that the dominant mode of modern literary vision is the ironic. The ironic mode, Frye argues, allows us to feel superior to the characters portrayed, who are restrained or limited usually by their own lack of intelligence or moral culpability. Rutherford uses this theory as a basis for his own argument: as readers, he claims, we can no longer understand war literature as representing an ideal, in which soldiers epitomize the best in human nature; nor can we easily appreciate realist literary representations of good or admirable acts in wartime.

Rutherford's study is concerned primarily with fiction, although it includes analyses of First World War poetry in the chapter, 'The Common Man as Hero: Literature of the Western Front'. His approach is indicative of several texts in the post-1945 period that consciously reconstruct a framework of heroic, military virtue within which to discuss war poetry. Among other works that mourn the modern suspicion of military roles and values is a more recent anthology, *Poets of the Great War* (1996), edited by Tonie and Valmai Holt. In this text, the editors describe their position in the following terms:

■ We sometimes fail to understand from our world-weary, cynical contemporary attitudes and values that the men of 1914 were simple, utterly sincere and intense in their sense of duty and patriotism. Not only did they speak and write in the language of high devotion and chivalry, they really felt that way.[10] □

For the Holts, the First World War poets who incorporated high ideals within their poetry did so as a simple reflection of their inner

natures: the poets themselves, as biographical subjects, are to be understood not merely as aspiring to patriotic duty and chivalry, but as literally embodying these values. The combination of the editors' keen
interest in an almost mythic heroism together with their biographical
and essentialist approach to the genre produces a number of problems:
aspects of army life or personal biographies that do not fit their vision of
martial masculinity are largely dismissed. Thus, for example, rereadings
of First World War poetry in the light of research into homoerotic sub-
cultures of military life are downplayed, as we will consider in the final
section of this chapter.

SHAPING NATIONAL IDENTITY

In the post-1945 period, as we discussed in Chapter One, literary and
cultural representations of both world wars have had an important
place in moulding and articulating British national identity. This process
of identity formation has sometimes taken place in nationalistic and
militaristic terms, using war poetry as another means of asserting British
interests. In an editorial for *PN Review* in 1983 the poet and critic Donald
Davie (1922–95) argues that in the context of the Falklands War (a conflict between Britain and Argentina over the contested territories of the
Falklands Islands or Malvinas, April–June 1982), there is a need to take
the idea of 'martial valour' more seriously.[11] There have also been far
subtler and less nationalistic uses of war literature as indicative of the
national character, and as a source of patriotic pride and belonging.

   In *The Voice of War: Poems of the Second World War* (1996) edited by
Victor Selwyn, the fifth anthology published under the auspices of The
Salamander Oasis Trust, the poems are prefaced with a selection of
prose pieces. These comprise: an introduction from Denis Healey (born
1917), the veteran British Labour politician who had been an army officer in the Second World War and had served as Minister of Defence
from 1964–70; a foreword by General Sir John Hackett (1910–97); an
article entitled 'The Second World War: an historical review' by Field
Marshal Lord Carver (1915–2001, a progressive military thinker who
argued against the possession of nuclear weapons as a defensive strat-
egy); another article entitled 'The sound of Oasis' by the actor Martin
Jarvis (born 1941); a piece entitled 'How I wrote my first poem' by
Spike Milligan (1919–2002), the comedian, novelist and poet; and 'The
world of the poets: a retrospective view' by Selwyn himself. The varied
professional affiliations of these individuals in the military, literary, dramatic, popular entertainment and political spheres, reflect the anthology's overall ethos of cultural cooperation and eclecticism. The
emphasis is, as Carver puts it, on an idea of the collective nature of the

war effort:

■ The Second World War, like the First, saw the whole nation in arms. Civilians at home were at times as much in the front line as those in uniform, London and the South East being subjected to bombardment by V1 and V2 rockets until Montgomery's forces [Viscount Montgomery, 1887–1976, British Field Marshal] had cleared their launching sites in France and the Low Countries. The whole life of the nation was devoted to the war effort.[12] □

This view is not confined to the two professional army men, but is echoed in a comment by Denis Healey in his introduction:

■ Very little class feeling could survive in the pressure cooker of the Second World War. The sense of common humanity overrode all else. Few fists were shaken at the politicians and the brasshats [a term used to refer to officers of high rank].[13] □

Other studies of British society in the Second World War have argued, conversely, that this image of social unity and dedication to the joint effort of winning the war belies many stark and unpalatable social trends, such as the rise in street crime and fraud.[14] In *The Voice of War*, however, poetry is firmly embedded within a narrative of the Second World War as a moment of national cohesion.

Integral to this vision of unity in *The Voice of War* is the portrayal of the freedom, independence and social optimism of the British people. In Selwyn's own contextualization of the anthology, 'The world of the poets', he describes high levels of literacy and a determined and uncompromised outlook:

■ Culture does not grow in a vacuum. All ability and inspiration can run into the sand without the soil to grow in and the climate to make it thrive. The Second World War saw a coincidence of factors – cultural, political and economic – that meant freedom of thought for those taking part. The war encouraged the independently minded, the voluntary organizations, particularly the women's without which the home front could not have worked. They needed no direction.[15] □

The inclusiveness of tone here is reflected in the poems selected for the anthology: a substantial proportion of these are written in dialect, reflecting the different regions of Britain; some are written in the vernacular; there are a number of women poets included; and many poets are from Commonwealth countries. Selwyn's reference to the resourcefulness of British society, and the willingness of those from many different walks of life to contribute to the war effort, is followed shortly afterwards by his account of the wartime hopes for a better life. He alludes here to William Beveridge (1879–1963), whose 1942 'Beveridge Report' set out the basis for the British Welfare State, and R(ichard) A(usten) Butler (1902–82), the British Conservative politician responsible for the 1944 Education Act:

> ■ ... the concern with establishing a different Britain led to Beveridge and welfare, Butler and education and the subject of a Churchill speech which would certainly surprise today's world. Entitled 'A Four-Year Plan for Post-War Britain', it looked ahead to state enterprise working with private enterprise. End the dole by having no unemployed. The speech was distributed to the troops. Our poets may have read it, as they did the plethora of service newspapers and magazines, in which mavericks had a field day. In this freedom poets wrote. Maybe it was an age of innocence. There was an essential belief in the goodness of people. People truly believed the world would be a better place. They could not envisage the technology and self-interest that would transform the material expectations of life and change attitudes fundamentally, and the Empire too.[16] □

Here, Selwyn situates war poetry within a retrospective construction of the Second World War as a golden age of just militarism and progressive liberalism. In the references to social and material betterment, we might recall not only Healey's reference to how little 'class feeling' could survive the conditions of war, but Orwell's wartime hopes of a more democratic and egalitarian post-war future (see Chapter Four). Selwyn's emphasis, and that of the contributors of the other prose pieces, is on poetry as symptomatic of the moral and social health of the wartime nation.

Kenneth Baker (born 1934), a British Conservative politician who held a number of Cabinet posts, including that of Home Secretary from 1990–92, and who is also a literary editor, takes a rather more functional approach to the relationship of war poetry to national identity in his *Faber Book of War Poetry* (1996). Like the generic war poetry collections of Bold and Eberhart and Rodman, this volume covers many hundreds of years of poetry on the subject of war. Baker's selection ranges widely in historical, national and literary terms, from Hebrew verse and anonymous Old Norse epic to twentieth-century British poets such as Philip Larkin (1922–85) and Geoffrey Hill (born 1932). Whilst he states that his aim is to 'paint a broad picture' of war,[17] Baker also emphasizes the centrality of the nation:

> ■ One of the most significant consequences of war is that it shapes a nation's identity. The power of the Greek states and of Imperial Rome depended first and foremost on military supremacy, and the national pride engendered by it is reflected in their poetry, whether it be on the small

scale of Simonides's elegy for the Spartans who died at Thermopylae [in a last stand against the Persians in 480 BC], or the vast one of Virgil's epic [*The Aeneid*] of the founding of Rome.[18] Myths concerning a nation's past are refined and embellished by its poets and used to galvanize the spirit of its people when faced with foreign aggression.[19] □

Baker sees two of the key functions of war poetry as giving voice to 'national pride' in military victories and enhancing the morale for war, particularly through the deployment of myths of the 'nation's past'. Whilst many other types of war poetry are included in Baker's anthology, the idea of poetry as 'galvanizing' a nation's people in times of conflict is of central importance. The point is not merely that some poets choose to embellish myths of national identity, but that nations utilize such poetry to prop up imperialist and defensive military enterprises, as Baker goes on to explain:

■ So medieval France needed its *Song of Roland* [anonymous eleventh-century French poem concerning legendary military feats], and expansionist Portugal its *Lusiads* [1572, an epic poem written by Portuguese poet and soldier Luis de Camoëns (about 1524–80)]. When a similar need arose in Elizabethan England, Shakespeare obliged by producing his history plays, chronicles of strife and bloodshed, loyalty and treachery, courage and cowardice; and he served the Tudor regime well by presenting its ancestors, the Lancastrians, and particularly Henry V, not only as successful warriors, but as the forgers of a united country. Henry V was a national hero, at one with St. George and England, but his son, Henry VI, was a tragic failure because his weakness led to a bloody civil war.

If Shakespeare was the myth-maker of a specifically English patriotism, later poets also helped to shape the 'Britishness' of the British nation.[20] □

It is important to note, here, that Baker's political background clearly influences his editorial perspective, as does Healey's in his prose piece in *The Voice of War*. Both speak from having worked within political institutions, indeed from having been Ministers in central government. Neither individual imposes an overtly party political agenda but rather signals, to some extent, their respective social and political values through their commentaries: for Healey it is his belief that in circumstances of extreme need, such as war, humanity is a force for good, breaking down social and cultural barriers; for Baker, it is his assessment of the mutual dependence in wartime of war poetry, myths of national identity and morale.

POPULAR POETRY AND PATRIOTISM

Earlier in this Guide, we considered examples of soldiers' verse and ballads of everyday army life, such as Kipling's *Barrack-Room Ballads*. These had become extremely popular in the late nineteenth century, exerting considerable influence on poetry of the subsequent Boer War and First World War. Some of these ballads, although written by non-combatants such as Kipling, were constructed as if spoken in the voice of the ordinary 'Tommy'. Many other volumes of popular soldiers' songs or ballads have been produced, some of which construct an imaginary soldier's voice in the manner of Kipling, and others which offer written (often adapted and bowdlerized) versions of traditional songs sung by soldiers, such as marching songs. These are often presented as popular expressions of soldierly spirit during wartime, articulating both cynicism and patriotism.

Soldiers' songs, ballads and verses have, however, existed in uneasy relation to the war poetry genre as it has developed during the twentieth century, being regarded as marginal at best by much orthodox critical opinion. In *War Poetry: An Introductory Reader*, Simon Featherstone explores this issue, pointing out that popular and oral forms of poetry have tended to be associated with working-class culture, whilst the war poetry canon is dominated by educated, officer-class poets and the lyric form. This critical focus upon a small group of educated individual poets has had a number of effects, Featherstone argues:

> ■ War poetry is still identified with a relatively small canon of writers and this inevitably distorts our view of the genre and its relationship with the mainstream commercial and ideological demands of the period. The pre-eminence of Owen, for example, when his work was largely unpublished until the 1920s, has frequently led to an overemphasis on the opposition to war in war poetry when the great bulk of contemporary material remained unshakeably patriotic throughout.[21] □

Featherstone points to the middle-class dominance of the genre both in terms of the poets selected and the critics who select. As a result, war poetry criticism tends to encapsulate a liberal, oppositional attitude to war, similar to that which Ceadel describes as a 'pacificist' approach (see Chapter Three). Featherstone further states that even those critics who have paid attention to the issue of working-class literature during wartime have, at times, mistakenly suggested that poems by officers with access to 'dominant literary culture and to metropolitan publishers' are instances of popular culture.[22]

In his chapter, 'Popular Culture', Featherstone explores the idea of popular working-class war poetry further by looking at poems printed in local newspapers during the First World War. These, he claims, 'suggest an alternative literary tradition existing alongside the more visible metropolitan mainstream'.[23] Turning to collections of soldiers' songs, Featherstone contrasts them with the supposedly unadulterated tradition of native English song promoted by Cecil Sharp (1859–1924) and by the English Folk Dance and Song Society that Sharp founded; Featherstone points out that soldiers' songs, unlike those that Sharp favoured, draw on an eclectic range of sources, including hymns and the tunes of Tin Pan Alley (the nickname, derived from the United States, of the publishing business that produced commercial popular music):

■ Soldiers' songs remained (and remain) curiosities. They do not fit into the category of war literature, but neither are they folk-songs in Cecil Sharp's purist terms – their indiscriminate use of tin-pan-alley and music-hall tunes, hymns, unclassifiable rhymes and the obscene traditions of the regular army put them outside the definitions of the English Folk Dance and Song Society. Yet it is that very mongrel quality that makes them part of the popular, rather than the mass culture of the war. The songs transform the musical and lyrical idioms of an established culture – whether it be that of the church, professional song writers, music-hall or army tradition – into an expression of the specific social circumstances of the war.[24]   □

Both the working-class poetry of the local newspapers and the soldiers' songs draw extensively and imaginatively, according to Featherstone, on existing idioms and conventions from dominant literary and musical traditions. Yet, importantly, soldiers' songs do not necessarily acquiesce in the values associated with such dominant traditions (such as intense and idealistic patriotism), often providing a comic, obscene or otherwise derogatory counterpoint to them.

The question of how far popular representations of soldierly experience are imbued with patriotism, militarism and pro-war sentiment is, as Featherstone indicates, complex. In his study *Fighting Songs and Warring Words* (1990), Brian Murdoch also argues for the need to consider the significance of what he refers to as 'lyrics – poetry and song'.[25] Murdoch, too, is aware that critical terminology often intertwines social and cultural assumptions with aesthetic value judgements: through, for example, a tendency to conflate the term 'verse' as a category for many working class or popular forms of poetry, with its use as a term to refer to an aesthetically inferior form of poetry. In the following passage from his Preface, Murdoch describes how he believes war poetry ought to be defined and approached, showing as he does so his particular interests in expressions of patriotism and in what he describes as 'popular' lyric forms:

■ Since wars are fought between nations, the study of modern war poetry ought surely to be comparative, even though there are enormous contrasts within and between national literatures. The greatness of – say – the English poets of the First World War who showed its horror is undeniable, but other attitudes to the wars in the lyric need not be neglected. It is of historical and sociological interest to consider the reception of a patriotic and pro-war poem in its contemporary context, however difficult it may sometimes be to appreciate literary effect in a work the morality of which is questionable. For the present-day reader with historical hindsight, however, the reading of and moral response to that same poem will be different, the very overtness of the patriotism causing the modern reader precisely to reject its implications. Poetry does not need to be expressly anti-war to make the point that wars, especially on the scale of those in the twentieth century, are bad.

To suggest that pro-war poetry can be an object of literary study in this way does not, incidentally, imply any revisionism, nor does it justify militarism as such. No one denies the catastrophic nature of the wars. This study intends only to suggest with some examples that the range of what is now normally understood as war poetry might be extended, with particular reference to the popular lyrics occasioned by the world wars. 'Popular' is a humpty dumpty word, it is true. However, some of the war poetry now accepted as canonical in English, for example, has become widely read only relatively recently, and then in limited contexts, while a great range of relevant material had (and sometimes still has) a popularity of a different and in some cases far wider kind. The word 'popular' can mean 'read and appreciated by a large number of people' (in its own time or since), 'made available to a wide audience', or 'produced by or for the ordinary soldier'.[26] □

Whilst Murdoch is in many ways setting out, like Featherstone, to open up the genre, he needs (as do all critics) to establish his definitional and methodological boundaries. In the passage above, he sets out his argument that examples of war poetry from different participating nations in any given war 'ought' to be compared, and that patriotic and pro-war poems, even if experienced as morally repugnant by a modern readership, should be appreciated for their 'historical and sociological interest'.

Murdoch's study includes a wealth of background information and commentary on war poetry, including a survey of war poetry anthologies. He is sensitive to the issue of working-class poets' access to publishing, and draws on a range of sources and traditions. It is interesting to note, however, in the passage quoted above, that a slight degree of defensiveness creeps into his commentary: 'To suggest that pro-war poetry can be an object of literary study in this way does not, incidentally, imply any revisionism, nor does it justify militarism as such.' Whilst arguing on the one hand for a fair appraisal and contextualized understanding of poetry with patriotic or pro-war elements, and a consideration of it as an important aspect of the genre, he is also very concerned not to be categorized as a pro-war or militaristic critic.

The fact that Murdoch foregrounds this issue reminds us how fundamental questions of political ideology and historical interpretation are to the war poetry genre. Murdoch's comment also suggests that the boundaries between critical selection, analysis and personal beliefs are sometimes blurred, misunderstood or misinterpreted, and (echoing a point of Rutherford's) that the post-war focus on anti-war poetry has cast studies of patriotic poetry in a suspicious light. In the next section, we will concentrate on the development of a body of anti-war criticism that has become, in educational contexts at least, the dominant approach.

PEACE, DEMOCRACY AND EDUCATION

THE PEACE MOVEMENT

In this subsection, we will be examining the appearance in the post-1945 period of a cluster of war poetry texts (both anthologies and critical studies) that expressed, or were strongly influenced by new formulations of anti-war thinking. This thinking, as we saw in the previous section, was at times pursued in conjunction with the acknowledgment or celebration of the heroism and military courage shown by ordinary soldiers. The broad anti-war orientation of the anthologists and critics considered in this section does not tend to take pacifism as its primary goal, or left-wing resistance as its premise; few of the post-1945 texts are concerned with opposing war as part of a radical challenge to the political and social system, as some of the 1930s poets were. There is often, however, a keen interest in selecting and presenting war poetry as a means of narrating wars, and as an illustration of the potential for moral, cultural and democratic progress in civilization.

A distinct strain of anti-war thinking did not emerge immediately after the Second World War, and several of the early post-war texts express slightly conflicting views on the significance of wartime culture. As we saw in Chapter Four, Stephen Spender's stated motivation for his 1946 study *Poetry Since 1939* was his concern that much literature published during the Second World War had not yet been brought to critical and public attention. In a sense, Spender's study is presented in a type of documentary spirit, as though a gap or lack in cultural knowledge is simply being filled. Alan Ross (1921–2001), also a poet during the Second World War, produced his study *Poetry 1945–1950* in 1951, aiming to continue the story of poetry where Spender's study concluded. Ross was concerned with surveying the poetic output of a specific, post-war period and, to some extent, relating it to underlying trends and techniques in English poetry, including those in evidence during the war itself. Both Spender and Ross, however, register a degree of tension between their recognition of the war as a self-contained and meaningful literary period, and their desire to extricate poetry from the war's impact and confines; to avoid ascribing too much significance to the conditions and themes of war. Both Spender and Ross reflect a post-war moment, in which British society under austerity measures needed to acknowledge the cultural events of the war and its immediate after-math, yet at the same time make a symbolic departure from wartime concerns and themes. Both individuals are also influenced by the suspi-cion (as discussed in Chapter Three) that the literature of war needs to be placed within parentheses, to be seen as an interruption of, aberra-tion from or unique aside to 'normal' literary and cultural development.

In the 1960s and early 1970s, however, a number of anthologies were published that foregrounded a renewed interest in the two world wars, and in war poetry as a genre. These included: Brian Gardner's *Up the Line to Death: The War Poets 1914–1918*, in 1964; Ian Hamilton's *The Poetry of War 1939–45* and Ian Parsons' *Men Who Marched Away* in 1965; Gardner's *The Terrible Rain: The War Poets 1939–45*, Charles Hamblett's *I Burn for England: An Anthology of the Poetry of World War II* and Ronald Blythe's anthology of Second World War prose and poetry *Components of the Scene*, all in 1966; and Maurice Hussey's *Poetry of the First World War* in 1967. Further consideration of war literature was made through the dis-cussion of Spanish Civil War poetry in the 1964 *Poetry of the Thirties* edited by Robin Skelton, and in Maurice Sperber's *And I Remember Spain: A Spanish Civil War Anthology* (1974). This substantial burgeoning of interest took place in a period of considerable social and political change. For the post-war generation, greater educational opportunities and a growth in mass communications meant a higher level of aware-ness of international conflicts. In particular, the tension surrounding the Suez Crisis (1956)[27] and widespread revulsion at the progress of the Vietnam War (1954–75)[28] began to galvanize a new peace movement and an interest in the political and historical representations of war. For some anthologies of this period, there is an underlying concern with the representation of wars as historical events; for others, the selection and presentation of poetry is a commemorative act and a generalized expression of anti-war sentiment.

In Gardner's anthology, the spirit in which the poetry of the First World War is selected and presented is made clear in the introductory note:

■ This book is intended as a tribute to those who fought, and died, in the First World War. There have been many accounts of that unparalleled tragedy, and here is yet another: one written by the men who lived through it.

Those who wish to ponder, with or without prejudice, on tactics and strat-egy, or to know How It Happened, must turn to other volumes. This account has nothing to do with that: it is traced on the emotions of men at war. Each poem has been selected because it tells part of the whole story.

A large proportion of the poets here represented died in battle nearly fifty years ago; but not all of them died, and some are most happily very much with us. To the surviving poets of the war, I can only convey my gratitude for allowing me to cross their great and precious past, and ask them to forgive me my trespass.[29] □

It is very clear in this extract that Gardner is not simply concerned with the war as a subject of academic study, although he acknowledges that there is a 'story' to be told. Here, the war is a set of profoundly emotional experiences for the many living war survivors. Yet the reverential, even hymn-like tone of the piece, ending on a comment reminiscent of the Lord's Prayer, 'forgive us our trespasses', is not merely a case of observing veteran sensitivities. The First World War, in Gardner's terms, is 'that unparalleled tragedy': despite the relative proximity of the Second World War, he clearly implies that no other historical event rivals the sense of rupture and loss caused by the 1914–18 conflict.

Gardner's articulation of the special significance of the First World War goes beyond an introductory emphasis on casualty statistics or bereaved families; his view of the war informs both the structure of his anthology and the type of poetry selected. As already discussed in Chapter Two, Gardner organizes the poetry under headings that suggest a particular narrative of the war, and the poems are selected to illustrate the war's 'phases'. The predominant mood in the anthology's final section, for example, headed 'At Last, at Last!', combines sombre relief and bitterness, including Kipling's 'A Dead Statesman', 'Back' by Wilfrid Gibson, 'A Dirge for Victory' by Lord Dunsany (1878–1957), from which the quotation heading the chapter is taken, and Herbert Read's 'A Short Poem for Armistice Day'. Indeed, the entire collection is prefaced by the famous Wilfred Owen quotation discussed in Chapter Three: 'Above all I am not concerned with Poetry. My subject is War, and the pity of War. The Poetry is in the Pity.' Isolated from any contextual information about Owen or his views on poetry and war, the quotation seems primarily designed to prepare the reader for a particular emotional response of sadness and compassion.

Maurice Hussey's anthology, like Gardner's, makes a strong case for the exceptionally tragic status of the First World War. In his Preface, Hussey depicts the war in terms of a central shift from the ideal to the disillusioned:

■ The poetry represented in this book, the work of many hands, may for a moment be approached as that of one composite writer, the English war poet. This man's mind can be seen developing as the conduct of the war makes certain ideas less and less tenable. The first mood, a patriotic prompting, drove the young writer from school or college to join the colours; it attains poetic form in the stilted rhetoric and the radiant assurance of untested ideals. In the second place, he begins to find reasons for becoming tentative in his patriotism and withdrawing into a more meditative position; he learns to look into his heart and write with a greater honesty. At another point, either after the Battle of the Somme in 1916 or in 1917 – with the appointment of Field Marshal Haig to the supreme position in the British Army – the bloodshed and misery intensify: the outcome seems no more certain nor more swiftly attainable. Protest against the continuance of hostilities makes the old romanticism both blind and morally objectionable. There emerges from all the experience a moment in which the writer ceases to be the moralist and accepts the state of war as the inevitable condition against which the individual's struggle is fruitless.[30] □

The basic element in this account of the First World War, which is very similar in structure to Gardner's, is that the moral awareness of the soldier is awakened and forever altered by the experience of battle. The concluding comment in the quotation above, again in a manner similar to Gardner, suggests an overall distrust and dislike of war, albeit without any commitment to a precise ideological position such as pacifism. As we saw in Chapter One, this type of approach and narrative structure is still prevalent in a range of representations of the First World War today. Hussey's use of a 'composite' war poet figure, based upon the idea that the war poet role emerges from a common set of experiences, has also endured.

Gardner, Hussey and other anthologists of First World War poetry were instrumental in developing a broadly pacific stance in relation to the war poetry genre, one that emphasized the poetry as part of the tragic narrative arc of the war. These anthologists were also implicitly exploring and debating the boundaries of the war poetry genre, arguing for its importance as a literary category, drawing from a wide range of poets and championing specific figures. Hussey, for example, includes Americans such as Robert Frost, populist patriotic poets such as William Watson, and modernists such as James Joyce. His anthology includes combatants, civilians and retrospective views of the war, and he argues even-handedly for the recognition of poets with very different approaches to poetic form and theme. When it comes to the anthologies of Second World War poetry, although a similarly broad anti-war perspective is sometimes taken, the selection of poets and discussion of the poetry's significance are placed within a rather different representative tradition.

Representations of the respective world wars derive in part from contrasting perceptions of the moral and pragmatic imperatives involved. Whilst many literary critics agree that the First World War descended, as Sassoon put it, into a war of 'aggression' in which unnecessary lives were lost, the Second World War tends to be seen as the just or unavoidable war. In Charles Hamblett's *I Burn for England*, the introductory text is prefaced with the opening lines of the poem 'Defined Attitude', by John Cromer (born 1916):

■ Against the thought of war,
Against the talk of war,
Against war.[31] □

Yet, despite this, Hamblett acknowledges that it had been necessary for the war to be 'got on' with. Indeed for the 1960s anthologists, the Second World War did not lend itself to being seen as a cause for moral outrage in the same way as the First World War. Most of the Second World War anthologies of this period display similar strains of thought: whilst in general war should not be sought out or welcomed, engagement in the Second World War was necessary and inevitable.

In the Second World War anthologies published in the 1960s and 1970s, then, editors cannot, in general, present the poetry of that war simply as culminating in a mood of disillusionment. Whilst the characteristic First World War themes of commemoration and tragedy are still used, they are deployed in quite different ways. In Blythe's *Components of the Scene*, for example, the definitive poetic experience of the Second World War does not derive from the trauma of battle, but emerges from the enforced retreat to an intense inner world:

■ The writers of 1939–45 fully accepted engagement in the struggle but rejected the suspension of private life advocated by the various propaganda machines. This was the condition by which their conscience permitted them to fight, as well as forsake the indignation of the poets of 1916–18. Their work was not addressed to great audiences or to the nation, but to another individual. Eventually, as the war intensified and its strangely fragmented pattern added to the impression of world insanity, the quiet urbanity of its literature provided a climate in which the urgent dialogue of the human condition could take place.[32] □

In *The Terrible Rain* anthology, however, whilst Gardner echoes Blythe's view that Second World War poets reluctantly accepted the war, he does not make the same emphasis on internal and philosophical poetic modes, commenting that he, '… could not, I hope, be expected to include those poems which penetrated exclusively into the poet's mind, rather than studied the lie of the human land around them …'[33] These two quotations seem to stress different perspectives on the poetry of the Second World War, Blythe apparently emphasizing the importance of a psychological exploration of experience, and Gardner the socio-historic. Yet both highlight the 'human condition', or the 'human land' as the indisputable focus of the poetry. In the next subsection, we will consider how a number of Second World War anthologies position this idea of a poetry of the 'human condition', to convey an ethos of egalitarianism, democracy and internationalism.

DEMOCRACY AND INTERNATIONALISM

In Maurice Wollman's *Poems of the War Years: An Anthology* (1950) the stated editorial aim is to make 'much good verse' which has been 'published since September 1939' available; it is a critical and editorial ambition, as we saw in the previous subsection, typical of the post-war era.[34] To this end, Wollman includes 100 poets, covering a wide range of poetic movements, and establishes a broad definition of war poetry: 'all were written under the threat of war or under the impact of war'.[35] Here, the considerable variety of war poets is emphasized: whether combatants, service people or poets writing 'of a winter afternoon' in wartime, they are all viewed by Wollman as writing under the defining 'condition' of war.[36] In Wollman's introduction, therefore, poetry is presented as one of many cultural forms that cannot help but be coloured by war, and in the same way, humanity is equal in its subjection to the experience of being at war.

Within this editorial framework, not only does war reveal the universality of the human condition, but it also causes poetic practice to undergo a process of democratization. Wollman goes on to say:

■ The War destroyed much that had impaired and clogged English poetry of recent years. Diminished was the private vocabulary and allusion of restricted acquaintanceship; the personal was often absorbed into the universal. Diminished were the psycho-analytical subtleties and probings; the emotions of one were the reactions of many. Diminished were the affectations and artificialities of the esoteric; the poet felt for his fellow men. Diminished were the hesitancies, the fumbling, the incertitudes; the poet now more frequently faced reality, grim though it might be, and accepted it, in 'the wakeful anguish of the soul,' with fortitude ...[37] □

As Gardner and others were later to highlight in their own terms, Wollman sees Second World War poetry as reaching towards a kind of universality: the poetry is characterized as unadorned and authentic (as opposed to affected and artificial), and as brave and certain in quality. The Second World War, according to this line of thought, seemed to diminish the 'psycho-analytical subtleties and probings' of earlier poetry, by which Wollman is probably referring to the psychoanalytically influenced poetry of the Auden group. As we saw in Chapter Four, the reputation of Auden and his poetry had suffered a great deal from his emigration to America in 1939.

On one level, it is difficult to reconcile the poetic values that both Wollman and Gardner celebrate with some of the poets they select: for example, Herbert Read, David Gascoyne (1916–2001), Dylan Thomas, Henry Treece and Vernon Watkins all explore, to varying degrees, complex interior worlds. These poets frequently draw upon myth, dream and the subconscious in representing wartime experiences. Yet the point that Wollman, Gardner and others are making is that the experiential, emotional content of poetry should not be focused exclusively inwards through coded language and complex references to the poet's private sense of self. According to this point of view, poets are responsible for channeling thoughts, experiences and emotions outwards, translating them into accessible poetic language and ideas: they have, that is to say, a social role.

In a number of Second World War anthologies, this emphasis on poetry as providing a point of access into the human condition is given a specifically international scope. The international theme is rarely couched in overtly political terms, being more typically subsumed within what is presented as a humanistic emphasis on the shared nature of suffering in war. In 1959, for example, another generic anthology of war poetry, *Ohne Hass und Fahne/ No Hatred and no Flag/ Sans Haine et sans Drapeau* was published by the joint editorial team of Wolfgang G. Deppe, Christopher Middleton and Herbert Schönherr. This anthology, focusing upon a selection of war poems of the twentieth century, makes its internationalist statement not only through editorial analysis and statements of principle, but also through language itself, being a completely trilingual publication in German, English and French. In *Ohne Hass und Fahne*, the editors are keen to state that their motives in pursuing such a trilingual project are not 'political': they are not, they insist, seeking to make a case for a new world order. Yet the anthology is clearly motivated by a broadly anti-war impulse, and in particular by the desire of a group of European intellectuals to overcome barriers in communication and understanding:

■ The poems chosen show a variety of attitudes to war. There are some poets who feel no compulsion to accuse or to appeal; they seem detached, though their statements are self-explanatory. Other poets consider the forces at work and oppose them decisively; these poets too have written good poems. One feature is shared by them all: they are all engaged in a struggle with a reality which has become the distinguishing stigma of our century, a reality which even such an outstanding member of the French

Resistance as LOUIS ARAGON called a 'tragic illusion' [Aragon (1897– 1982) was a prominent French poet, novelist, essayist, journalist and political activist].

The short biographical notes may help readers to understand the poems and their authors. It might even be hoped that these notes will encourage readers to read further, further in works by foreign authors too. That attitude which is indicated in the title of this book can be acquired by just such a penetration of the barriers of language, by a voyage into the interior spirit of a foreign literature, and thus into the spirit of the nation to which that literature belongs.[38] □

Here, it is immediately apparent that the 'variety of attitudes' to war selected by Deppe, Middleton and Schönherr, are distinctly circumscribed. The attitudes under discussion include 'detached', observational perspectives and explicitly oppositional views, but not, for example, support for war or pride in fighting for one's country. The spirit behind the book is, as for many of the 1960s anthologies, to identify points of social and cultural concord, and to place poetry at the centre of a struggle against the twentieth-century 'stigma' of war. In the case of Deppe, Middleton and Schönherr, there is also a particular concern with proving the existence of a 'community of ideas and a community of action' in Europe.[39]

In the *Ohne Hass und Fahne* anthology, the issue of poetry translation is necessarily at the heart of the text. This is clearly acknowledged in the editorial introduction, in a discussion of the search for 'proper' poetry translations that can 'mediate between the languages'.[40] Whilst acknowledging the difficulty of truly literary translations, the editors argue that it is possible to overcome linguistic and cultural barriers between nations. It is interesting to reflect on this ambition from an early twenty-first-century perspective: the selection of British poets includes a number of names that have become firmly established in the war poetry canon, including Owen, Sassoon and Rosenberg, Auden, Day Lewis and Spender, and the slightly less well-known Keyes and Lewis. Yet of the French and German poets, most have remained at the margins of British awareness, or receded entirely from view. A small number of the French poets, such as Apollinaire (1880–1918), Aragon, Eluard (1895–1952) and Péguy (1873–1914), are still occasionally included in translation in generic war poetry collections, but of the German poets, only Bertolt Brecht (1898–1956) has received any sustained attention. Indeed, of the other generic war anthologies we have considered that contain poetry in translation, few include any substantive representation of German war poets; those that do tend to confine themselves to the radical Socialist Brecht or the Romantic Rainer Maria Rilke (1875–1926).

One of the prime exceptions to this observation is the more recent
Poetry of the Second World War: An International Anthology (1995), edited by
Desmond Graham (1995).[41] This collection, like *Ohne Hass und Fahne*,
articulates an ambitious international agenda, including poetry from
Romania, the Soviet Union, Canada, New Zealand, Poland and many
other of the nations involved in the Second World War. Graham's
anthology includes a number of German poets, including Günter Eich
(1907–72) and the famous German poet and novelist Günter Grass
(born 1927), both of whom served in the German Army. Graham, like
many other post-1945 anthologists, sees his anthology as a testimony to
the range of human experience in the war, and places this in a particular
intellectual and political context:

■ The Second World War and Auschwitz have often been said to have
silenced the poet, to have gone beyond words; to be too big to encompass,
too terrible to find expression for: the war could not, above all, be
expressed in poetry, that celebrating art form, that musical manner of
speech, that making of beautiful things. Time has shown, or rather, the
poets have shown, quite the opposite to be the case. The need to break
silence, to give witness, to relieve memory, to lament, cry out and question,
has placed the Second World War in the centre of much of the poetry written during it and afterwards. The scale of the task has meant that it has
needed time; though some did write contemporaneously, even in the most
terrible circumstances. But poetry, with its artifice, its traditions of ways of
saying and making fictions, has proved a positive aid to reaching towards
the experience of the war.
   The poems of that experience are gathered in this anthology. What
emerges is a poetry capable of conveying the vast and terrible sweep of the
war. A poetry in which human responses and experiences echo each other
across boundaries of culture and state.[42] □

Graham refers at the beginning of this extract to the idea that the geno-
cidal aim and ambition of the Nazi 'Final Solution' could not be represented, the horror and rupture to the understanding of civilization and
humanity being so great. This relates to the famous dictum of the
philosopher Theodor Adorno (1903–69) that '[to] write poetry after
Auschwitz is barbaric',[43] being a notion which has caused much debate
and many different interpretations. Through both his introductory comments and poetry selections, Graham implicitly refers to this dictum and
asserts that there must be poetry after Auschwitz; that poetry must be
understood as a means to 'break silence, to give witness, to relieve
memory, to lament, cry out and question'. In this context it can be seen
that for Graham, the inclusion of poetry from Germany and its allies
during the Second World War is a vital part of a process of questioning
and remembering history.

Although this discussion of democratic and internationalist tendencies in anthologies has placed more emphasis on anthologies than on criticism, and on the Second World War than the First, this is by no means a comprehensive account. Also of interest are a number of First World War critical studies of the post-1945 period that have incorporated non-British poets. In Bernard Bergonzi's third edition of *Heroes Twilight: A Study of the Literature of the Great War* (1996), Bergonzi includes a useful update on critical developments since the first edition of his book in 1965.[44] This notes in particular the publication of studies such as Elizabeth A. Marsland's *The Nation's Cause: French, English and German Poetry of the First World War* (1991) and *The Lost Voices of World War I*, edited by Tim Cross (1988),[45] which included prose extracts and poems by writers from many of the countries involved in the war.

EDUCATIONAL APPROACHES

Critics and anthologists of the post-war period have not only approached war poetry as an opportunity to cross international boundaries, or to forge an appreciation of the 'common European mind', but have also seen it as occupying an important place in education. As Simon Featherstone points out, war poetry was used in schools long before the Second World War, although until the 1950s it was the nationalist and imperialist work of poets such as Laurence Binyon that tended to be favoured.[46] By the 1960s, Featherstone argues, in parallel with the continuing increase in reputation and popularity of the 'protest' poets of the First World War, the conception of the role of war poetry within education was changing:

■ Soon the influence of Owen's and Sassoon's anti-militarist stance permeated the secondary sector of education. New emphases on relevant modern material, the encouragement of classroom discussion and interdisciplinary study, along with a strong examination bias towards practical criticism, led to changes in the kind of poetry taught in schools. The old-style patriotic ballads were exchanged for poems which provoked argument and encouraged students to take up social and political issues.

Many English Literature textbooks of the 1960s and 1970s have a section on war, and in these sections by far the most popular poets are Owen and Sassoon. Their criticisms of war and nationalism had made them inappropriate for school reading before this time, but in the increasingly liberal educational climate of the 1960s, their concerns became those of a newly radical teaching establishment. Owen and Sassoon wrote about youth and war, and these were issues that educational theory saw as relevant and appealing to adolescents (with some justification). They also appealed to those teachers recently qualified from higher education, who had been involved in the Campaign for Nuclear Disarmament [a non-party political British organization advocating the abolition of nuclear weapons worldwide, founded 1958] and later in the anti-war campaigns concerning US involvement in Vietnam. The link between modern and historical issues is made in many of the textbooks.[47] □

Featherstone argues here that the gradual embedding of Owen and Sassoon into the secondary school curriculum was the result of a number of factors, including a more liberal and child-centred educational philosophy, an emphasis on the techniques of practical criticism (discussed in some detail in Chapter Three) and a teaching profession which was becoming more politically radical and, in particular, more anti-war in orientation.

In a school textbook of the period, *War Poetry: An Anthology* (1968), edited by D. L. Jones (a Senior English Master at St. Albans Boys' Grammar School), an explicitly pedagogical framework is established.[48] Jones's introduction is divided into two sections: one 'Mainly for the Teacher' and the other 'Mainly for the Students'; and there is commentary by the editor on each of the poets included. The poetry covers a period beginning with Chaucer and concluding with contemporary poets such as Peter Porter (born 1957), Charles Causley (1917–2003) and Ruthven Todd (1914–78). Of the twentieth-century poetry included there are, in addition to a range of work from the two world wars, several poems of the Spanish Civil War and two poems which are described as concerning 'the war which hasn't happened, the nuclear war'.[49]

In his introductory section for 'the teacher', Jones identifies war as a subject that appeals to young people and can be discussed at a 'reasonably adult level'.[50] He also discusses the pedagogical application of his book in the classroom, identifying the need to lay a foundation in the patterns of rhythm and sound used in poetry (known as prosody) and in the characteristic practical criticism method of close reading.[51] Yet, Jones writes, it is of 'greater importance' that students should consider the nature of the poetic content or message. Jones clearly views the choice of subject matter as significant in historical, political and personal terms: he sees war poetry as raising issues and problems that students will perceive as relevant to them:

■ The subject of war was chosen because it was desirable to have a unifying theme in a short and concentrated course and because war is a topic which attracts the interest, and may hold the attention, of young people living in the kind of world with which the twentieth century has confronted them. Perhaps the initial appeal is greater to boys than to girls, but I should expect the responses of girls to the predominantly masculine world with which war poetry is concerned to be of particular interest compared with those of boys.[52] □

Here, although Jones articulates the gender assumptions of his day in assuming that war as a subject will be of less interest to girls than boys, he also displays the progressive intent of his text by indicating that, despite this, girls' responses are likely to be 'of particular interest'. The underlying thinking in this quotation appears to be an association of femaleness with opposition to militarism, a notion that will be referred to again in the final subsection of this chapter. Jones's approach is consistently characterized by the importance placed on the full and thoughtful teacher-led discussion of responses.

Jones incorporates a number of judgements of a social and political, as well as literary, nature in his commentaries on the war poems themselves. In his discussion of 'The Soldier', he places Brooke's ardent love of England in the context of his social privileges: Brooke was, Jones comments, blessed 'more liberally' than 'many who were to die'.[53] In Sassoon's poetry, on the other hand, 'is heard for the first time the authentic voice of the ordinary, unheroic soldier, for Sassoon, like Wilfred Owen, wrote on behalf of the inarticulate many'.[54] This is a highly debatable point if we consider the difference in class, and in regional and experiential backgrounds, between the officer Sassoon and the private soldiers who reported to him. Yet Jones is here emphasizing that Sassoon, unlike many other members of the officer class, wrote poetry from a position of concern for all soldiers. Commenting on a poem by Edward Thomas, Jones writes:

> ■ In *This Is No Case of Petty Right or Wrong*, he [Edward Thomas] reaches a conclusion about patriotism which we feel is valid because it has been arrived at by a process of clear-sighted truthfulness – one which may make Brooke's *The Soldier* appear comparatively facile; for Thomas dismisses the wartime propaganda and concentrates upon what he himself holds to be good and of lasting value.[55] □

The conclusion about patriotism here, Jones, argues, is one that 'we' feel is valid. Jones's pedagogic use of the collective pronoun introduces the point as though it were incontrovertible; the student is asked to join the editor in recognizing the 'truth' of Thomas's milder patriotism, which draws a liberal distinction between hatred of the Kaiser and tolerance of the German people.

Jones concludes his book with a discussion of 'The Responsibility' by Peter Appleton (born 1925):

> ■ The immensely complicated nature of modern society and the scientific nature of modern warfare increase the individual's feeling of being out of touch with any immediate responsibility for what happens, and this poem, while illustrating the complexity of the situation, brings home to us the uncomfortable reality of the burden we all have to bear.[56] □

This type of emphasis on individual awareness of wider social and political questions is, as Featherstone implies, characteristic of much English teaching in the 1960s and 1970s. There is a great stress on personal responsibility, and on the need to understand contemporary military phenomena such as nuclear weapons with massive destructive capability.

In a later example of a war poetry anthology designed for 'young people', *In Time of War* (1989), the editor, Anne Harvey, admits to having 'suffered doubts about the wisdom of offering young readers poetry on such a bleak subject. Why not put past wars behind us and concentrate on making the world a peaceful place?'.[57] Here, Harvey may be implicitly addressing the growing trend of the late 1980s and 1990s towards the idea of 'protecting' children and depoliticizing education, yet she describes the decision to go ahead on the basis of a positive response to her plans from the educational community. Harvey includes a number of disturbing poems, some of which are written from a comparative European perspective, and several of which are about the Holocaust, such as 'Massacre of the boys' by Tadeusz Rozewicz (born 1921), written in 1948. Although the selection is interspersed with a number of illustrations such as images of wartime posters, there is no editorial commentary on the style or content of any of the poems. The final poem in the collection is Day Lewis's 'Will it be so again?', the last stanza of which concludes:

■ Shall it be so again?
Call not upon the glorious dead
To be your witnesses then.
The living alone can nail to their promise the ones who said
It shall not be so again.[58]   □

Despite the neutrality of the introduction, and the absence of analysis or elaboration, the poetry selection and its manner of conclusion again clearly affirms a broad liberal-humanist and anti-war ethos.

CULTURAL HISTORICISM AND FEMINISM

WAR EXPERIENCE AND THE CANON

The growth in interest in war poetry from the mid-1960s onwards is evident not only through the increase in anthologies, such as those discussed above, but also through the substantial number of critical studies that have been published. Many of these are based upon case studies of individual war poets rather than being organized according to philosophical, historical or technical poetic issues. In Chapter One, we noted the tendency to interpret war poetry in terms of the poetic subject's 'experience' of war, with the biography of poets often being treated as accessible and knowable in comparison to the ambiguities of poetic imagery and the complexities of condensed and codified poetic language. The tendency towards using the war poet as an organizing principle in anthologies and studies can also be related back to the fame and mythification of Owen and Brooke. In Chapter Two we saw how Brooke's death was received by a range of public figures as symbolic of the deaths of all young British men in the course of the war; in Chapter Three, we observed how Owen became a focal point for anti-war thinking. These were early examples of the power of the war poet image to mobilize cultural and political (as well as literary) responses, and they were crucially reinforced by the selective reproduction of both poetry and photographs, consolidating Brooke as the beautiful, passionately patriotic aesthete and Owen as the compassionate, dutiful conscience of war.

In this Guide, we have already considered a number of examples of critical studies that focus upon individual war poets, such as Silkin's *Out of Battle: The Poetry of the Great War*, discussed in Chapter Two. In this study, some 14 First World War poets are analysed in detail, including chapters on 'Rudyard Kipling and Rupert Brooke', 'Edmund Blunden and Ivor Gurney', 'Herbert Read, Richard Aldington and Ford Madox Ford' (1873–1939) and a chapter each on Sassoon, Owen and Rosenberg. Silkin's extended introduction invites the reader to consider a set of remarkable individual characters and achievements, and to note the relationship of these individuals to the tradition of war poetry dating back to the Romantic period, and earlier. As Simon Featherstone points out in *War Poetry: An Introductory Reader*, Silkin not only provided detailed and extremely influential analyses of a range of First World War poems and poets, but along with Paul Fussell (whose work we will consider again later in this section) formulated a particularly important part of the continuing arguments about how we think about the two world wars.[59] Silkin's approach, Featherstone argues, is based on the idea of 'a developing consciousness of the realities of war as a determining factor in the poetry'; Silkin is also clearly concerned with the development of a war poetry canon. However in his discussion of *Out of Battle*, Featherstone points out that Silkin is reluctant to see the historical, social and political contexts of war poetry as 'determining forces'; he is, Featherstone suggests, more keen to emphasize the 'autonomy of poetic creation'.[60]

The tension that Featherstone identifies here, between consideration of individuals as autonomous artists and the recognition (and theorization) of the relationship between individual poets and wider contexts (historical, social, political and cultural), colours much post-1945 war poetry criticism. This can also be seen in more recent work on the poetry of the First World War, such as Jon Stallworthy's informative and accessible *Anthem for Doomed Youth* referred to in previous chapters of this guide. Stallworthy's text illustrates the remarkable level of continuity in the war poetry canon: of the 12 poets discussed by Stallworthy, all but the Irish poet Francis Ledwidge are covered in Silkin's 1972 study. Like Silkin, Stallworthy provides a great deal of interesting and relevant contextual information on his selected poets, placing them against a backdrop of historical factors and literary influences. Yet Stallworthy implies in his introduction that poets are ultimately selected and judged on their intrinsic and autonomous character as artists and individuals; their capacity, as he puts it, to be 'true to their different forms of experience'.[61] This is a difficult idea to test out in relation to war poetry: how do we assess the authenticity of a poem if we have not had the same experience ourselves? We might read biographical and historical studies to help us to relate a poet's representation of war to other kinds of account, but can we ever know precisely how close a poem is to the personal experience of a poet? Despite these problems, the ideas of an individual poet's authenticity and 'truth to experience' continue to be key criteria by which war poetry is judged.

The focus upon individual poets is not exclusive to analyses of First World War poetry. Studies of Second World War poetry such as Linda Shires's *British Poetry of the Second World War*, and comparative work such as *Spirit Above Wars: A Study of the English Poetry of the Two World Wars* (1976) by A. Banerjee, both use a similar basic structure involving a contextualizing introduction and chapters that concentrate usually on one or two poets, although Shires also includes a chapter, 'Where are the War Poets?' investigating broader poetic tendencies and groupings of the period. Both Banerjee and Shires illustrate the gradual post-1945 development of a Second World War canon, comprising a core of three male combatant poets, Keith Douglas, Sidney Keyes and Alun Lewis, with Dylan Thomas, Roy Fuller, Alan Ross and Edwin Muir forming an outer circle. For both Shires and Banerjee the notion of the poets' war experience is an important element in the consideration of their literary approaches and themes.

Shires, in particular, draws extensively on psychological and biographical perspectives, as can be seen in the following discussion of Keith Douglas:

■ Keith Castellain Douglas was born in Tunbridge Wells, Kent, on 24 June 1920. From his youth he loved shapes and colours, then words and images. An only child and independent, he actively seized upon creative self-amusements. Placed in a boarding school at the age of six because of family problems, Douglas flourished in reading and writing early. When he was eight his father, a career soldier, left the family to live with another woman, and Keith Douglas never saw him again. Like Sidney Keyes, Douglas was deeply affected by the broken relationships of his childhood, and they made their way directly into his war poetry. Similarly, Douglas was able to understand and grasp the complexities of war better for having been exposed early to suffering and disjunction.

Two images, expressed in various forms, weave in and out of Douglas's poems. The first is that of an uncaring father, a distanced God who governs men's lives and reduces them to puppets on the stage of life. The other major image is that of a beast 'so amorphous and powerful that he could be a deity'.[62] It seems clear that the two images of uncaring father and beast are related, outer and inner forms of the same ruling deity. Variously named as Devouring Time, Death, the beast, God, the power he describes is 'inefficient' or cruel. Implacably, this devilish manipulator breaks and severs the relationships that Douglas seeks. His strong response to its domination was exacerbated by his need for order, his attraction to justice, and the real absence of his father.[63] □

Here, Shires correlates poetic characteristics with biographical details: Douglas's broken relationships 'made their way directly into his war poetry'. Indeed, the imagery identified by Shires as especially significant is presented as a type of psychological profile; thus when Shires writes of 'the devilish manipulator' that 'breaks and severs the relationships that Douglas seeks', the biographical representation of Douglas seems almost to be conflated with the poetic texts themselves.

Whilst many critics have continued to focus predominantly upon the individual war poet figure, the study of war poetry has also been challenged and extended by the development of new approaches in literary studies, and by a range of social and cultural changes. Bernard Bergonzi highlights some of the factors that have impacted upon the development of the war poetry genre in the third edition of his *Heroes Twilight: A Study of the Literature of the Great War* (1996).[64] In the Preface to this edition, Bergonzi discusses the modifications to his own thinking since the first edition of his book in 1965, noting in particular the greater sophistication of critical approaches to the genre. He describes how he has revised some of his 'original assumptions, particularly about the extent to which the poetry of the war expresses a clear disjunction between early idealism and later disillusionment'.[65] He also points out that he has expanded his discussion of some poets, notably Edward Thomas and Ivor Gurney, following extensive research on their work and lives by literary scholars. Thirty-one years after his first edition, Bergonzi writes:

■ *Heroes' Twilight* has unavoidably become a different book from the one I originally wrote even where the text remains unchanged. The context in which it is read has altered with time. When it first appeared the First World

War was well within living memory, many of the writers I discussed were alive, and some were still actively working. Now they have all gone, and so has direct memory, and discussion of the war and the writing it generated is divided between scholarship and mythology (modes which can interact in unexpected ways).[66] □

Here, Bergonzi argues that the study of war poetry underwent a significant change as the last poets who had lived through the war died. Critics of First World War poetry, Bergonzi writes, had to move away from reliance upon and respect for the 'real' testimony of survivors; they had to turn to historical analysis and to consider the imaginative and mythic landscapes of the war. Such developments impacted on the genre as a whole, feeding into critical approaches to Second World War poetry as well.

In the final two subsections of this chapter, we will consider further some of the many contrasting approaches that emerged during the period of genre development from the mid-1960s onwards. The first of these sections looks at the move to collect and re-evaluate women's poetry of both world wars, and considers readings of the homoerotic elements in First World War poetry. The final section concludes with an examination of two critical texts that have attempted to forge a different type of theoretical approach to the poetry of war, arguing against the focus on individual poets and a passively constructed 'backdrop' of history. In both these subsections the debate continues about the constitution and status of the war poetry canon.

WOMEN WAR POETS AND THE HOMOEROTIC

In 1978, Catherine Reilly published her *English Poetry of the First World War: A Biobibliography* and eight years later followed this with her *English Poetry of the Second World War: A Biobibliography*. Both texts contain a huge amount of information on poetry publications of the two world wars, including basic biographical details on thousands of poets; they have been used extensively by those researching into war poetry ever since. Yet, as Reilly points out in *The Virago Book of Women's War Poetry and Verse*:

■ Women's writing in general tended to be undeservedly neglected until Virago Press and other feminist publishing houses made available a large corpus of meritorious but little-known work by women. Until then anthologies of the poetry of both wars had been published over the years but the contributions were largely by men. The term 'war poet' was applied initially to the soldiers fighting in the trenches of France and Flanders. These anthologies often included poetry by such well-established literary lions as Thomas Hardy, Rudyard Kipling, D. H. Lawrence [1885–1930] and W. B. Yeats, all non-combatants. So it appeared that the business of war was still regarded as primarily a masculine concern, even though women would have an increasingly active part to play in twentieth-century war-fare.[67] □

The Virago anthology is the combined edition of two separate, previously published texts: *Scars Upon My Heart: Women's Poetry and Verse of the First World War* (1981) and *Chaos of the Night: Women's Poetry of the Second World War* (1984). The poems printed in these anthologies are by women from a wide spectrum of war experience: civilians, auxiliaries and war workers of all kinds, bereaved wives and mothers and stalwart patriots, very few of whom had been widely read beforehand. In the passage above, Reilly argues that this poetry has been 'undeservedly neglected': as we have noted elsewhere in the Guide, these anthologies are part of a move, stimulated by the development of a range of feminist approaches to literature and history, to identify and re-evaluate what were becoming viewed as lost or neglected female perspectives. The anthologies are also designed to challenge the stereotype of war as primarily a 'masculine concern'.

The questions of what might be special about women's war poetry, and how it should be evaluated, have produced a variety of responses. In the Virago anthology, Reilly bases her assessment on an essentialist view of gender in which men and women are distinguished by contrasting intrinsic qualities. Women, Reilly argues, 'always excel when writing about human emotions'.[68] Later in her introduction, however, she observes that to an extent, 'any war poem is a statement against war'.[69] These suggestions, of the intrinsic nature of female sensitivity on the one hand, and the inherently anti-militarist nature of war poetry on the other, raise further problems, however. As we discussed in Chapter Two, not every poem selected for the Virago anthology can in fact be read as a 'statement against war'. Judith Kazantzis acknowledges this issue in her preface to the anthology, arguing that the sentimental and jingoistic women's poems need to be understood in historical context, rather than dismissed on the basis of their unpalatability to the modern reader.

The idea that women excel in the representation of human emotions is also difficult to square with the authoritarian and nationalistic urgings of poets such as Jessie Pope, an example of whose work we also considered in Chapter Two. These tensions stem in part from the post-1945 linkage between war poetry and anti-war thinking that we have already examined, but also from an ideological affiliation between some branches of feminism and anti-militarism. A more extended analysis of the complex relationship between the women's movement, militarism and representations of war can be found in a number of further historical and critical works, including *Militarism versus Feminism: Writings on Women and War* edited by M. Florence, C. Marshall and C. Ogden (1987)[70] and in N. Khan's *Women's Poetry of the First World War* (1988).[71]

Both Reilly and Kazantzis also emphasize that the war poems in the Virago anthology have an important role in offering female (although predominantly middle-class) perceptions of social conditions and culture in wartime. In Reilly's terms, the poems provide 'significant social comment on these periods of twentieth-century history'.[72] For Kazantzis:

■ The grind, along with the joking, is there: working-class poverty, middle-class war-shortages, officers' last leaves, wistful rural backwaters seen at all income-levels levels and tenderly described in the Georgian tradition; Jingoism rampant; London both grim and feckless; hospitals; soldiers wounded and unwounded; public schools; anxious mothers contemplating their small sons; varieties of war work, including the ubiquitous socks – all done from a middle-class viewpoint, despite the sallies into Kiplingesque Cockney.[73] □

Kazantzis here details the historical importance of the non-combatant perspective of women's war poetry, its exploration of contemporary urban and rural landscapes, its susceptibility to the discourses of war-lust and its capacity to show the effect of war upon the fabric of society. Here the argument for a specific women's anthology coalesces most effectively around the need to see beyond the viscerality and horror of battle itself.

Early on in her preface, Kazantzis makes explicit reference to the attitude of poets such as Sassoon, who wrote of the hypocrisy of women in wartime. As we discussed in Chapter Two, Sassoon's 'Glory of Women' made bitter accusations concerning women's ignorance and romanticization of war in the face of rising death tolls and horrifically mutilated returning soldiers. Yet as Martin Taylor argues in the introduction to his anthology *Lads: Love Poetry of the Trenches* (1998), poets such as Sassoon and Owen need to be understood not just in terms of a misogyny legitimated by the gender assumptions of the time, but in the context of the intensity in relationships between men.[74] Developing an argument made by Fussell,[75] Taylor discusses the 'phenomenon' of homoerotic relationships in the First World War, and the light this casts upon war poetry. By 'homoerotic' Taylor refers to the widespread nature of passionately intense and romantic feelings between men that were not necessarily physically expressed. As Taylor writes:

■ Much of the best of First World War poetry is characterized by a strong homoerotic element, but it is a consideration that requires very careful treatment if its complexities are to be fully understood. Sentiments that appear to the modern reader to be overtly homosexual were written and published, without embarrassment or censure, in an age that could still remember the fall of [Oscar] Wilde [1854–1900, playwright, novelist and poet] and the scandal of Cleveland Street. And expressions of love for one's comrades did not only appear in the elevated medium of verse, but also in the more prosaic form of letters and personal diaries. Most reflections on the First World War experience contain some anecdote revealing an affection between fighting-men that went beyond the bounds of ordinary comradeship. The pervasiveness of the emotion is matched only by its unselfconsciousness. This qualification is not intended to diminish the homoerotic element of First World War literature, but simply to warn readers against adopting too unguarded an approach.[76] ☐

Taylor's argument is that the homoerotic element in war poetry needs to be carefully constructed in cultural and historical context: it must be understood as often, but not always, sexually innocent. However, in the Holts' *Poets of the Great War*, discussed earlier in this chapter, the subtlety of this position is overlooked in the editors' observation concerning Taylor's anthology. In the introduction to their anthology, the Holts comment that it 'somewhat stretches credulity in discovering a gay in every communal bathing stream and behind every shell-shattered tree', implying a sexual reductiveness that is not present in either Taylor's or Fussell's argument.[77]

The poets in Taylor's anthology include such frequently anthologized figures as Sassoon, Owen, Gurney, Read and Nichols, all of whom we have considered in the context of separate debates in this Guide, and many other less well-known poets. The framework within which Taylor presents the poetry also draws on the well-established war poetry paradigm of narrating war through section headings. In his anthology, however, Taylor adjusts the narrative slightly to reflect his rereading, so that sections entitled 'The Call' and 'Somewhere in France' are followed by 'Mates', 'Youth in Arms' and 'The Greater Love'.

In his introduction, Taylor argues that the nature of the romantic friendships prevalent within memoirs and literature of the First World War period was specific to the historical moment. During the war, the intense, loving nature of the relationships between men could be and was articulated; as Taylor shows with his selections of poetry, there are many instances in which relationships are expressed in terms of physical admiration or attraction. Yet, as Taylor points out, the significant shift in the way that sexual and social behaviour between men was conceptualized and judged in the post-war period, particularly in the light of work by psychologists questioning the 'threshold between friendship and homosexuality', meant that the concept of a romantic friendship became more problematic.[78] Some retrospective accounts of the war in the 1920s and 1930s, such as Robert Graves's *Goodbye To All That* and Richard Aldington's *Death of a Hero* (1929) are thus distinctly defensive about male friendships, making overt distinctions between loving or comradely attachment, and homosexual desire.

MEMORY AND MYTH

As we have already noted, Paul Fussell is one of the post-1945 critics widely recognized as having shifted the terms by which we understand and discuss war poetry. Fussell's *The Great War and Modern Memory*, first published in 1975, places great emphasis on the unique nature of the war, but also on the need to understand the war through a range of (often interconnecting) literary and cultural traditions and practices. Fussell discusses in detail the way in which the war has been constructed as ironic and satirical, not only through literary texts but also through memory, and shows the considerable influence that First World War representations have had upon subsequent war writing.

Memories of the 'Great' War, Fussell writes, have become powerfully associated with ironic deflation of hope, or rupture of expectations. Considering a personal recollection of the first day of the Battle of the Somme, 1 July 1916, by the novelist Henry Williamson (1895–1977), Fussell comments:

■ What assists Williamson's recall is precisely the ironic pattern which subsequent vision has laid over the events. In reading memoirs of the war, one notices the same phenomenon over and over. By applying to the past a paradigm of ironic action, a rememberer is enabled to locate, draw forth, and finally shape into significance an event or a moment which otherwise would merge without meaning into the general undifferentiated stream.[79] □

Fussell argues, here, that memories are not free flowing, uniform phenomena but selected, prioritized and structured. Literary texts about the First World War are similarly influenced and given shape by the 'paradigm of ironic action'. He develops his theme by comparing the use of irony in two works, one about the First World War and one about the second: R. C. Sherriff's play *Journey's End: A Play* which we discussed in Chapter Three, and Joseph Heller's Second World War novel *Catch-22* which, as mentioned earlier in this chapter, is a satire on the absurdity of war. Fussell writes that Heller's description of a character's death:

■ ... works because it is undeniably horrible, but its irony, its dynamics of hope abridged, is what makes it haunt the memory. It embodies the contemporary equivalent of the experience offered by the first day on the Somme, and like that archetypal original, it can stand as a virtual allegory of political and social cognition in our time. I am saying that there seems to be one dominating form of modern understanding; that it is essentially ironic; and that it originates largely in the application of mind and memory to the events of the Great War.[80] □

Here, Fussell's use of the ironic as the 'dynamics of hope abridged' reminds us of Northrop Frye's use of the 'ironic', as we saw earlier in this chapter in the discussion in 'The spirit of the soldier'. It is this dominant paradigm of 'hope abridged' against which Rutherford and others argue, seeing it as precluding any appreciation of the heroic or virtuous.

In addition to the pervasiveness of the ironic mode of understanding, Fussell examines the production of myth in wartime, the literariness of the First World War and the use of military rhetoric. Through these and other strategies of inquiry, he provided what were, in the mid-1970s, novel perspectives upon the 'experience' of war, and challenged orthodox understandings of war literature of various kinds. Analysing a number of key literary and cultural traditions in which First World War poets were steeped, for example, Fussell expounds on the specifically British obsession with pastoral:

■ Recourse to the pastoral is an English mode of both fully gauging the calamities of the Great War and imaginatively protecting oneself against them. Pastoral reference, whether to literature or to actual rural localities and objects, is a way of invoking a code to hint by antithesis at the indescribable; at the same time it is a comfort in itself, like rum, a deep dug-out, or a woolly vest. The Golden Age posited by Classical and Renaissance literary pastoral now finds its counterpart in ideas of 'home' and 'the summer of 1914.' The language of literary pastoral and that of particular rural data can fuse to assist memory or imagination.[81] □

Fussell brings his broad-based analysis of pastoral 'comfort' to bear in discussing war poems such as Owen's 'Exposure', and he points to the ironic application of pastoral in later poetry such as Keith Douglas's 'Cairo Jag', where 'gun barrels split like celery/ the metal brambles have no flowers or berries ...'. Thus Fussell examines literary texts within a wide range of literary, historical, rhetorical and cultural contexts, and stresses the complex ways in which texts (and the traditions they invoke) interrelate and influence one another.

Fussell's First World War study has been influential, and was followed in 1989 by his Second World War study, *Wartime: Understanding and Behaviour in the Second World War*. Yet the emphasis given by Fussell to the uniqueness of the First World War as an event, and its mythical and literary nature, has also been the subject of criticism. According to

Simon Featherstone, Fussell does not fully resolve the relationship between the 'actuality' of war experience and the mythical and literary nature of the war:

■ Fussell's work, then, veers between an analysis of war writing as a complex set of rhetorical strategies for expressing the inexpressible and a celebration of the literature as a special kind of experiential writing. The latter purpose carries the weight of Fussell's own experience as a soldier in the Second World War, a personal involvement in the subject-matter which is never made explicit in *The Great War and Modern Memory*, although it is undoubtedly the emotional core of the work.[82] □

Here, Featherstone highlights the fact that Fussell himself fought in the Second World War, and that personal experience of this importance and relevance needs to be, on some level, acknowledged or accounted for within his work. Featherstone also points out that Fussell, like many other war poetry critics, gives very little consideration to the range of non-combatant perspectives on war, including those of women writers. Whereas some critics might defend their concentration on male writers by defining war poetry as exclusively that of combatants, Featherstone points out that Fussell's aim is to broaden the analysis of war literature and war culture. This, he argues, sits uneasily with the marginalization of women and other critical non-combatant voices in his text.

In *War Poetry: An Introductory Reader*, which combines criticism with a discrete anthology section including prose and poetry of both world wars, Featherstone takes a broadly cultural, literary-historical and politically sensitive approach, focusing in particular on a number of limitations and exclusions from other critical studies. A number of Featherstone's cogent and helpful arguments are referred to throughout this Guide, and particularly in this chapter. These include, for example, a discussion of popular culture (involving an analysis of working-class war poetry in local newspapers during the First World War) and a commentary on the uses of war poetry within education. Featherstone also incorporates a discussion of gender and war poetry, including an analysis of H. D., Hilda Doolittle, as a war poet, and discussions of selected artistic and intellectual milieux, including the 'provincial radicalism' of Herbert Read, the Jewish radical culture from which Rosenberg emerged, the treatment of war by Scottish poets, and the exile poet communities of India and Egypt in the Second World War.

Featherstone is particularly concerned, therefore, with researching and discussing areas of the genre that have sometimes been treated as marginalia. He is also a keen advocate of the need to bring some of the theoretical complexity and rigour of English studies over the last thirty or so years into discussions of war poetry. Featherstone argues that until the 1970s, the critical orthodoxy about war poetry derived from F. R. Leavis's view that the First World War poets were a side issue compared with the poetic developments of Pound and Eliot. Whilst critics such as Silkin and Fussell (and many others discussed in this Guide) challenged this view, bringing the study of war poetry into a more scholarly realm and developing it as a substantive academic genre in its own right, there is, Featherstone writes, a need to explore and extend further the potent social, political and cultural analysis of war poetry.

Several other critical studies have been produced during the 1990s that show how far this process of extending the analysis of war poetry is underway. In particular, it has been evident over the last decade that interest in the Second World War as a literary period has become even more firmly established. Adam Piette's study *Imagination at War: British Fiction and Poetry 1939–1945*,[83] for example, offers an analysis of wartime culture based on the tensions between 'public' and 'private' discourses. Piette's aim is to refocus the analysis of wartime culture through perceptions of 'the private imagination':

■ One voice tells us that the wartime coalition and wartime acts of Parliament reveal a nation at one moving towards new ideas of the state based on social justice; the private voice shows deep fissures and rifts in the society, violent modifications across right and left that nevertheless forced the two wings drastically apart. The private story is the story this book hopes to tell.[84] □

Mark Rawlinson takes a different approach, in his recent innovative study *British Second World War Literature* (2000). Rawlinson's method is to investigate the literature of war not only in relation to cultural history, but also in terms of a detailed analysis of philosophical theories of war. Rawlinson focuses primarily on fiction but his theoretical approach and broad range of literary and cultural references offer many points of connection with the poetry of the Second World War.

This chapter has traced a number of the main critical themes and approaches to war poetry in the post-1945 period, demonstrating how the acts of critical selection and interpretation can produce dramatically different analyses. Often, particularly in the context of educationally oriented texts, we have seen how these analyses are anti-war in orientation, whilst in many popular anthologies we have seen how admiration and celebration of martial courage and patriotism persists. We have also seen how apparently divergent readings can be made of the same material, and how critics and anthologists use literary, historical and biographical information to build an interpretive framework within which to 'understand' the poetry. All these discussions of post-1945 critical work build on (and often modify and challenge) a number of basic assumptions about the genre of war poetry that developed during 1914–45. As we continue to be reminded, through memorial services and in newspapers and anthologies, of poetry's 'special' role in commemorating and warning us about war – its horror and 'pity' – it is salutary to recall that such sentiments have been put forward since the first half of the twentieth century.

Conclusion

The interest in war poetry, as we have seen in this Guide, shows no sign of abating. As we noted in Chapters One and Five, new war poetry anthologies such as Hollis and Keegan's *101 Poems Against War* are still being produced, whilst several older anthologies, such as Gardner's *Up The Line to Death*, continue to be reprinted. In one historical period after another, and for one editor after another, war poetry seems to exert an irresistible attraction. With each new anthology produced, there is a sense of a new project unfolding, whether this involves placing the poetry within an overt anti-war framework, using it as an illustration of patriotic feeling or declaring that it helps us celebrate, in a more general sense, the values and qualities associated with the armed forces.

From the critical material contained in this Guide, it is possible to see that what might seem at first to be an easy and unproblematic category – 'war poetry' – is one that has rarely stood still at any point in the twentieth century. As a genre, war poetry needs to be studied with reference to its shifting nature; by the way it has been reconstructed and reinterpreted at so many different points in twentieth-century history. For each new generation of poets, critics and readers, the significance attached to war poetry, and the cultural and political values and beliefs associated with it, have been in a process of transition. These changing perceptions of war poetry have, of course, been informed by experiments with poetic technique, developments in aesthetic theory and innovations in literary criticism, yet they have also been informed by different desires for a return to 'tradition', for social change or for new political agendas.

We have considered, on many occasions in this Guide, how often editors and critics imply or declare that war poetry is a natural and inevitable part of life. This idea is reinforced on many levels in British culture through the incorporation of war poetry into monuments and memorials and through war poetry's use in many different historic and imaginative representations of the world wars. We have also noted that this type of declaration is often closely followed by a very specific view of the political necessity or morality of war itself. The references to a wide range of poetry and critical material in this Guide demonstrate that no one view of war poetry has yet been accepted as inevitable or incontestable, even though some prominent critical trends can be identified during different historical periods. Whilst the many pedagogical anthologies and critical works in the post-1945 period present their anti-war stance as if it were the definitive position on the poetry of war, other texts assert, just as confidently, that war continues to function as an opportunity for the assertion of national identity, and the celebration of military values.

This Guide has attempted to provide an overview of some of the paradoxes and key approaches that have characterized the genre at different points in the twentieth century. It has also attempted to expose, rather than obscure, the divergent and often contradictory meanings that have been drawn out of war poetry by critics. Whilst, as we have seen, war poetry has become heavily laden with different memories, myths and ideological associations, particularly in relation to the role of the two world wars in British history, it is, at the same time, still very much available to be reconstructed and reinvested with significance: by the next anthologist, the next critic, or perhaps, inevitably, by the next war.

Notes

CHAPTER ONE

1 Excerpt used in the Act of Remembrance from 'For the Fallen', Laurence Binyon, quoted in 'A Service of Remembrance: IRAQ 2003', St. Paul's Cathedral, Friday 10 October 2003.

2 J. M. Winter, *The Experience of World War I* (New York: Oxford University Press, 1995), p. 226.

3 This was referred to in a lecture given by K. Thornton, delivered jointly to the Ivor Gurney Society, Edward Thomas Fellowship and the Wilfred Owen Association at the Art Workers Guild, Queen Square, Bloomsbury, London on Friday 1 November 1996.

4 B. Bergonzi, 'The Problem of War Poetry', *Heroes' Twilight* (Manchester: Carcanet Press Limited, 1996), p. 215. First delivered as the Byron Foundation Lecture, University of Nottingham in 1990.

5 *The Way to the Stars* (1945), directed by Anthony Asquith. See discussion in 'Unity and dissonance' in Chapter Four.

6 The Salamander Oasis Trust is a registered charity founded in 1976 by editors and poets to collect, preserve and promote poetry of the Second World War. See 'Shaping national identity' in Chapter Five.

7 See the Preface to Sean Day-Lewis's biography *C. Day-Lewis: An English Literary Life* (1980). The surname was originally hyphenated, but he changed his writing name to C. Day Lewis in the 1920s.

8 W. B. Yeats, *The Oxford Book of Modern Verse 1892–1935* (Clarendon Press, 1936), and see the discussion in Chapter Three, 'Yeats and the difference of war poetry'.

9 Ezra Pound and T. S. Eliot were primary proponents of new approaches to poetry that later became known as 'Modernism', of which further discussion can be found in Chapter Three, 'Modernism and war poetry'.

10 J. Williams, *Twentieth-Century British Poetry: A Critical Introduction* (London: Edward Arnold, 1987), p. 27.

11 Imagism, a movement concerned with developing greater precision in poetic diction and imagery, and Georgian poetry, which tended to focus upon a rural English identity, are both considered further in Chapter One, 'War poets and literary contexts'.

12 Williams (1987), p. 35.

13 Williams (1987), p. 65.

14 Piette (1995), p. 36.

15 C. F. E. Spurgeon, *Poetry in the Light of War* (Oxford: The English Association, 1917).

16 R. Eberhart and S. Rodman, *War and the Poet: An Anthology of Poetry Expressing Man's Attitudes to War From Ancient Times to the Present* (New York: The Devin-Adair Company, 1945), p. v.

17 C. Reilly, *English Poetry of the Second World War: A Biobibliography* (London: Mansell Publishing, 1986), p. vii.

18 T. S. Eliot's Introduction to D. Jones, *In Parenthesis*, 2nd edn (London: Faber, 1961), p. vii.

19 T. Kendall, '"The Pity of War?"' in *PN Review*, Vol. 30, No. 1 (September–October 2003), pp. 30–2.

20 Kendall (2003), p. 32.

21 Dennis Welland, *Wilfred Owen: A Critical Study* (London: Chatto, 1960).

22 J. Silkin, *Out of Battle: The Poetry of the Great War* (London and New York: Ark Paperbacks, 1987). First published 1972.

23 Silkin (1987), p. 75.

24 Silkin (1987), p. 104.

25 [*Shires's note:*] Stephen Spender, 'Poetry for Poetry's Sake', *Horizon*, XIII, 1946, pp. 243–5. Also see G. S. Fraser, 'Dylan Thomas', *Essays on Twentieth Century Poets* (Leicester: Leicester University Press, 1977), p. 193.

26 L. Shires, *British Poetry of the Second World War* (London and Basingstoke: The Macmillan Press Ltd, 1985), pp. 45–6.

27 See N. Jones, *Rupert Brooke, Life, Death and Myth* (London: Richard Cohen Books, 1999).

28 N. de Somogyi, ed., *The Little Book of War Poems* (Exclusive Editions, 2001), for Marks and Spencer plc.

29 de Somogyi (2001), p. 8.

30 de Somogyi (2001), pp. 8–9.

31 P. Barrett and K. B. Collison, eds, *The Happy Warrior: An Anthology of Australian and New Zealand Military Poetry* (Hartwell, Victoria: Sid Harta Publishers, 2001), p. 13.

32 Barrett and Collison (2001), book jacket.

33 M. Hollis and P. Keegan, eds, *101 Poems Against War* (London: Faber and Faber Limited, 2003).

CHAPTER TWO

1 B. Gardner, ed., *Up the Line to Death: The War Poets 1914–1918* (London: Methuen Paperbacks, 1976). First published in 1964 by Methuen & Co. Ltd. There have been nine reprints of this text between 1964 and 1995.

2 A. Motion, 'Afterword', *101 Poems Against War*, M. Hollis and P. Keegan, eds (London: Faber and Faber Ltd., 2003), pp. 135–6.

3 Hollis and Keegan (2003), p. 136.

4 Hollis and Keegan (2003), p. 136.

5 Silkin (1987), pp. 1–2.

6 For the full elaboration of this argument, see Silkin's Introduction (1987), pp. 1–31. On p. 7, Silkin makes one of a small number of direct comparisons, when he writes that Coleridge 'anticipates the attacks made by Sassoon and Owen on those at home who are unable through lack of imagination, or who refuse, to consider what those who are fighting endure'.

7 A. Bold, ed., *The Martial Muse: Seven Centuries of War Poetry* (Oxford: Wheaton, 1976), pp. 14–15.

8 Bold (1976), p. 55; also see the discussion in the subsection on pacifism and protest in this Guide.

9 Bold (1976), p. 56.

10 C. Carrington, ed., *The Complete Barrack-Room Ballads of Rudyard Kipling* (London: Methuen & Co. Ltd., 1973), p. 39.

11 See Carrington's Introduction (1973), pp. 2–3.

12 S. Featherstone, *War Poetry: An Introductory Reader* (London: Routledge, 1995), p. 26.

13 H. Newbolt, *Admirals All and Other Verses* (Mathews, 1898).

14 M. Van Wyk Smith, *Drummer Hodge: The Poetry of the Anglo-Boer War (1899–1902)* (Oxford: Clarendon Press, 1978), pp. 6–7.

15 Carrington (1973), p. 32.

16 J. Wain, *The Oxford Anthology of English Poetry* (Oxford: Oxford University Press, 1986), pp. 566–67.

17 Van Wyk Smith (1978), p. 109.

18 C. F. E. Spurgeon, *Poetry in the Light of War*, The English Association pamphlet, No. 36 (January 1917), p. 3.

19 R. O. A. Milne, the Marquess of Crewe, *War and English Poetry*, The English Association pamphlet, No. 38 (September 1917), p. 3.

20 Milne (1917), p. 25.

21 Milne (1917), p. 25.

22 Milne (1917), p. 25.

23 [*Williams's Note:* J. Reeves, ed., *Georgian Poetry* (Penguin Books, 1962), p. xv.]

24 Williams (1987), p. 13.

25 *Des Imagistes* (London: Poetry Bookshop, 1914).

26 *Some Imagist Poets: An Anthology* (New York: Kraus Reprint Co., 1969), p. vi. First published by Houghton Mifflin Company, 1915.

27 Featherstone (1995), pp. 100–4.

28 E. Marsh, *Georgian Poetry 1911–1912* (London: The Poetry Bookshop, 1912), title page.

29 S. Sassoon, *The Old Huntsman and Other Poems* (London: Heinemann, 1917), p. 71.

30 S. Sassoon, *Selected Poems* (London: William Heinemann, 1925), p. 49.

31 S. Sassoon, *War Poems* (London: Faber and Faber, 1983), p. 104.

32 A. Curtayne, *The Complete Poems of Francis Ledwidge* (Martin Brian, 1974), p. 189.

33 R. G. Thomas, ed., *The Collected Poems of Edward Thomas* (Oxford: Clarendon Press, 1978), pp. 325–7.

34 For a detailed account of perceptions of foreign military threats, see I. F. Clarke, *Voices Prophesying War 1763–1984* (London: Oxford University Press, 1966). Chapters Three and Four are particularly relevant background to the First World War; p. 142 lists a number of fictional works from the period immediately preceding the First World War that imagined German invasion intentions.

35 R. Brooke, *1914 and Other Poems* (London: Sidgwick and Jackson Limited, 1915), p. 15.

36 A reader's letter, 'Our Poets', *The Times*, 20 October 1914, p. 9.

37 'The Day of the Young', *The Times*, 24 October 1914, p. 7.

38 *The Times*, 24 October 1914, p. 7.

39 R. Service, *The Rhymes of a Red-Cross Man* (London: Fisher Unwin, 1916), pp. 15–16. This anthology includes many other overtly patriotic poems.

40 L. Binyon, *The Four Years: War Poems Collected and Newly Augmented* (Mathews, 1919), p. 40.

41 C. Reilly, *The Virago Book of Women's War Poetry and Verse* (London: Virago, 1997), p. 88. 'The Call' is commented on in N. Khan's *Women's Poetry of the First World War* (Hemel Hempstead: Harvester Wheatsheaf, 1988), pp. 18–19.

42 See Katzantsis's Preface in Reilly (1997), pp. xxi–xxx.

43 Reilly (1997), p. xxiv.

44 D. Roberts, *Minds at War: The Poetry and Experience of the First World War* (Burgess Hill: Saxon Books, 1996), pp. 54–67.

45 Roberts (1996), p. 54.

46 Roberts (1996), pp. 54–5.

47 Roberts (1996), p. 58.

48 Bold (1976), p. 127.

49 Reilly (1997), p. 88.

50 'A Call to Arms', *The Times*, 8 September 1914, p. 9.

51 C. Ricks, *The Poems of Tennyson* by Alfred Tennyson (London: Longman Group Limited, 1969), pp. 1034–6.

52 See G. B. Shaw's *Man and Superman: A Comedy and Philosophy* (Constable: 1903).

53 B. Russell, *Principles of Social Reconstruction* (London: Allen and Unwin, 1920), pp. 62–3. First published in 1916.

54 Featherstone (1995), p. 55.

55 See M. Ceadel, *Pacifism in Britain, 1914–1945: The Defining of a Faith* (Oxford: Clarendon Press, 1980), p. 38ff for a discussion of the workings of tribunals in the First World War.

56 R. Hart-Davies, *Siegfried Sassoon's Diaries, 1915–1918* (London: Faber and Faber, 1983), p. 177.

57 Sassoon (1925), p. 31.

58 See R. Graves, *Goodbye To All That* (London: Penguin, 1957), p. 174, where some of Sassoon's military feats are described, earning him the nickname 'Mad Jack'.

59 R. Brooke, *Poems* (London: Sidgwick, 1911).

60 Printed in *1914 and Other Poems* (1915).

61 Review of *1914 and Other Poems* in *Poems by Rupert Brooke* (London: Sidgwick and Jackson Ltd., 1917), end page.

62 D. Hibberd, ed., *Poetry of the First of World War: A Casebook* (London: Macmillan Press Ltd., 1981), p. 13.

63 Hibberd (1981), p. 13.

64 Extract from a letter of 2 August 1924 in M. Newbolt, ed., *The Later Life and Letters of Sir Henry Newbolt* (London, 1942), pp. 314–15.

65 J. Stallworthy, *Anthem for Doomed Youth: Twelve Soldier Poets of the First World War* (London: Constable, 2002), p. 101.

66 Hibberd (1981), p. 44.

67 Sassoon (1925), p. 42.

68 Gardner (1976), pp. 141–2.

69 R. K. R. Thornton, *Ivor Gurney: Collected Letters* (The Mid Northumberland Arts Group & Carcanet Press, 1991), p. 81.

70 Letter from Isaac Rosenberg to Mrs Cohen, quoted in D. Hibberd, ed., *Poetry of the First World War: A Casebook* (London: The Macmillan Press Ltd., 1981), p. 33. Source: G. Bottomley and D. Harding, eds, *The Collected Works of Isaac Rosenberg* (London, 1937).

71 M. Schmidt, *Lives of the Poets* (London: Phoenix, 1999), p. 609.

72 Letter from Charles Sorley, 28 April 1915, quoted in Hibberd (1981), p. 39. Source: *The Collected Letters of Charles Sorley* (Cambridge, 1919).

73 J. C. King, *The First World War* (Macmillan Press Ltd., 1972), 'Trench Life', pp. 197–233.

74 King (1972), pp. 219–28.

75 W. Churchill, obituary of Rupert Brooke, *The Times*, 26 April 1915. Churchill had also gained a reputation himself as a notable prose writer on war, through works such as *The River War* (1899).

76 F. Cornford, 'Youth', *Collected Poems* (London: The Cresset Press, 1954), p. 19.

77 'William Watson, War-Eater' by 'Attila' in *The New Age*, 17 December 1914, p. 178.

CHAPTER THREE

1 A. St. John Adcock, ed., *For Remembrance: Soldier Poets who have Fallen in the War* (London: Hodder, 1918).

2 J. Drinkwater, ed., *Patriotism in Literature* (London: Williams & Northgate, 1924), p. 43.

3 Drinkwater (1924), p. 63.

4 For Drinkwater, as for many other war poetry anthologists particularly in the 1920s, the poet's military identity was of primary importance.

5 F. Brereton, ed., *An Anthology of War Poems* with an introduction by E. Blunden (Collins, 1930).

6 F. W. Ziv, ed., *The Valiant Muse: An Anthology of Poems by Poets Killed in the World War* (Putnam's, 1936).

7 A. Calder, ed., *The People's War: Britain 1939–1945* (London: Pimlico, 1992), p. 498.

8 M. Ceadel, *Pacificism in Britain, 1914–1945: The Defining of a Faith* (Oxford: Clarendon Press, 1980). See Part I, Chapter Four, 'The Great War'.

9 S. Spender, *The Thirties and After: Poetry, Politics, People (1933–75)* (Glasgow: Fontana, 1978), pp. 15–16.

10 M. Roberts, ed., *New Signatures: Poems by Several Hands*, 3rd edn (London: The Hogarth Press, 1934). First published in 1932.

11 M. Roberts, ed., *New Country: Prose and Poetry by the Authors of New Signatures* (Freeport, New York: Books for Libraries Press, 1933).

12 Roberts (1933), p. 11.

13 Roberts (1933), p. 13.

14 Roberts (1933), p. 17.

15 G. Grigson, 'Faith or Feeling', *New Verse*, 2 (March 1933), p. 15.

16 Spender (1978), p. 19. Spender's chapter 'Background to the Thirties' provides a useful retrospective overview of the allegiances and key poetic events of the decade.

17 Roberts (1933), p. 21.

18 As the chapter goes on to explore, Owen came to be seen as the epitome of the heroic and humane observer of the First World War.

19 Ceadel (1980). Ceadel's excellent analysis of pacifism through both world wars identifies a number of different strands within it: in the interwar period, he describes the two leading tendencies as pacifist (those opposed to war on any terms) and pacificist (those who believe war should be reserved only for the most extreme of circumstances). See Ceadel, Part II, chapters 6–8.

20 Ceadel (1980), p. 102.

21 E. M. Remarque, *Im Westen Nichts Neues* (1929) was translated as *All Quiet on the Western Front* (London: Putnam, 1929) and went through many impressions in the same year.

22 Sassoon wrote six autobiographical volumes in all: *Memoirs of a Fox-Hunting Man* (1928); *Memoirs of an Infantry Officer* (London: Faber, 1930); *Sherston's Progress* (London: Faber, 1936); *The Old Century and Seven More Years* (1938); *The Weald of Youth* (1942) and *Siegfried's Journey* (London: Faber, 1945).

23 D. Jones, *In Parenthesis*, 2nd edn (London: Faber, 1961), p. ix.

24 Graves (1957), p. 137.

25 Graves (1957), p. 175.

26 See J. Stallworthy, *Anthem for Doomed Youth: Twelve Soldier Poets of the First World War* (London: Constable, 2002), p. 89.

27 E. Blunden, ed., *Poems by Wilfred Owen* (1920).

28 G. Walter, ed., *Rupert Brooke & Wilfred Owen* (London: Everyman Paperbacks, 1997), p. xxi.

29 E. Blunden, ed., *The Poems of Wilfred Owen: Edited with a Memoir by Edmund Blunden* (London: Chatto, 1931).

30 This quotation is as included in Day Lewis's essay, but is printed 'Nor my titanic tears, the seas, be dried' in Hibberd, 1973.

31 This is as in Day Lewis's essay, but is printed 'Now, he is old; his back will never brace'; in Hibberd, 1973.

32 This is as in Day Lewis's essay, but is printed 'Heart, you were never hot' in Hibberd, 1973.

33 C. Day Lewis, *A Hope for Poetry*, 6th edn (London: Blackwell, 1944), pp. 14–17.

34 E. Marsh, *Collected Poems of Rupert Brooke, with a Memoir* (London: Sidgwick & Jackson, Ltd., 1928), p. ix.

35 Marsh (1928), pp. xiv–xv.

36 Marsh (1928), p. xxiv.

37 In the quotation from her review of Marsh, Roth's reference to Novello, a popular and commercially successful composer, seems intended to illustrate Marsh's cultural superficiality and, by association, to denigrate Brooke.

38 Q. D. Leavis, 'The Background of Twentieth Century Letters: reviews by Q. D. Leavis', *A Selection from Scrutiny*, Vol. 1 (1968), pp. 163–6.

39 T. Eagleton, *Literary Theory: An Introduction* (Oxford: Basil Blackwell Ltd., 1983), p. 25.

40 Eagleton (1983), pp. 28–9. Eagleton refers to Chris Baldick's D.Phil thesis, which was the basis of Baldick's book *The Social Mission of English Criticism 1848–1932* (Oxford: Clarendon Press, 1983).

41 Eagleton (1983), pp. 29–30.

42 Graves (1957), pp. 238–9. Graves notes that some of the elder dons had regarded all soldiers as 'noble saviours' during the war, but regained their hauteur when peacetime resumed.

43 I. A. Richards, *Principles of Literary Criticism* (London: Routledge & Kegan Paul Ltd., 1960), p. 3. First published in 1924.

44 Richards (1960), p. 2.

45 There were 19 volumes of *Scrutiny* running from 1932 to 1953, with a 20th issue appearing in 1963. The periodical published many notable critical essays during this time, although it had a tendency to be dismissive of contemporary literature.

46 The 1918 *Collected Poems* has the following version of these two lines:

■ 'Now God be thanked Who has matched us with His hour,
And caught our youth, and wakened us from sleeping'. □

47 H. L. Elvin, 'Eagles and Trumpets for the Middle Classes', *Scrutiny*, Vol. 1, No. 2 (September 1932), pp. 162–3.

48 W. B. Yeats, ed., *The Oxford Book of Modern Verse 1892–1935* (Oxford: Clarendon Press, 1936), pp. xxxiv–xxxv.

49 Jones (1963), p. xv.

50 Eliot in Jones (1963), pp. vii–viii.

51 Day Lewis (1934), p. 17.

52 See note 4.

53 See Cunningham's chapter in F. Gloversmith, ed., *Class, Culture and Social Change: A New View of the 1930s* (Sussex: The Harvester Press, 1980), p. 47. The italics in this extract are Cunningham's.

54 M. Sperber, *And I Remember Spain: A Spanish Civil War Anthology* (London: Hart-Davis, MacGibbon, 1974), pp. 203–20.

55 Cunningham, in Gloversmith (1980), p. 47.

56 'Manifesto', *The Left Review*, Vol. 3, No. 8 (September 1937), pp. 445–6.

57 E. Rickword, 'John Cornford 1913–1937', *The Left Review* Vol. 3, No. 2 (March 1937), pp. 67–8.

58 R. Campbell, *Light on a Dark Horse: An Autobiography (1901–1935)* (London: Hollis & Carter, 1951), p. 226.

59 Campbell (1951), p. 317.

60 R. Campbell, *Flowering Rifle: A Poem from the Battlefield of Spain* (London: Longmans, Green and Co., 1939), p. 9.

61 Campbell (1939), p. 31.

62 See R. Skelton, ed., *Poetry of the Thirties* (Harmondsworth: Penguin, 1964), p. 146.

63 See Skelton (1964), p. 133.

64 Review article by S. Spender, 'New Poetry', *Left Review*, Vol. 3, No. 6 (July 1937), pp. 358–61.

65 W. H. Auden, 'The Public vs. the Late Mr. W. B. Yeats', *Partisan Review*, Vol. 6, No. 3 (Spring 1939), pp. 46–51.

66 Sperber (1974), p. 221.

67 Spender (1978), pp. 17–18.

68 G. Orwell, *Inside the Whale and Other Essays* (Harmondsworth: Penguin, 1962), pp. 38–9.

69 S. Weintraub, *The Last Great Cause: the Intellectuals and the Spanish Civil War* (London: W. H. Allen, 1968), p. 45.

70 Weintraub (1968), p. 47.

CHAPTER FOUR

1 See P. Tomlinson's 'To the Poets of 1940', *Times Literary Supplement*, 30 December 1939, p. 755; also C. W. Brodribb's 'Poets in War', *Times Literary Supplement*, 8 August 1942, p. 391.

2 See the discussion of Owen's reputation in Chapter Three.

3 Tomlinson (1939), p. 755.

4 See R. Hewison, Chapter One, *Under Siege: Literary Life in London* (Newton Abbot: Readers' Union Ltd., 1978), pp. 5–26.

5 H. Treece, 'Growing up in wartime', *How I See Apocalypse* (New York and London: AMS Press, 1979), pp. 5–6. Reprint of the 1946 edition, published by L. Drummond, London.

6 Treece (1979), pp. 7–8.

7 Treece (1979), p. 12.

8 This is referred to by the contemporary writer and poet Laurence Durrell, in the introduction to Douglas's prose work *Alamein to Zem Zem* (London: Faber and Faber, 1966), p. 11. First published in 1946 by Edition Poetry London.

9 See Lewis's poem 'All Day it has Rained', in B. Gardner, ed., *The Terrible Rain: The War Poets 1939–45* (London: Magnum Books, 1977), p. 36, and in several other Second World War anthologies.

10 'My feeling for Wilfred Owen began by being intensely personal. He was there, in my room. A great poet was in my room. I never had any doubt of his greatness. And he was speaking to me.' P. Dickinson, *The Good Minute* (London: Victor Gollancz Ltd., 1965), p. 119.

11 C. Day Lewis, 'Where are the War Poets?', quoted and discussed in the introduction to R. Skelton, ed., *Poetry of the Forties* (Harmondsworth: Penguin Books, 1968), p. 19.

12 S. Keyes, 'War Poet', in R. Blythe, ed., *Components of the Scene* (Harmondsworth: Penguin Books, 1966), p. 171.

13 R. Fuller, *The Strange and the Good* (London: Collins Harvill, 1989), pp. 206–7.

14 Fuller (1989), pp. 224–5.

15 A discussion of reactions to Auden's departure can be found in 'Turning Points', P. Hendon, ed., *The Poetry of W. H. Auden* (Cambridge: Icon Books Ltd., 2000), pp. 82–110.

16 This referred to the 1930s as a 'low, dishonest decade' and went on, 'We must love one another or die'. This poem is quoted in full in E. Mendelson's *W. H. Auden: Selected Poems* (London: Faber and Faber, 1979) and discussed in Hendon (2000), pp. 133–4.

17 [*Woolf's note:*] Mr Auden ... says:

■ Half-boys, we spoke of books and praised
The acid and austere, behind us only
The stuccoed suburb and expensive school. □

(Poems XXIV (To Christopher Isherwood),
Look, Stranger!, Faber and Faber, 1936)

18 [*Woolf's note:*] *In Germany, in Russia, in Italy, in Spain:* the 1930s saw the rise of the Nazi Party in Germany, Stalin's purges of the Communist Party, Mussolini's Abyssinian War (1935) and the Spanish Civil War (1936–39).

19 V. Woolf, 'The Leaning Tower', in R. Bowlby, ed., *A Woman's Essays: Selected Essays Volume One* (Harmondsworth: Penguin Books, 1992), p. 167.

20 Woolf (1992), p. 178.

21 G. Orwell, 'England Your England', *Inside the Whale and Other Essays* (Harmondsworth: Penguin Books, 1962), p. 85.

22 Orwell (1962), pp. 68–9.

23 E. Rickword, see 'Notes on Culture and the War', 'War and poetry: 1914–18' and 'Poetry and Two Wars' in *Literature in Society: Essays and Opinions, Volume 2* (Manchester: Carcanet Press, 1978).

24 Rickword (1978), p. 137.

25 Rickword (1978), p. 157.

26 C. Reilly, *English Poetry of the Second World War: A Biobibliography* (London: Mansell Publishing Ltd., 1986), p. vii.

27 It is interesting to note here, that whereas Reilly sees the routine danger of war as a possible reason for an increase in war poetry, Henry Treece, in the extract discussed in the previous section cites this as a reason for the early *lack* of war poetry. This illustrates the

quite distinct analyses that can be made of the same social and cultural phenomena, especially from different historical perspectives.

28 Reilly (1986), p. xii.

29 Reilly (1986), p. xiv.

30 A. Calder-Marshall, *The Book Front* (London: The Bodley Head, 1947), p. 30. Further accounts of wartime publishing can be found in chapter two of Hewison (1978).

31 J. Symons, *Notes from another Country* (London: London Magazine Editions, 1972), pp. 66–7.

32 D. Graham, ed., *Keith Douglas. A Prose Miscellany* (Manchester: Carcanet Press, 1985), p. 119.

33 S. Spender, *Poetry Since 1939* (London: Longmans Green & Co., 1946), p. 58.

34 C. Connolly, Editorial, *Horizon* (May 1940).

35 G. Rees, 'Letter from a soldier', *Horizon*, Vol. I, No. 7 (July 1940), pp. 467–71.

36 Spender (1946), p. 58.

37 Spender (1946), pp. 22–3.

38 Spender (1946), pp. 50–8.

39 Spender (1946), p. 59.

40 T. S. Eliot was an editor at Faber and Faber throughout the war years, and Herbert Read, prolific writer, critic and poet, was a director of George Routledge and Sons.

41 *Penguin New Writing* was one of the most commercially successful literary magazines of the war period. See J. Whitehead's 'John Lehmann's *"New Writing"*, An Introductory Essay', in *John Lehmann's 'New Writing', An Author-Index 1936–1950, Studies in Comparative Literature*, Vol. 13, p. 15.

42 For a fuller description of the tensions between these roles, see the third of 5 volumes of autobiography by C. W. Gardner, *The Dark Thorn* (London: Grey Walls Press, 1946).

43 Louis MacNeice worked at the BBC as a feature writer and producer from 1941–49, and Dylan Thomas wrote propaganda film scripts. See Reilly (1986).

44 D. Stanford, *Inside the Forties: Literary Memoirs 1937–1957* (London: Sidgwick and Jackson, 1977), p. 80.

45 J. Lehmann, *I Am My Brother* (London: Longmans Green & Co. Ltd., 1960), pp. 41–2.

46 S. Jennett, 'The Price of Books', *Life and Letters Today* (January 1945), p. 10.

47 Stanford (1977), p. 81.

48 A. P. Wavell, ed., *Other Men's Flowers* (London: Jonathan Cape, 1944), p. 17.

49 The English Association, *England An Anthology* (London: Macmillan & Co. Ltd., 1944), p. 1.

50 The English Association (1944), p. v.

51 The English Association (1944), p. vi.

52 M. J. Tambimuttu, *Poetry in Wartime* (London: Faber and Faber, 1942), p. 5.

53 O. Williams, *New Poems 1944: An Anthology of American and British Verse* (New York: Howell, Soskins Publishers, 1944), p. 3.

54 Williams (1944), p. 61.

55 K. Rhys, *Poems of the Forces* (London: Routledge, 1941), p. xvi.

56 Mass-Observation, *War Begins at Home*, T. Harrisson and C. Madge, eds (London: Chatto & Windus, 1940), p. 4.

57 R. Graves, 'The Poetry of World War II', *The Common Asphodel* (London: Hamish Hamilton, 1949), p. 312.

58 Mass-Observation (1940), p. 5.

59 R. Nichols, *An Anthology of War Poetry 1914–18* (Redhill: Love and Malcomson Ltd., 1943), p. 22.

60 Nichols (1943), p. 34.

61 See 'Some autobiographical statements', in I. Hamilton, ed., *The Poetry of War 1939–1945* (London: Alan Ross Ltd., 1965), pp. 155–72.

62 M. Meyer, *The Collected Poems of Sidney Keyes* (London: Routledge, 1988), p. xv.

63 K. Douglas, *Alamein to Zem Zem* (London: Editions Poetry London, 1946), p. 15.

64 Hamilton (1965), pp. 155–72.

65 S. Featherstone, *War Poetry: An Introductory Reader* (London: Routledge, 1995), p. 84.

66 A. Calder, *The People's War: Britain 1939–1945* (London: Pimlico edition, 1992), p. 268.

67 C. Reilly, *The Virago Book of Women's War Poetry and Verse* (London: Virago Press, 1997), p. vii.

68 'Other New Publications', *Times Literary Supplement*, 29 April 1944, p. 215.

69 D. Sheridan, ed., *Among You Taking Notes: The Wartime Diaries of Naomi Mitchison 1939–1945* (London: Phoenix Press, 2000), p. 41.

70 Tambimuttu (1942), p. 122.

71 Tambimuttu (1942), p. 120.

72 P. Ledward and C. Strang, *Poems of This War, By Younger Poets* (London: Cambridge University Press, 1942), pp. 30–1.

73 See discussion of the process of mythification of the Blitz as 'glossified and sanctified', Hewison (1977), pp. 36–7.

74 Calder (1992), p. 521.

75 Rhys (1941), p. 84.

76 [*Fussell's note:*] *Roosevelt and Hopkins: An Intimate History* (New York, 1948), p. 438. [The square brackets in the quotation are Fussell's.]

77 [*Fussell's note:*] *The Licentious Soldiery*, p. 66. [The square brackets in the quotation are Fussell's.]

78 [*Fussell's note:*] *A Cackhanded War*, 13, p. 228.

79 [*Fussell's note:*] *Collected Poems* (London, 1966), pp. 152–3.

80 [*Fussell's note:*] Mary Lago and P. N. Furbank, eds, *Selected Letters of E. M. Forster* (Cambridge, Mass., 1984; 2 vols.), II: p. 170.

81 P. Fussell, *Wartime: Understanding and Behaviour in the Second World War* (New York and Oxford: Oxford University Press, 1989), pp. 130–1.

82 There were three anthologies produced under the auspices of the Apocalyptics during the war years: *The New Apocalypse* (1939), *The White Horseman* (1941) and *The Crown and Sickle* (1945). The poetry tends to use dramatic, even violent successions of images, influenced by myth and psychological theory.

83 J. F. Hendry and H. Treece, eds, *The Crown and the Sickle* (London: P. S. King & Staples Limited, 1945), p. 10.

CHAPTER FIVE

1 S. Featherstone, *War Poetry: An Introductory Reader* (London & New York: Routledge, 1995), p. 38.

2 R. Nichols and J. Tennyson, eds, *An Anthology of War Poetry 1914–18* (Redhill: Love and Malcomson Ltd., 1943).

3 Eberhart and Rodman (1945), p. ix.

4 Eberhart and Rodman (1945), p. v.

5 Eberhart and Rodman (1945), p. vii.

6 Eberhart and Rodman (1945), p. v.

7 A. Rutherford, *The Literature of War: Studies in Heroic Virtue* (Basingstoke: The Macmillan Press Ltd.,1989), p. 1. First published in 1978.

8 [*Rutherford's Note:*] N. Frye, *Anatomy of Criticism* (Princeton, 1937), pp. 33–4.

9 Rutherford (1989), p. 3.

10 T. Holt and V. Holt, eds, *Poets of the Great War* (Barnsley: Cooper, 1996), p. 2.

11 D. Davie, 'Editorial', *PN Review*, 34, 10 (2) (1983), 1–2.

12 V. Selwyn, ed., *The Voice of War: Poems of the Second World War* (London: Penguin Books, 1996). First published by Michael Joseph, 1996, p. xvii.

13 Selwyn (1996), p. xi.

14 See D. Thomas, *An Underworld at War: Spivs, Deserters, Racketeers and Civilians in the Second World War* (John Murray, 2003). Other critics such as Adam Piette in *Imagination at War* (1995) have argued that many 'private' recollections of the war contrast starkly with public narratives of the war as cohesive and positive; see the final section of Chapter Five.

15 Selwyn (1996), p. xxiv.

16 Selwyn (1996), p. xxv.

17 K. Baker, ed., *The Faber Book of War Poetry* (London: Faber, 1996), p. xxiii.

18 Simonides's elegy can be found in Baker (1996), p. 561 and extracts from Virgil's epic can be found on pp. 353–4 and p. 505.

19 Baker (1996), p. xxiv.

20 Baker (1996), pp. xxiv–xxv.

21 Featherstone (1995), p. 38.

22 Featherstone (1995), p. 39.

23 Featherstone (1995), p. 39.

24 Featherstone (1995), p. 43.

25 B. Murdoch, *Fighting Songs and Warring Words* (London and New York: Routledge, 1990), p. xi.

26 Murdoch (1990), pp. ix–x.

27 The Suez Crisis was a military confrontation over the Suez Canal, which links the Mediterranean and Red Seas, providing the shortest sea route from Europe to the East. In 1956, the canal was nationalized by President Nasser of Egypt, leading to attacks by Israel, Britain and France. The latter were forced to withdraw following international pressure.

28 War between communist North Vietnam and South Vietnam, which was backed by the United States.

29 Gardner (1976), p. xix.

30 M. Hussey, ed., *Poetry of the First World War* (London: Longmans, Green and Co. Ltd., 1967), p. xv.

31 C. Hamblett, ed., *I Burn for England: an Anthology of the Poetry of World War II* (London: Leslie Frewin, 1966), p. 11.

32 Blythe (1966), p. 13.

33 Gardner (1977), p. xxiv.

34 M. Wollman, ed., *Poems of the War Years: An Anthology* (London: Macmillan and Co. Ltd., 1950), p. xxxvii. First published in 1948.

35 Wollman (1950), p. xxxvii.

36 Wollman (1950), p. xxxvii.

37 Wollman (1950), p. xxxviii.

38 Deppe, Middleton and Schönherr, *Ohne Hass und Fahne/ No Hatred and No Flag/ Sans haine et sans drapeau* (Hamburg: Rowohlt, 1959), p. 13.

39 Deppe, Middleton and Schönherr (1959), p. 14.

40 Deppe, Middleton and Schönherr (1959), p. 14.

41 D. Graham, *Poetry of the Second World War: an International Anthology* (London: Chatto & Windus, 1995).

42 Graham (1995), p. xv.

43 Theodor W. Adorno, 'Cultural Criticism and Society', in *Prisms*, trans. Samuel and Shierry Weber (London: Neville Spearman, 1967), p. 34.

44 B. Bergonzi, *Heroes Twilight: A Study of the Literature of the Great War* (Manchester: Carcanet Press Ltd., 1996). First edition published 1965; second edition 1980.

45 T. Cross, ed., *The Lost Voices of World War 1: An International Anthology of Writers, Poets and Playwrights* (London: Bloomsbury, 1988).

46 Featherstone (1995), p. 10.

47 Featherstone (1995), p. 10.

48 D. L. Jones, ed., *War Poetry: An Anthology* (London: Pergamon Press, 1968).

49 Jones (1968), p. 136.

50 Jones (1968), p. 1.

51 Jones (1968), p. 2.

52 Jones (1968), p. 2.

53 Jones (1968), p. 81.

54 Jones (1968), p. 86.

55 Jones (1968), p. 88.

56 Jones (1968), pp. 137–8.

57 A. Harvey, ed., *In Time of War* (London: Penguin Books Ltd., 1989), p. 7. First published in 1987.

58 Harvey (1989), p. 135.

59 Featherstone (1995), p. 19.

60 Featherstone (1995), p. 20.

61 Stallworthy (2002), p. 9.

62 [*Author's Note:*] Keith Douglas, 'Note on Drawing for the Jacket of Bête Noire', in Graham (ed.), *The Complete Poems of Keith Douglas*, p. 120.

63 Shires (1985), pp. 117–18.

64 Bergonzi (1996), Preface, pp. 1–7.

65 Bergonzi (1996), p. 1.

66 Bergonzi (1996), pp. 1–2.

67 C. Reilly, ed., *The Virago Book of Women's War Poetry and Verse* (London: Virago Press, 1997), p. vii.

68 Reilly (1997), p. viii.

69 Reilly (1997), p. ix.

70 M. Florence, C. Marshall and C. Ogden, eds, *Militarism versus Feminism: Writings on Women and War* (London: Virago, 1987).

71 N. Khan, *Women's Poetry of the First World War* (Brighton: Harvester, 1988).

72 Reilly (1986), p. viii.

73 Reilly (1986), p. xxiii.

74 M. Taylor, *Lads: Love Poetry of the Trenches* (London: Duckworth, 1998). First published in 1989.

75 P. Fussell, *The Great War and Modern Memory* (New York & London: Oxford University Press, 1975).

76 Taylor (1998), p. 16.

77 Holt and Holt (1999), p. 3.

78 Taylor (1998), p. 29.

79 Fussell (1975), p. 30.

80 Fussell (1975), p. 35.

81 Fussell (1975), p. 235.

82 Featherstone (1995), p. 22.

83 A. Piette, *Imagination at War: British Fiction and Poetry 1939–1945* (London and Basingstoke: Papermac, 1995).

84 Piette (1995), p. 5.

Bibliography

ANTHOLOGIES
All collections of more than one poet's work are listed under the overall heading 'anthologies'. These are subdivided below, according to which war or period the poetry primarily deals with. Collections that cover more than one war are listed under 'general war anthologies' and those that do not primarily deal with war are listed under 'other general anthologies'.

FIRST WORLD WAR ANTHOLOGIES
Adcock, A. St. John, ed., *For Remembrance: Soldier Poets Who Have Fallen in the War* (London: Hodder, 1918).

Brereton, F., ed., *An Anthology of War Poems* (London: Collins, 1930).

Clarke, G. H., ed., *A Treasury of War Poetry: British and American Poems of the World War 1914–1919* (London: Hodder & Stoughton, 1919).

Cross, T., ed., *The Lost Voices of World War I: An International Anthology of Writers, Poets and Playwrights* (London: Bloomsbury, 1988).

Gardner, B., ed., *Up to the Line to Death: The War Poets 1914–1918* (London: Macmillan & Co. Ltd., 1976).

Holt, T. and Holt, V., eds, *Poets of the Great War* (Barnsley: Cooper, 1996).

Hussey, M., ed., *Poetry of the First World War* (London: Longmans, Green & Co. Ltd., 1967).

Nichols, R., *An Anthology of War Poetry 1914–18* (Redhill: Love and Malcomson Ltd., 1943).

Parsons, I. M., ed., *Men Who March Away: Poems of the First World War* (London: Chatto & Windus, 1965).

Reilly, C., ed., *Scars Upon My Heart: Women's Poetry and Verse of the First World War* (London: Virago Press, 1981).

Taylor, M., ed., *Lads: Love Poetry of the Trenches* (London: Duckworth, 1998).

Ziv, F. W., ed., *The Valiant Muse: An Anthology of Poems by Poets Killed in the World War* (New York: Putnam's, 1936).

1930s AND SPANISH CIVIL WAR ANTHOLOGIES
Roberts, M., ed., *New Signatures: Poems by Several Hands* (London: The Hogarth Press, 1934).

Roberts, M., ed., *New Country: Prose and Poetry by the Authors of New Signatures* (Freeport, New York: Books for Libraries Press, 1933).

Skelton, R., ed., *Poetry of the Thirties* (Harmondsworth: Penguin Books Ltd., 1964).

Sperber, M., ed., *And I Remember Spain: A Spanish Civil War Anthology* (London: Hart-Davis, MacGibbon, 1974).

1940s AND SECOND WORLD WAR ANTHOLOGIES
Blythe, R., ed., *Components of the Scene* (Harmondsworth: Penguin Books Ltd., 1966).

Deppe, W. G., Middleton, C. and Schönherr, H., eds, *Ohne Hass und Fahne/ No Hatred and No Flag/ Sans haine et sans drapeau* (Hamburg: Rowohlt, 1959).

Gardner, B., ed., *The Terrible Rain: The War Poets 1939–45* (London: Magnum Books, 1977).

Graham, D., ed., *Poetry of the Second World War: An International Anthology* (London: Chatto & Windus, 1995).

Hamblett, C., ed., *I Burn for England: An Anthology of the Poetry of World War II* (London: Leslie Frewin, 1966).

Hamilton, I., ed., *The Poetry of War 1939–1945* (London: Alan Ross Ltd., 1965).

Hendry, J. F., ed., *The New Apocalypse: An Anthology of Criticism, Poems and Stories* (London: Fortune Press, 1940).

Hendry, J. F. and Treece, H., eds, *The White Horseman: Prose and Verse of the New Apocalypse* (London: Routledge & Sons, 1941).

Hendry, J. F. and Treece, H., eds, *The Crown and the Sickle* (London: P. S. King & Staples Limited, 1945).

Ledward, P. and Strang, C., eds, *Poems of This War, By Younger Poets* (London: Cambridge University Press, 1942).

Reilly, C., ed., *Chaos of the Night: Women's Poetry of the Second World War* (London: Virago, 1981).

Rhys, K., ed., *Poems of the Forces* (London: Routledge, 1941).

Roscoe, T. and Winter Were, M., eds, *Poems by Contemporary Women* (London: Hutchinson, 1944).

Sackville-West, V., ed., *Poems of the Land Army: An Anthology of Verse by Members of the Land Army* (London: Michael Joseph, 1945).

Selwyn, V. ed., *The Voice of War: Poems of the Second World War* (London: Penguin Books, 1996).

Skelton, R., ed., *Poetry of the Forties* (Harmondsworth: Penguin Books, 1968).

Tambimuttu, M. J., ed., *Poetry in Wartime* (London: Faber and Faber, 1942).

Williams, O., ed., *New Poems 1944: An Anthology of American and British Verse* (New York: Howell, Soskins Publishers, 1944).

GENERAL WAR ANTHOLOGIES

Baker, K., ed., *The Faber Book of War Poetry* (London: Faber, 1996).

Barrett, P. and Collinson, K. B., eds, *The Happy Warrior: An Anthology of Australian and New Zealand Military Poetry* (Hartwell, Victoria: Sid Harta Publishers, 2001).

Bold, A., ed., *The Martial Muse: Seven Centuries of War Poetry* (Oxford: Wheaton, 1976).

De Somogyi, N., ed., *The Little Book of War Poems* (Exclusive Editions, 2001).

Drinkwater, J., ed., *Patriotism in Literature* (London: Williams & Northgate, 1924).

Eberhart, R. and Rodman, S., eds, *War and the Poet: An Anthology of Poetry Expressing Man's Attitudes to War From Ancient Times to the Present* (New York: The Devin-Air Company, 1945).

English Association, The, *England An Anthology* (London: Macmillan & Co. Ltd., 1944).

Harvey, A., ed., *In Time of War* (London: Penguin Books Ltd., 1989).

Hollis, M. and Keegan, P., eds, *101 Poems Against War* (London: Faber and Faber Limited, 2003).

Jones, D. L., ed., *War Poetry: An Anthology* (London: Pergamon Press, 1968).

Reilly, C., ed., *The Virago Book of Women's War Poetry and Verse* (London: Virago, 1997).

Wavell, A. P., ed., *Other Men's Flowers* (London: Jonathan Cape, 1944).

Wollman, M., ed., *Poems of the War Years: An Anthology* (London: Macmillan and Co. Ltd., 1950).

OTHER GENERAL ANTHOLOGIES

Marsh, E., ed., *Georgian Poetry 1911–1912* (London: The Poetry Bookshop, 1912).

Pound, E., ed., *Des Imagistes* (London: Poetry Bookshop, 1914).

Some Imagist Poets: An Anthology (New York: Kraus Reprint Co., 1969).

Wain, J., ed., *The Oxford Anthology of English Poetry* (Oxford: Oxford University Press, 1986).

Yeats, W. B., ed., *The Oxford Book of Modern Verse 1892–1935* (Oxford: Clarendon Press, 1936).

SINGLE AUTHOR POETRY TEXTS

These are sub-divided according to the relevant war. Texts that relate to more than one war, or which contain non-war related material, are listed under 'Other'.

FIRST WORLD WAR POETRY TEXTS

Binyon, L., *The Four Years: War Poems Collected and Newly Augmented* (London: Mathews, 1919).

Blunden, E., ed., *The Poems of Wilfred Owen, With a Memoir* (London: Chatto & Windus, 1931).

Brooke, R., ed., *1914 and Other Poems* (London: Sidgwick and Jackson Limited, 1915).

Brooke, R., *Poems by Rupert Brooke* (London: Sidgwick & Jackson Ltd., 1917).

Curtayne, A., ed., *The Complete Poems of Francis Ledwidge* (Martin Brian, 1974).

Hibberd, D., ed., *War Poems and Others: Wilfred Owen* (London: Chatto & Windus, 1973).

Jones, D., *In Parenthesis* (London: Faber, 1961).

Marsh, E., ed., *Collected Poems of Rupert Brooke, with a Memoir* (London: Sidgwick & Jackson, Ltd., 1928).

Sassoon, S., *War Poems* (London: Faber, 1983).

Service, R., *The Rhymes of a Red-Cross Man* (London: Fisher Unwin, 1916).

Thomas, R. G., ed., *The Collected Poems of Edward Thomas* (Oxford: Clarendon Press, 1978).

Walter, G., ed., *Rupert Brooke & Wilfred Owen* (London: Everyman Paperbacks, 1997).

SPANISH CIVIL WAR POETRY TEXTS

Campbell, R., *Flowering Rifle: A Poem from the Battlefield of Spain* (London: Longmans, Green and Co., 1939).

SECOND WORLD WAR POETRY TEXTS

Meyer, M., ed., *The Collected Poems of Sidney Keyes* (London: Routledge, 1988). First published in 1945.

Paulin, T., *The Invasion Handbook* (London: Faber, 2002).

OTHER POETRY TEXTS

Brooke, R., *Poems* (London: Sidgwick and Jackson Limited, 1911).

Carrington, C., ed., *The Complete Barrack-Room Ballads of Rudyard Kipling* (London: Methuen & Co. Ltd., 1973).

Mendelson, E., ed., *Selected Poems* (London: Faber and Faber, 1979).

Newbolt, H., *Admirals All and Other Verses* (London: Mathews, 1898).

Ricks, C., ed., *The Poems of Tennyson* (London: Longman Group Limited, 1969).

Sassoon, S., *Selected Poems* (London: William Heinemann, 1925).

Sassoon, S., *The Old Huntsman and Other Poems* (London: Heinemann, 1917).

REFERENCE GUIDES

Reilly, C., *English Poetry of the First World War* (London: Prior, 1978).

Reilly, C., *English Poetry of the Second World War* (London: Mansell Publishing, 1986).

WAR POETRY AND PROSE CRITICISM

Works of criticism that deal with more than one war, or that also deal with non-war related topics, are listed under 'Other'.

FIRST WORLD WAR RELATED CRITICISM

Bergonzi, B., *Heroes' Twilight: A Study of the Literature of the Great War* (Manchester: Carcanet Press Ltd., 1996).

Fussell, P., *The Great War and Modern Memory* (New York & London: Oxford University Press, 1975).

Hibberd, D., ed., *Poetry of the First World War: A Casebook* (London: Macmillan Press Ltd., 1981).

Khan, N., *Women's Poetry of the First World War* (Brighton: Harvester, 1988).

Milne, R. O. A., *War and English Poetry*, The English Association pamphlet No. 38, September 1917.

Roberts, D., *Minds at War: The Poetry and Experience of the First World War* (Burgess Hill: Saxon Books, 1996).

Silkin, J., *Out of Battle: The Poetry of the First World War* (London & New York: Ark Paperbacks, 1987).

Spurgeon, C. F. E., *Poetry in the Light of War*, The English Association pamphlet No. 36, January 1917.

Stallworthy, J., *Anthem for Doomed Youth: Twelve Soldier Poets to the First World War* (London: Constable, 2002).

Welland, D., *Wilfred Owen: A Critical Study* (London: Chatto, 1960)

SECOND WORLD WAR RELATED CRITICISM

Alldritt, K., *Modernism in the Second World War: The Later Poetry of Ezra Pound, T. S. Eliot, Basil Bunting and Hugh MacDiarmid* (New York: Lang, 1989).

Piette, A., *Imagination at War: British Fiction and Poetry 1939–1945* (London and Basingstoke, Papermac, 1995).

Rawlinson, M., *British Writing of the Second World War* (Oxford: Clarendon Press, 2000).

Ross, A., *Poetry 1945–1950* (London: Longmans, Green & Co., 1951).

Shires, L., *British Poetry of the Second World War* (London: The Macmillan Press Ltd., 1985).

Spender, S., *Poetry Since 1939* (London: Longmans, Green & Co., 1946).

OTHER WORKS OF CRITICISM

Banerjee, A., *Spirit Above Wars: A Study of the English Poetry of the Two World Wars* (London: The Macmillan Press Ltd., 1976).

Featherstone, S., *War Poetry: An Introductory Reader* (London: Routledge, 1995).

Graves, R., *The Common Asphodel* (London: Hamish Hamilton, 1949).

Hendon, P., ed., *A Reader's Guide to Essential Criticism: The Poetry of W. H. Auden* (Cambridge: Icon Books Ltd., 2000).

Murdoch, B., *Fighting Songs and Warring Words* (London & New York: Routledge, 1990).

Rutherford, A., *The Literature of War: Studies in Heroic Virtue* (Basingstoke: The Macmillan Press Ltd., 1989).

Rickword, E., *Literature in Society: Essays and Opinions, Volume 2* (Manchester: Carcanet Press, 1978).

Schmidt, M., *Lives of the Poets* (London: Phoenix, 1999).

Spender, S., *The Thirties and After* (London: Fontana, 1978).

Treece, H., *How I See Apocalypse* (New York & London: AMS Press, 1979).

Van Wyk Smith, M., *Drummer Hodge: The Poetry of the Anglo-Boer War (1899–1902)* (Oxford: Clarendon Press, 1978).

Williams, J., *Twentieth-Century British Poetry: A Critical Introduction* (London: Edward Arnold (Publishers) Ltd., 1987).

Woolf, V., edited by Bowlby, R., *A Woman's Essays: Selected Essays, Volume One* (London: Penguin, 1992).

ARTICLES IN NEWSPAPERS AND PERIODICALS

'Attila', 'William Watson, War-Eater', *The New Age*, 17 December 1914, p. 178.

'A Call to Arms', *The Times*, 8 September 1914, p. 9.

Connolly, C., *Horizon*, May 1940.

Churchill, W., 'Obituary of Rupert Brooke', *The Times*, 26 April 1915.

Davie, D., 'Editorial', *PN Review*, Vol. 34, No. 2 (1983).

Jennett, S., 'The Price of Books', *Life and Letters Today*, January 1945.

Kendall, T., ' "The Pity of War" ?', *PN Review*, Vol. 30, No. 1 (2003), pp. 30–2.

'Other New Publications', *Times Literary Supplement*, 29 April 1944, p. 215.

Reader's letter, 'Our Poets', *The Times*, 20 October 1914, p. 9.

Rees, G., 'Letter from a soldier', *Horizon*, Vol. 1, No. 7.

'The Day of the Young', *The Times*, 24 October 1914, p. 7.

Tomlinson, P., 'To the Poets of 1940', *Times Literary Supplement*, 30 December 1939.

Whitehead, J., '"New Writing", An Introductory Essay', in *John Lehmann's 'New Writing', An Author-Index 1936–1950* (Studies in Comparative Literature Vol. 13)

BIOGRAPHY AND MEMOIR

Dickinson, P., *The Good Minute* (London: Victor Gollancz Ltd., 1965).

Douglas, K., *Alamein to Zem Zem* (London: Faber and Faber, 1966).

Fuller, R., *The Strange and the Good* (London: Collins Harvill, 1989).

Gardner, C. W., *The Dark Thorn* (London: Grey Walls Press, 1946).

Graham, D., *Keith Douglas. A Prose Miscellany* (Manchester: Carcanet Press, 1985).

Graves, R., *Good-Bye to All That* (London: Penguin, 1957).

Hart-Davies, R., ed., *Siegfried Sassoon's Diaries, 1915–1918* (London: Faber and Faber, 1983).

Jones, N., *Rupert Brooke. Life, Death and Myth* (London: Richard Cohen Books,1999).

Lehmann, J., *I am My Brother* (London: Longmans Green & Co. Ltd., 1960).

Sheridan, D., *Among You Taking Notes: The Wartime Diaries of Naomi Mitchison 1939–1945* (London: Phoenix Press, 2000).

Stanford, D., *Inside the Forties: Literary Memoirs 1937–1957* (London: Sidgwick & Jackson, 1977).

Symons, J., *Notes From Another Country* (London: Editions, 1972).

Sorley, C. H., *The Collected Letters of Charles Sorley* (Cambridge: Cambridge University Press, 1919).

Thornton, R. K. R., ed., *Ivor Gurney: Collected Letters* (The Mid-Northumberland Arts Group & Carcanet Press, 1991).

WORKS OF HISTORICAL AND PHILOSOPHICAL CONTEXT

Adorno, T. W. *Prisms*, trans. Samuel and Shierry Weber (London: Neville Spearman, 1967).

Calder, A., *The People's War: Britain 1939–1945* (London: Pimlico Edition, 1992).

Calder-Marshall, A., *The Book Front* (London: The Bodley Head, 1947).

Ceadel, M., *Pacifism in Britain, 1914–1945: The Defining of a Faith* (Oxford: Clarendon Press, 1980).

Clarke, I. F., *Voices Prophesying War 1763–1984* (London: Oxford University Press, 1966)

Hewison, R., *Under Siege: Literary Life in London* (Newton Abbot: Readers' Union Ltd., 1978).

Harrisson, T. and Madge, C., eds, *War Begins at Home*, for Mass-Observation (London: Chatto & Windus, 1940).

King, J. C., ed., *The First World War* (London, melbourne: The Macmillan Press Ltd., 1972).

Orwell, G., *Inside the Whale and Other Essays* (Harmondsworth: Penguin Books, 1962).

Orwell, G., *The Lion and the Unicorn* (Harmondsworth: Penguin Books, 1982).

Russell, B., *Principles of Social Reconstruction* (London: George Allen & Unwin, 1920).

Thomas, D., *An Underworld at War: Spivs, Deserters, Racketeers and Civilians in the Second World War* (London: John Murray, 2003).

Winter, J. M., *The Experience of World War I* (New York: Oxford University Press, 1995).

NOVELS AND PLAYS

Barker, P., *Regeneration* (London: Penguin, 1992).
Barker, P., *The Eye in the Door* (London: Penguin, 1994).
Barker, P., *The Ghost Road* (London: Viking, 1995).
Heller, J., *Catch-22* (New York: Dell, 1973).
Hemingway, E., *A Farewell to Arms* (London: Arrow, 1994).
Manning, F., *Her Privates We*, unexpurgated edn (London: Serpent's Tail, 1999).
Shaw, G. B., *Man and Superman: A Comedy and Philosophy* (London: Constable, 1903).
Sherriff, R. C., *Journey's End: A Play* (London: Victor Gollancz Ltd., 1929).

Index